Understanding Social Media

Understanding Social Media

How to create a plan for your business that works

Damian Ryan

LONDON PHILADELPHIA NEW DELHI

First published in Great Britain and the United States in 2015 by Kogan Page Limited

2nd Floor, 45 Gee Street
London EC1V 3RS
United Kingdom
www.koganpage.com

1518 Walnut Street, Suite 1100
Philadelphia PA 19102
USA

4737/23 Ansari Road
Daryaganj
New Delhi 110002
India

© Damian Ryan, 2015

ISBN   978 0 7494 7356 3
E-ISBN   978 0 7494 7357 0

British Library Cataloguing-in-Publication Data

A CIP record for this book is available from the British Library.

Library of Congress Cataloging-in-Publication Data

CIP data is available.

Library of Congress Control Number: 2015002513

Typeset by Graphicraft Limited, Hong Kong
Print production managed by Jellyfish
Printed and bound by CPI Group (UK) Ltd, Croydon, CR0 4YY

CONTENTS

07 How to build a social media team – how to pick the right suppliers   160

60 HEADS ARE BETTER THAN ONE!

Not only is this a book about social media marketing, but it has been created using social media channels by social media people (60 of us) and has its genesis in one central belief: that social media is so universally important but is changing so rapidly that it makes no sense to think that one person is adequate to tell the entire story to others. Moreover, the very nature of the medium is such that it lends itself to collaboration among peers and, therefore, I believe the story is better told by many people – a coterie of writers and contributors working together to help digital marketers navigate their journey through this new and exciting world.

My role in all this has changed from author to curator. I hope readers will agree that this will prove to be the right strategy and will ensure a better quality product and, academically, a tool that will enable marketers to be that much more competitive when it comes to tackling the vast array of issues neatly bottled under the label... social.

Is it new? No.

Social media (we used to call it Web 2.0) has been around for 20 years, having started life with channels such as Geocities in 1994. It is, however, merely an enhancement and an obvious progression from the radical democratization of content and the universal shift in power from media to consumer.

For anyone who has read my previous work they will know I obsess about this democratization and, like that old spinning gramophone record, will endlessly cite Apple's empowerment of the publishing generation of the 1980s, leading to the web in the 1990s, where ordinary folk could command their own social network through the creation, production and distribution of published material – an explosion in new magazine titles and newsletters, proliferations of direct mail and the rise of Joe Public as someone with a respectful/ wishful share of voice.

No surprise, then, to see this newly viable but potently powerful hunger for change seeping its way into other media. Was it the growth in video recording devices and their inevitable collapse in price that brought about behemoths such as YouTube? No, I do not believe so. I believe it is that human desire to be heard as well as seen – and when distribution and community was mixed into the cooking pot with affordability and speed to market, well, the rest is just history.

And speaking of history – let's take it back a further notch in time. What is it that makes social media work so incredibly well that it now demands more share of the web than pornography?!

FOMO? Is it the fear of missing out on something that causes us all to spend incredible shifts of time creating, updating and nurturing various online profiles (which, incidentally, seem to wildly contradict themselves across a variety of social media channels)? Do we struggle with authenticity as we use the medium to determine what part of our personality we want to project?

Or is it just that humans like shiny things? No need to delve into the primal attraction of media (or elements) that uses light to engage a human rather than coloured paper or an accompanying vibration of radio sound waves... one ride on the London Underground during rush hour will show anyone where media now lives. On mobiles, on tablets, on laptops... all the little faces lit up as they are engaged in what McLuhan used to call 'hot media', that which requires a limit of sensory engagement – are we absorbing less as we reach out more? I sometimes think so.

And what of our 21st-century lifestyles – smaller families, bigger houses, more stuff than ever and a global population that is 10 times what it was 100 years ago, with a planet that reportedly can sustain about half of us. Have we increased our use of social media to give us more share of voice? Will it matter how many friends we have? Is this a weird new form of natural selection? (SHUDDER).

One thing is for sure, social media legitimizes isolation. Years ago I wrote a piece marvelling at how Starbucks and Facebook seem to have at least one thing in common – and that is their incredible ability to allow people to be on their own but together with other people on their own. Yet does one's use of social media measure their capacity to manage solitude? Should marketers selling family planning solutions seek out those with the least amount of friends?

And what would Marshall McLuhan think?

(See **http://en.wikipedia.org/wiki/Tetrad_of_media_effects**.)

He would have a field day with social media – he would gloat over its enhancement of the modest telephone call. He would be thrilled to see the retrieval of the old-fashioned pen-pal experience and he would undoubtedly bow his head in memory of the obsolete letter-writing era and wonder, as I do, where on earth will this go next – what will social media become and what media is ahead in our future into which it will inevitably reverse?

Will Facebook be around in 50 years' time? I can sense about 80 per cent of you shaking your head (sorry Mark!). Well, what about in 20 years' time? Or 10?

Things happen fast online. We are a collective of 2 billion people that is about to become 6 billion people over the next five years, as emerging markets get on board and help to show us all the way forward. Online brands that existed 20 years ago are long forgotten now, such is the fickle nature and increasingly sophisticated demands of online consumers.

And now we're wearing tech – this should come as no surprise either. Nike wristbands and Jawbone have been paving the way for years. Google glasses, I suspect, have some way to go as applications pursue tech.

I wrote about virtual assistants in *Understanding Digital Marketing* in 2011 – the idea was actually spawned from watching an old episode of *Knight Rider*! We are heading towards an entirely and unfathomably powerful era where social media, big data and wearable technology will combine – VAs will think for us, understand our preferences, realize our budgets, direct us, remind us, and bring us more opportunities to have as much time as possible for doing whatever we need to do in order to pay for the tech in the first place. I'm just not sure why we would want to make this wearable when we could go the whole hog and have a VA surgically implanted – neural media, now there's got to be another book in that, right?

I believe that social media is at the heart and will be front and centre of this technical revolution in the coming years. Whether or not Facebook will offer implants remains to be seen, but they and other leading channels have sparked a mind-shift in what media will mean and what consumers will want from both media and marketers in the years ahead.

However brilliantly we continue to innovate, marketers must be mindful of a rising dissent among consumers when it comes to 'overtargeting' or 'intrusive' behaviour by advertisers. In 2014 we saw the advent of Ello – a new social media network that promises not to sell advertising or trade consumer data with brands. Whether or not this will become a genuine competitor to Facebook remains to be seen but Ello has raised US $500 million in venture capital already and, at the time of writing, is receiving 45,000 requests per hour for membership!

This is why it is important that digital marketers do their best to understand social media and it is why you are now holding a book that will help you to do just that.

ABOUT DAMIAN RYAN

Damian is also the author of *Understanding Digital Marketing*, now the bestselling academic book of its kind, which is listed as number one in the genre on Amazon and is now required reading by over 100 universities and colleges. An estimated 100,000 marketers have now read at least one of his books. He is also author of *The Best Digital Marketing Campaigns in the World*, a sister publication to *Understanding Digital Marketing* and, of course, *Understanding Social Media*.

Damian is also founder and chairman of the Global Academy of Digital Marketing (GADM) (**www.gogadm.com**), a new collaborative movement comprised of digital marketers seeking knowledge, case studies, contacts and credible data to help them prosper. GADM is expected to go live in March 2015 to an estimated founder membership of over 40,000 senior digital marketers representing the world's leading brands.

Aside from his passion for digital media and digital marketing, Damian is also a partner with Mediaventura, the UK's leading corporate finance firm for the marcoms and martech sectors.

Damian lives in London, is the proud father of two daughters and when he's not working he enjoys Sunday lunches with friends, movies, music, climbing, golf, generally going out and having fun. More recently he's been spending lots of time with his girlfriend Tamara, especially in San Sebastian!

Damian can be contacted at **dryan@mediaventura.com** or through social media (*quelle surprise!*):

uk.linkedin.com/in/understandingdigital/
Twitter: **damianryan1**

ACKNOWLEDGEMENTS

Despite this being the book with my least amount of actual writing contribution to date, it has been the one with the greatest number of challenges. The revolutionary nature of the collaborative content proved too much for the faint of heart at times – I managed to confuse loads of people, most likely irritated many more and went through a steady stream of editorial assistants in the process. So you can't make an omelette without breaking a few eggs right?!

As ever there are lots of people to thank for the realization of this project. Miranda Glover who performed trojan work in the latter stages of the project as contributing editor. Also the guys at Upfront: Jody Osman and Emma Levett in particular. Thank you to Beckie Rowe. And thanks to the team at Kogan Page: Helen Kogan, Melody, Geraldine, Anna, Philippa, Megan and Sonya.

Later on in the book you will read more details of the 60 or so other writers who collaborated together on the creation of this book, some of whom I have worked with before but there are many new names too – and I am so grateful and proud that they gave their time, passion and energy, so wilfully deployed to help you (the reader) understand more about social media.

Thanks also to all those who contributed case studies – there are some really useful and entertaining campaigns to enjoy here.

I am particularly proud to see my lovely niece Danielle Ryan of Ryanair get involved in the book's creation; other contributors will forgive me for singling her out! In fact I'd like to extend that by dedicating this book to some of the other wonderful women in my life; my two charming daughters who now take great pleasure in introducing me to the coolest new apps, my Mum who turns 80 in 2014, my fabulous sisters (Frankie, Senay and Junko) and my darling

Tara who, despite the miles between us, is an inspiration and has my heart. We'll be sipping 'billie' soon!!

Finally I'd like to invite all readers to take part in future collaborative writing projects – please get in touch with us at **www.gogadm.com**.

Damian Ryan
Author-curator, Understanding Social Media

Also available by Damian Ryan:

The Best Digital Marketing Campaigns in the World II

In the second collection of *The Best Digital Marketing Campaigns in the World*, Damian Ryan presents an international showcase of the most successful digital marketing campaigns in recent history.

Full of behind-the-scenes insights into campaign strategy, implementation and results, it explores how businesses and agencies, large and small, have harnessed social media, blogs, video, e-mail, mobile and search to boost their brand and engage with consumers. Covering a wide range of world-class, award-winning campaigns including Red Bull and Stratos, Peugeot: Let Your Body Drive, and Students Beans' Freshersfields.com, *The Best Digital Marketing Campaigns in the World II* is an inspirational showcase of digital creativity. Providing a fascinating snapshot of the digital landscape and a privileged insight into some of the freshest, most creative thinking in the industry, this is a must-read for everyone studying or working in marketing and advertising.

ISBN: 978 0 7494 6968 9
Published by Kogan Page

Understanding Digital Marketing, 3rd edition

The world of digital media is changing at a phenomenal pace. Constantly evolving technologies are transforming not just how we access our information but how we interact and communicate with one another on a global scale.

Understanding Digital Marketing is a comprehensive and accessible guide to the world of digital marketing. One of the best-selling books in the industry, this third edition has been entirely updated to reflect key developments within the digital marketing sphere. New chapters cover topics such as online marketing metrics, content strategy and internal stakeholder management. The book also demonstrates how to harness the power of digital media and use it to achieve the utmost success in business.

Understanding Digital Marketing deals with key topics in detail, including:
search marketing, social media, Google, mobile marketing, affiliate marketing, e-mail marketing, customer engagement and digital marketing strategies.

Understanding Digital Marketing will help readers to:

- choose online marketing channels to get their products and services to market;
- understand the origins of digital marketing and the trends that are shaping its future;
- achieve the competitive edge to keep them ahead of the pack.

Essential reading for practitioners and students alike, and including in-depth insider accounts of digital marketing successes from top brands such as Harley-Davidson, Help for Heroes, MercadoLibre and the UEFA Europa League, *Understanding Digital Marketing* provides readers with tools to utilize the power of the internet to meet current and future business objectives.

ISBN: 978 0 7494 7102 6
Published by Kogan Page

Getting started – how to create a compelling social media programme 01

Welcome to the digital crossroads!

Many digital marketers (like you and me) find ourselves at the crossroads. We know that social media works in some way, but making it work for us and convincing our financial bosses to invest in a programme can often be challenging when, to the uninitiated, social media can suggest more about time-wasting and less about improving the bottom line for a business. Social means 'fun', right? Well, actually, getting social right is serious business, critical to the success or failure of your company or organization's future success. These days, if you don't have a social media strategy it would be fair to say that you don't have a strategy at all. Social is core.

Social media obsolesces call centres and customer care initiatives. It also retrieves from our recent past. Where we would previously have upheld the monetary value of vouchers and discounts, now social media offers a very different kind of reward – the human connection between diaspora. But what social media will reverse itself into is still relatively unknown. I have always predicted, for example, that Facebook will have its own television channel but in the style of a traditional format rather than a digital format. We have yet to see.

Some key rules to 'owning' your social media output can be defined, even if we are working within constantly moving parameters. These are business rules that are sound both inside and outside of the social media context:

- Rule one: understand your audience. How do they use social? How can your product or service be part of that discussion in a positive and proactive way?

- Rule two: test everything and find out what works – start small, test everything and go from there.

- Rule three: give it time.

- Rule four: if you want to measure success make sure you can, otherwise repeat rule three.

A question I often hear from organizations is: 'Who do you think should "own" the programme?' My answer varies, dependent on the scale, nature and make-up of the business. Yet, again, the same principles remain. Give ownership of your social media programme to the person or the people in charge of customer experience. Believe me when I say that 'customer experience' is going to be the great leveller and the ultimate definer of failure or success in the years ahead. I am intrigued as I watch the battle take place from the side-lines – like the proverbial Irish hurler on the ditch... big players such as Accenture, PricewaterhouseCoopers (PwC) and Deloitte want to own that space on behalf of their clients. Agencies recognize that this is the future too and are arming themselves for one hell of a ding dong – inside organizations we will undoubtedly see the discussion take place between 'marketing' and 'information technology'. Who do I think will win?

The person or group that becomes proficient with social media and understands digital marketing! Customer experience is the only currency that will make a real difference in the competitive world. Keep an eye on changing trends, new channels and emerging technologies by appointing someone in your team to keep on the ball, or outsource the job to a digital agency with the latest knowledge, or preferably do both.

Although the future is, broadly, unknown, there are clearly some new technological advances that are moving rapidly into the mainstream. Wearable technology is becoming important, but the move towards machine-to-machine and machine-to-device networks is fast taking us into deeper territory than this. Old media also has a role to play in future channels. Television should not seek to retain audience on its device; it should embrace the audience by offering all devices and provide an access-all-areas policy. For my money, the ultimate social media is neurologically based; but that really is in our future. Science fiction is rapidly becoming science fact. To explore more on this topic, read the extraordinary book *Virtually Human* by Martine Rothblatt (St Martin's Press, New York, 2014), for example, which takes us far beyond today's realms, into a world where artificial consciousness and 'uploading' drive a new dimension in human evolution.

But for now, back to today! When you start planning the next iteration in your social media programme, remember that there is no difference between a social media strategy and a digital strategy. The key is to go where your audience is.

In this chapter we are fortunate to have elicited three very different contributing perspectives. Each has a unique experience of employing social media. Danielle Ryan implements a social media programme for RyanAir; Richard Costa-D'sa, managing director and partner, of Jam, advises clients on their social media strategies; and Jemima Gibbons delivers social media programmes and workshops for start-ups. What is interesting is where, at this crossroads, the crossovers between their varied activities lie. The same questions come up over and over again.

Who are your customers? Where are you going to find them? The list of social media channels is endless and intimidating but it doesn't have to be. Understanding your brand, your objectives, your target customer base, when they are online, and what makes them tick, will help you to determine which social media channels will work most efficiently for you and your brand, product or service. In order for social media to work hard for you and your business, you must define what your objective actually is:

- Is it to drive awareness of your product or service?
- To drive traffic to your website?
- To optimize sales conversion?
- To create trust amongst your target group?
- To create an additional platform for customer care?

Or is it all of these and more? Those who will succeed over the next five to ten years need to take a step back and start to understand the broader importance of being a business with social thinking at its heart.

Let's hear what our experts have to say.

Danielle Ryan, digital channel and conversion manager, Ryanair

In today's digital world we must 'look social', but actually being social is a different ball game, one that requires planning and thought. There is no denying that our everyday lives are now engulfed by social media; we love to talk, we love to laugh and we love content. Not only is social media a great way to reach your target audience efficiently, or to share real-time, relevant, rich content, but social media forms part of our customers' user experience.

Breaking it down, user experience is about any interaction we have with brands, products or services that stimulates our emotions and ultimately our perceptions, online or offline, in a good or bad way. It is what makes our customers feel good; it drives loyalty, trust and ultimately the desire to spend with us instead of with a competitor. Nowadays, even if your brand doesn't have a Facebook page, for example, there is no getting away from the fact that an existing or potential customer could form a negative perception of your brand based on a post they have read, a video they have watched or a photograph they have seen, which has been posted or shared by a friend. Being social allows you to steer these conversations and perceptions in a way that suits you. It also provides you with a channel to reach out to customers directly, rather than having to wait for them to reach out to you.

Defining your target market

Who are your customers and where are you going to find them? The list of social media channels is endless and intimidating but it doesn't have to be. Understanding your brand, your objectives, your target customer base, when they are online, and what makes them tick, will help you to determine which social media channels will work most efficiently for you and your brand, product or service.

Defining your objectives

I'll put up my hands and say that there have been times when I have been guilty of 'social media – the afterthought'. Shameful, I know, but we have all been there. You're launching a new proposition, the landing page is about to go live and you realize something is missing – the share functionality, those cute little social media icons at the bottom of the page. You scurry over to the developer's desk or hurriedly open your content management system (CMS) to ensure they are added before someone else notices, but why? What are we trying to achieve by prompting our customers to 'tweet', 'share' or 'pin'? More importantly, what are we trying to achieve by adding yet another call to action to a landing page?

You should define your KPIs, your social media strategy should be measurable, and without understanding your return on investment (ROI) there is no way of knowing whether a particular channel is worth your time, effort and resource.

Tips

Top tips for creating a compelling social media programme

- Invest in resources to manage your social media channels.

- Understand your target audience and localize.

- Stay true to your brand values and tone of voice.

- Don't dilute your content and messaging – find a channel that works for your brand and your customers and get that one right before introducing more.

- Respond to customer queries in a timely manner.

- Remember – right time, right place, right customer.

- Share moments and plan ahead as much as possible. For example, the Oreo ad during the Super Bowl blackout – although absolutely brilliant, my guess would be that it didn't just happen that quickly, there was probably a team of people and designers on hand, getting ready and planning for any eventuality that could occur on the night, the result of which seriously paid off.

- Give your customers a good reason to join you (and to stay with you).

- Remember how cluttered these social media channels actually are. Ask yourself why someone would take notice of your post over a cute kitten, a funny video, or photos of their Saturday night out with their friends.

- Use social media as part of your overall marketing mix and not just in isolation.

Richard Costa-D'sa, managing director and partner, Jam

There are a number of reasons why clients come to see us. A few ask how they can get a bigger social presence, others how they can create content that people want to share. In those singular, blinkered objectives lies the inherent missed opportunity. It is clear that the emergence of social over the past few years has enlightened businesses to a new, more exciting reality. Those that are going to succeed over the next five to ten years need to take a step back and start to understand the broader importance of being a business with social thinking at its heart.

This is not about bigger social communities or top-ranking mobile apps, but much more about shaping your business around consumers and not traditional business structures. Look at the fastest growing and most successful businesses in the past five years (aside from the social platforms, of course) – brands such as Airbnb and Uber. What have they got in common? They are close to their customers and place customer experiences at the heart of their brand and products, using social media and technology as their levers. In fact, look at those businesses with the greatest valuation and you quickly see a correlation between their value and their social/cultural traction. Brands are winning the war through adding value to customers' lives in credible ways and making their customers' lives that bit better in the process. It is about more relevant content, more useful 'things' and less 'ads'.

These businesses have not got where they are through following the paradigm of advertising that was created and has not adapted in the past 20 years, but by reshaping it around the ever-evolving world of social and placing it at its core.

However, before I get into how businesses can succeed through building a compelling social media programme, let's first define the parameters of what I mean by social (which by the time you read this may even be a defunct word, and simply called digital). Social is a space where consumers, technology and media consumption have collided to create the most connected individuals the world has ever known. Where one-to-one communication is expected, where brands are created and destroyed each day by as little as 140 characters, where doing nothing as a business is simply not an option.

Well, that's the scary part out of the way. There is something much bigger in play, though. Never has a brand had a better opportunity to get closer to its customers, to collaborate and build futures together – to beta, to fail and do it again.

So, back to my earlier point; you have to set up your business for success. Create programmes with owners. Without it you get caught in a spiralling vacuum towards a 'like' number war, or worse still, launching more and more social platforms as new ones appear and tickle the fancy of the chief marketing officer (CMO).

To do this you get into the heart of the business. You write something bigger than a social strategy – as this simply does not capture the depth of the opportunity at hand. It is about placing social and its levers at the heart of the business – just look at brands such as Coca-Cola and Ford, for example, who have recently reshaped their structures and communications around social.

Given that I am writing this for just a small section in this book, let me outline the crib-notes version. Broadly speaking, there are five key steps to do this, as set out below.

Placing your social programme within the broader business context

Put the work in context. What is the bigger picture? What is the business trying to achieve? What are its three-year, five-year and seven-year plans? Then understand in which parts social can help to reframe. Remember this is not about being the biggest brand in social, or the most amusing brand on YouTube. This is about growing genuine business impact; average revenue per user (ARPU) and market share.

Too often we see the brief arrive without this in place. It has to be done – as it becomes the guiding beacon towards success, with the work built upon the requirements of the business, not a channel or individual marketer.

Auditing (what's our social impact to date?)

We often take over work from clients, lift up the lid and see in the first 30 seconds why they have booked a meeting. Hundreds of social pages, lots of pieces of content, lots of different parts of the business engaging consumers every day, *but* no common language, shared goals or, in many cases, impact.

And this is inherently where social has traditionally fallen down. Put simply, it could sit in many different parts of a business. It is not just marketing, it is also research and development (R&D). It is not just recruitment, it is also information technology (IT). So what you get is lots of 'owners' and lots of objectives driven by departments, not the business as a whole.

So this first phase is about understanding the lie of the land. This is done through a combination of desk research, but is importantly supplemented by interviews with all parts of the business (Marketing, Public Relations, Human Resources, R&D, IT, etc). This is where you get to understand the micro-pressures as well as the macro ones that help the framework within which the road map must work.

Ask yourself:

1 What have you done to date and what has worked?

2 What are people saying about you?

3 How are you performing?

4 What tools have you got?

5 How are you measuring success?

Creating a plan (understanding your social levers)

The reality is that social has such a wide-reaching benefit to support a business that I could write a whole book on it, but here are a few things that you will need to think about:

- *Social commerce*: how are we using social to drive more sales? Whether that is through social recommendations or things like slingshot, social is the new shop window where you can help your consumers to the till.

- *Social CRM*: what tools are you using to help connect the one-customer view? How are you building your social data into your traditional CRM platforms? The future is one-to-one personalized communications. Start now.

- *Social customer services*: in the next few years, the call centre as we have known it over the previous 30 years will have completely disappeared. Consumers will expect you to be listening to them where and when they are talking, not when you are ready to listen.

- *Social software*: there are so many pieces of technology these days that it makes it almost impossible to cut through the clutter. However, you can and must. These tools are the key to unlocking the potential – whether that is buzz listening tools or social data optimizers, they are the catalysts to success.

These are just some of the ways... think about PR and social, social platform strategies, dot-com and social integration. You will end up with probably around 30 tools that are bespoke to your business. Don't be scared by this. No one said it would be easy.

The reality is that you then need to prioritize. Although the building blocks can be run in parallel, you simply will not be able to do them all in time. Look back to the bigger objectives and pull out the one- to three-year delivery plan. Chunk it up and don't try to bite off too much. Remember, it is meant to be achievable, not a noose around your neck. It is also meant to be iterative. Even from the time I have written this to the time you read it, the space will have changed. It is about having a road map that keeps to its core principles and objectives, but can use different building blocks to get there. The broad themes will remain, the details won't.

Ownership (who gets the reins?)

So you have got yourself probably 30 building blocks that underpin your social business. Next you need to understand the person or team that will lead the delivery of your road map. This really depends on your business: the size of the organization, the appetite, the social maturity and the structure. However, it broadly fits into two established schools of thinking: the hub and spoke model or decentralized experts.

The hub and spoke model

The hub and spoke, as the name suggests, outlines a core central team that oversees the development of the above road map and essentially becomes a centralized social team in charge of delivering best practice, reporting, ideation etc. It is usually made up of people who will help you to deliver your building blocks, but as a start, a core team consisting of: a leader (head of social business), analyst, social marketing managers, community lead and media expert. Each of these people will have specific backgrounds and skills to help manage the road map, and each team created will be bespoke to the road map of that business. Brands such as Starbucks and McDonald's adopted this model in the infancy of social and have seen huge successes, not just in engagement with their customers but, importantly, in consistency of message, innovation and revenue.

Decentralized experts

In time, all businesses will run social through decentralized teams, where the social expertise is inherent in all employees, thus allowing the skills of social to flourish within different departments. Chief marketing officers (CMOs) will be digital natives; the chief information officer (CIO) will be looking at social tools as much as internal operations. However, to start you need a centre of excellence and focus.

Buy-in (who is going to support you?)

So you have outlined the road map based upon business priorities, and the team structure that the road map dictates and, believe it or not, you are only 10 per cent of the way there. What comes next is probably the hardest part: the bit where you have to win hearts and minds to make it happen; where it becomes less of a vanity, tick box exercise and becomes the blueprint for your business. This is the bit where good partners can only help you to a certain degree, with inspiration sessions, internal business sell-ins etc. However, the drive for change within any business has to come from within. The road map needs to be managed and stakeholders brought along on that journey. I have seen many businesses fail at this final stage. It is easy to talk about road maps and objectives, but it is hard to take businesses (especially established ones) on these new paths.

Tips

1   Make it ambitious. Talk in business metrics not social ones: ARPUs and EBITDA (earnings before interest, taxes, depreciation and amortization), not likes and downloads.

2   Involve all parts of the business up front. The stakeholder interviews and follow-ups are a chance to build rapport, not create fights for ownership.

3   Get a board level sponsor. It is the only way that you can take it from a road map to a plan with investment behind it. It is the chief executive officers (CEOs) talking on stage now about social media success stories – the likes of Mark Fields of Ford and Ana Botin of Santander – not the social media manager any more.

4   Surround yourself with brilliant partners, not salespeople. You will meet a lot of 'Holy Grail' solutions on this journey: you need people who can help you to cut through it all.

5   Build a team that is passionate about change; people who won't ever forget the bigger picture, but are ready to be flexible and understand that they won't always be the experts.

I feel bad in part for getting you only 10 per cent of the way, but the bit that comes next is the fun bit. It is the bit that turns the words into genuine change and, in the end, money on to the bottom line of your business – and hopefully makes people's lives that little bit better in the process.

Jemima Gibbons, social media strategist, writer and blogger

It is a well-worn cliché, but social media really is different from any other marketing channel you will use. In fact, the impact of social is such that it changes the way your other channels function: PR, advertising, experiential marketing, digital marketing, direct marketing and sponsorship can all be amplified (or restrained) by what you say or do on social media.

Your listening post

Social is powerful – and different – because it is driven by conversations, not campaigns. That means that the first part of any social media programme needs to focus on listening – to your customers and potential customers, your market and your competitors. This is a crucial point – the first action you need to take is passive, not dynamic. Listening is the essential – but often neglected – first step in creating your compelling social media programme.

This initial passive action is something that many businesses and individuals struggle with. Our natural urge is to rush headlong into social media, shouting our message from the virtual rooftops – only to get frustrated and discouraged when we realize that no one is paying us any attention. But in social (unlike other media) you are not paying for someone else's proven eyeballs – you build your own network, from scratch.

Once your presence on specific social networks is established, you will also be able to leverage the networks of other people. But first you need to establish who you are, prove your commitment and start to build meaningful relationships. This is why a compelling social media programme – built on the right foundation (aka listening) is so important.

Key questions you need to ask include:

- Who are my existing customers and what do they want?
- Who are my potential or target customers?

- Do I need to segment my customers and target customers into different groups and, if so, what are the key characteristics of each group?
- What are my customer (segment)s talking about?
- Where do my customers like to hang out online?
- What type of content do they like to consume and share?
- What are my competitors doing on social media?
- How successful are they?

Working the data

As you gather information, try to compile it into useable data that enables comparisons and benchmarking. You may find that spreadsheets work better than documents.

The great thing about social media – older, established platforms at least – is that the majority of content and profiles are publicly accessible. You can easily compare key metrics such as number of followers and the engagement rate between your own social media profiles and those of your main competitors. If you do not consider yourself to have any competitors, take five similarly sized organizations (in any sector) whose social media content you admire, and benchmark yourself against them.

There is also a number of free tools you can use to extract key data, pinpoint relevant conversations and identify influencers.

Patience is a virtue

Like the telephone or fax, social media benefit from positive network externalities – a positive network effect. In simple terms, this means that as each new user joins the network, they add value, and that value increases exponentially. Social networks become more valuable, the more users they have. In the same way, the more people that your brand or business can connect with, the more powerful your network will become.

Social media is not difficult – but the rules are different. Once you are aware of those rules, and know how to play by them, you will start to see the benefits – you will see how addictive it is as a business development, sales and marketing tool – once you really start gaining traction, you'll never look back.

Nurture your network and it will reward you, but be negligent and you will get nothing in return. A common misconception around social is that it is free. Social is not free. The networks and tools may be free (even the most expensive monitoring programmes offer free trials or freemium models), but the time and human resources that you will put into building your social presence are not.

Before you even embark on developing a social media programme, you need to think carefully about what you are ready or able to invest: an easy rule of thumb for a small company could be one hour per person per week. You might find that you have the budget to take on a full-time person devoted to social media, or a team. Once you have (realistically) agreed your resources, assign a cost to them. Later on you can use this to effectively find out (and monitor) how much you pay for each social interaction over time.

Setting your goals

Once you have assigned resources, look at your business goals for the next quarter, year (or whichever period you need to set a programme for) and decide where and how social media can help you to achieve them. You need to translate each business objective into a social media objective. So, for example, if a key business goal in the next 12 months is to increase sales by 10 per cent, there are a number of social media activities that can help you to reach that target: you could use social media to generate more leads, drive more traffic to your website, raise brand awareness or even directly increase sales (if you have social commerce set up).

Once you have defined your social media goals, set a numerical target or KPI against each goal. You may think that social is a creative process, and it is, but you need to set up strong parameters to ensure that every piece of content you create is working – the KPIs will define what 'working' means to you. Your targets should be ambitious but achievable – high enough to motivate you and your team, but not unrealistic.

The strategic game plan

From your earlier listening exercise, you should know enough about your market to know the type of content you should create, and where you should be creating it. Now you are ready to write a tactical plan. These are the questions you need to answer:

- What social networks should we focus on? (Choose two or three to start with.)
- What type of content should we be creating?
- What type of content should we be curating/sharing?
- What are our main topics? (Choose three or four ideally.)
- What is our tone of voice? (Very important but often overlooked – choose three words to describe your tone of voice and make sure that all team members are familiar with them.)
- Who do we want to be connecting with?
- What are our long-term objectives with social media?
- What are our quick wins?

Chapter conclusions

Achieving social media impact depends on your business understanding its key objectives, target market and creating authentic approaches that will make your audience believe in you. To achieve persistent engagement, work out exactly who your customers are, where you are going to find them and how your communications can add genuine value. The list of social media channels is ever-growing. Choose selectively based on your audience type and behaviours. Understand your brand's objectives in relation to your target groups. A social conversation should be a real conversation, not used as a bland opportunity for a marketing promotion. Work out what you want the conversation to achieve before you enter into it – and stay on message. Is the purpose to drive awareness of your product or service? To drive traffic to your website? To drive sales conversion? To create trust amongst your target group? To create an additional platform for customer care? Or is it all of these and more? Those who are going to succeed over the next five to ten years need to take a step back and start to understand the broader importance of being a business with social thinking at its heart.

CASE STUDY   Topman/Google

Client

Topman.

Provider

Google.

Brief

Launch world's first international shoppable Hangouts and debuts +Post Ads.

Overview

As one of the most fashion-forward brands in UK menswear, Topman is in the habit of making a huge statement at the British Fashion Council's event London Collections: Men. In 2014 the brand occupied the leading edge again by launching a packed programme of activity on Google+.

The approach

The ground-breaking initiative connected users more directly to products and unique experiences accessible only via social media. Through a YouTube livestream of the fashion show, the brand gave fans an exclusive opportunity to follow front-row celebrities, influencers and Topman designers during the event.

Viewers were able to access the catwalk and behind the scenes with co-hosts MTV presenter Becca Dudley, fashion expert Darren Kennedy and YouTube stars Jim Chapman and Marcus Butler. Footage from wearable cameras – positioned on British Fashion Council ambassadors, Topman personal shoppers, fashion photographers, and the show's PR and production teams – gave watchers a remarkable insiders' view. As a centrepiece to the innovative experience, Topman debuted the first-ever international shoppable Hangouts on Google+. With trends falling into the categories of Country Living, Simply Dapper and Sartorial Pop,

FIGURE 1.1   Topman and Google – the world's first international shoppable hangout

customers were able to buy multiple looks as worn by the hosts directly via the shoppable Hangouts app. Topman promoted the initiative extensively both online and offline, through the windows of their London flagship store at Oxford Circus (Figure 1.1) and with posters and billboards in the interior of the store, while a homepage takeover on the Topman website featured the live hangout. Not only was the real-time coverage projected in pubs in the London Soho area, but it was featured on stage at the fashion show itself.

Topman used the new interactive social ad format +Post Ads to promote the activity, too. This brand-friendly format was designed to make it easy to take a piece of Google+ content and quickly transform it into a lightbox ad that can run across over 2 million sites in the Google Display Network. Topman used the format to let all their fashion fans follow the news around the London Collections: Men show, before, during and after it took place, allowing followers to view the live hangout.

The results

The +Post Ads outperformed expectations, achieving an average engagement rate of 2.6 per cent. Meanwhile, the average viewing time of Topman's live Google+ coverage clocked in at 8 minutes 36 seconds. The shoppable Hangouts was another huge success, with an astounding 85 per cent of unique viewers clicking through to engage with products.

Overall, the total social reach of the activity is estimated at over 14 million (this represents the cumulative number of impressions of all posts from the owned media channels of Google, Topman, Joey Graceffa, Jim Chapman, Marcus Butler, Becca Dudley and Darren Kennedy). And because fashion week is all about creating buzz, the significant media coverage was another big win, with the story being picked up by style leaders including the British Fashion Council, *Fashion Times*, Fashion United, London Collections: Men, Fashion Beauty Insight and *PAUSE* magazine.

About Topman's positive results

- +Post Ads achieved average engagement rate of 2.6 per cent.
- Average 8 minutes 36 seconds viewing time of live Google+ coverage.
- 85 per cent of unique viewers clicked from shoppable Hangouts to engage with products.
- Total social reach estimated at over 14 million.

Client testimonials

'Working with Google so closely on our partnership during London Collections: Men and testing new display formats using our Google+ content was an exciting digital proposition for Topman. The results have been very positive with a strong engagement rate, and we look forward to running future campaigns on this platform.'

Callum Watt, digital marketing manager, Topman

'We're excited to be working with Google+ to showcase Topman's continued involvement at the forefront of London Collections: Men. Whilst taking users behind the scenes via exclusive access is great, the ability for them to then shop in real time for what our hosts are wearing on camera is a brilliant digital innovation.'

Jason Griffiths, marketing director, Topman

Rules governing the relationship between search and social

OUR CHAPTER PLEDGE TO YOU

When you reach the end of this chapter you will have the answers to the following questions:

- What emerging factors categorize the growing interdependency between search and social?
- How deeply is search influenced by social?
- Why is fresh content so important to search?
- What tools can help us to optimize our keyword selections?
- Where should we be 'talking', aside from on our own channels, to amplify the impact of our messages?
- How can we best engage with the blogosphere and how can it help us?
- How should our search/social media activity coexist in practical terms?

The new world of the three S's

We are moving towards the world of the three S's: content online is snackable, searchable and social. Most companies are yet to integrate their digital marketing efforts to address this change. Social media impacts on search results because sharing amplifies content and gives it searchable legs. If, for example, a tweet about a new indie film is shared 20 times and a blogger then picks up on it and writes about it, the content will become searchable. This renders the careful planning of content journeys across the social sphere critical to effective marketing of a product or service. Fresh content is the critical vehicle that carries your message from social to search. Producing regular, new content for your website and ensuring it is linked and tagged with your keyword will drive search engines back to your site more regularly, so that they might, for example, index new product pages or changes more rapidly. Google prefers to deliver new content for many search queries, providing you with an opportunity to get your blog and social posts keyword rankings, which otherwise would be very difficult to attain. If you are creating content but failing to optimize it for search then you are not even beginning to integrate search and social. Without integration you will miss opportunities to generate substantial traffic and sales with organic and paid search.

To do this successfully you first need to do your research. Pinpoint the keywords that work for you then look for gaps in your existing content. Everything you publish for your brand should be designed to be shared socially, so always include like and share buttons that make it easy for your followers to make recommendations – it is essential extra, and free, marketing for your offer. If people find you through search and like what they get, they may well share it with their friends.

As well as producing great, pertinent content that is on message and timely for your audience, you need to generate genuine engagement with those influencers whose comments, links, likes and shares will help it find its way into the top search results. By that I don't mean sending blanket e-mails out to bloggers. Get their true attention by reading their blog, following them on Twitter, retweeting their messages and commenting on their Facebook pages. Once you get into a two-way conversation with them, they are more likely to want to share some of the content you offer them, or to a link to a page that you have shared.

Historically, search engines have used links from other websites to identify the topic of a page and to measure its importance and authenticity. But in the past couple of years we have witnessed its widespread abuse in the form of orchestrated, artificial link-building. It is therefore no surprise that search engines are turning to social to help them deliver better results. Google+ should be monitored closely for opportunity. It may not yet have a direct impact on our rankings, but that is likely to change. Your Google+ profile image already appears in search results, for example. That alone could help to improve your organic search click-through rate. The rules governing search and social may not be set in stone but the relationship is both strong and growing... and it is definitely not going away. Every social media network has some type of search functionality. As social media usage has risen, so has the volume of searches on these networks (YouTube is the second largest search engine behind Google; and Twitter receives around 2.1 billion queries per day).

It is worth contemplating how search engine optimization (SEO) principles can be used to impact ranking directly on the various social media channels. They may not be as clear and researched as Google ranking factors, or as straightforward to implement (Facebook has stated that their News Feed has 100,000 ranking factors, which makes Google sound simple), but there are still many ways in which you can increase visibility of your brand and content within the social media channels themselves.

In this chapter, we are fortunate to present two very different views on the rules governing the relationship between search and social. Joseph Morgan uses both to engage with customers for global brands, while Elaine Lindsay advocates smart content management to small and medium-sized enterprises (SMEs) to help them focus on social that counts. The case studies share a broader experience of using content in social spaces to engage with target groups and amplify message effectively, whether by building shareable apps or creating Facebook campaigns.

Joseph Morgan, director of strategy, Matter Of Form, The Brand Interactions Agency™

Search and social media are two of the fastest-changing mediums in the communication landscape; affected (as all communication is) by both macro and micro trends. Each area is surrounded by much of the same debate: what data is being collected? How is the data being collected? Is it ethically right to monetize people's supposedly private information? The list is extensive.

Some question whether search and social are actually two sides of the same coin, both serving our insatiable desire to extract more information from the world around us, and are inevitably destined perhaps to share the methods in which they go about achieving the same objective. For example, is Twitter a social or search platform? What about YouTube? Ultimately, the marketing communications industry features two types of people: 1) generalists who (try to) visualize the bigger picture, describing scenes of blurred lines and blending media channels; and 2) specialist niche players, who report the ongoing fragmentation of their areas of interest into deeper and deeper subcategories.

In truth, both trends are happening at once. At a broader level, different core strands of popular media are converging; but at a more granular level these central strands are also producing smaller off-shoots, which are branching off exponentially into further esotericism.

The reality is that convergence can be temporary, cyclical and subject to mass change, caused by a multitude of variables that, while undoubtedly interesting, would not be helpful to digress into in this chapter.

This brings us to the point of this contribution to the chapter: the task of discerning some of the top-level rules that govern the relationship between search and social. And as you may have picked up on from the casual (yet not so subtle) narrative penned thus far, it is not one that is answered with much confidence or clarity.

Rather, it is plagued by ambiguity, guesswork and lack of information. So let's start at the beginning, with what we know. You will be glad to hear that your reading thus far has not been in vain; we do know that there is a relationship between search and social. However, the exact nature of this relationship varies over time, and often depends on which 'expert' one canvasses for opinion (ourselves included).

In fact, the actual dynamics of the bond apparently reaches so far into the complex sphere of always-changing technical wizardry that not even Matt Cutts, Google's head of webspam and popular blogger on all things SEO-related (**http://www.mattcutts.com/blog/**) knows the complete extent as to what the connection is between the two – which, perhaps quite oddly, forms the basis for the first rule that we should put onto paper:

1 *The relationship between social and search is complex and always changing. You will never know it all.*
Yes, when written down in plain English it can all seem a bit depressing: there is not any one person alive who can truly define the relationship between search and social. However, there is a little light at the end of the tunnel should you be of a positive disposition; because, whilst we must accept our fallibility in terms of comprehending and making sense of the relationship, we must also recognize that the field in which we are competing is somewhat equalized by a ubiquitous lack of supreme knowledge. And so begins the addictive, never-ending game of learning and optimization, which we cordially invite you to join.

Which leads us to rule number 2:

2 *The only rules are the latest rules. Compete by educating yourself through fast-moving, up-to-the-minute mediums.*
The search engines and social networks are constantly updating their modus operandi; meaning that books such as this one are of course useful for overall guidance, but are not updated quickly enough to keep you fully abreast of the information you need to know in order to compete and succeed. Even hard-copy mediums that are more regularly published, such as magazines and press, are too often out of date by the time you read them. To navigate this fast-moving field the best advice is to regularly get online and read a

broad spectrum of the most up-to-date blogs and news sources, such as:

- SEO Moz: **http://moz.com**;
- Search Engine Watch: **http://searchenginewatch.com**;
- Occam's Razor: **http://www.kaushik.net/avinash/**;
- Social Media Examiner: **http://www.socialmediaexaminer.com**;
- Jeff Bullas: **http://www.jeffbullas.com**;
- Addictive Mobile Weekly Fix (sign up for their weekly e-mail): **http://www.addictivemobile.com/blog/**;
- and, of course, our website: **http://matterofform.com/**.

The next rule on our polylateral list of rules concerns what sits at the heart of not just search and social, but at the crux of all media and communication, and this is content. At the time of writing, the word 'content' and the practice of 'content marketing' is getting a lot of press, so please know that using these commonly used buzzwords in this chapter hurts us just as much as it hurts you. However, sometimes there is a kernel of truth and validity that lies at the nexus of the hype, and with search and social the issue of content will always be a significant topic of discussion (as it arguably should always be).

The simple fact is that regardless of the relationship between search and social, both mediums will always rely on relevant content to fuel their success and usage. A search engine or social platform that cannot find and deliver relevant content to users is a platform that is likely not long for this world.

This does not mean that one should produce content and throw it everywhere across the various social networks and search engines, it means that one must have an understanding of what content the user or users you are looking to communicate with are looking for, and find a way to meet this need across the varying mediums, crafting the execution(s) in line with the various formats and cultures seen across the landscape. Successful Tumblr content is presented very differently to that of Google, Bing, Facebook, Vine, Pinterest, Instagram and so on. To design relevant content one must develop a process for identifying what users are looking for; helping you to create, curate, format and distribute such content into the search and social sphere, whilst ensuring it contributes to your agenda in some way.

Common methods for finding such insight are keyword research (the practice of looking at the popular search terms around particular topics or websites), using tools such as Google Adwords (**www.google.com/adwords/**) or conducting social listening (viewing trends in conversation over social networks) with digital products such as followerwonk.com, sysomos.com and so on.

At Matter Of Form we use our proprietary content engine framework to help formalize the process of canvassing and compiling different data inputs and research, and developing that information into relevant content themes and strategies for creation, curation and deployment. We see this as an ongoing, circular process; used to constantly iterate on existing approaches and capitalize on new trends or change, as and when it happens – which lands us squarely on rule number 3.

   3 *Develop a method for creating, curating, formatting and*
   distributing the most relevant content for your audience(s),
   across the most appropriate platforms and channels.
   For business owners and agencies, the choice of how
   to engage in these activities, either for self-promotion or
   for clients, is a common one (if one buys the argument
   that one must be engaged at all). Is the right choice to
   bring these capabilities 'in-house', work with specialist
   agencies in each of the domains, or find a partner with an
   all-in-one solution?
      Our recommendation on this point would be to keep your
   social, content and search efforts as close as possible. Even
   agencies that promise an integrated offering will likely split
   out the three elements across their place of work. Some may
   argue that this is not the case, and that their triumvirate happily
   snuggles around the fire at Christmas, but unfortunately it is
   predominantly not true. Having worked in digital for many
   years, we can testify that even the more progressive
   organizations will only keep two out of the three together
   (typically content and social in a newsroom-style affair), but
   inevitably one of the teams (search) are left in the basement

doing things that no one else understands or has the patience to really listen to. Which segues us neatly into the fourth provocation: a piece of advice relevant to those looking for an agency partner to handle the work, or looking to do it themselves.

4 *Structure your team so that search, social and content effortlessly cross-pollinate each other's work; ensure cross-disciplinary agents connect the dots and provide the macro-generalism to the micro-specialists.*

Rule number 4 is important, because if we know that there is a relationship between search, social and their chief enabler, content – and we recognize that agility is critical to staying up-to-date with the dynamic movements of the three domains – then it makes no sense to silo off the various faculties into different teams, because they can (and should) help each other to build better, more relevant and more successful work.

At Matter Of Form we have always kept search, social and content together, employing both cross-functional generalists to leverage the opportunities thrown-up by ongoing media macro-convergence, and specialists who better understand the intricacies of the different platforms, how best to use them, and the fragmentations thereof.

This brings us to our closing statement, and the last rule we would like to explicate. However, arguably this final rule is not a rule, it is a law. It is simple yet cardinal, and you should never forget it. The search and social roadside is filled with players who were tempted by the dark side of the force: those who chose to take a cheeky sip from the golden chalice or a quick chow-down on the magic beans. But they all suffer at the hands of the platforms eventually. And whether it is buying back-links, keyword-stuffing your pages, purchasing likes and followers, or engaging in any other form of subterfuge, please do not be seduced by the alluring call of the search and social sirens. You will be blacklisted – and you (or your clients) will not like it. The fifth rule therefore is:

5 *Never cheat. It doesn't pay (for long).*

Elaine Lindsay, international speaker and media consultant

'I'm craving steak. What was that new restaurant? I know I saw it the other day in my stream, not sure what platform; I think it was my friend Patricia Wall who mentioned it. Wait a minute, maybe it was one of her friends? I can't remember. That's okay because the search engines will find it for me.'

Back in 2011, I predicted that social platform interactions would start to have an impact on search results. By 2012, Google had started to prove my prediction. These days, everything happening on social has an effect on search results.

Now I make a point of responding to posts that have something interesting, such as a restaurant or funky shoes, as my response will be the trigger for the search engines to include related information the next time I'm asking them to trigger my memory of a restaurant. This works for my friends too, as my social network activity affects their search results just like their social activity can affect mine. Plussing or commenting on any post is like building a scrapbook online. I don't have to look back through the scrapbook of my platforms for my comments, because the search engines are integrating many social interactions for me. In fact, if I'm clever with my search phrase, it could bring up the actual post that mentioned the restaurant to remind me of the name. I hope the restaurant in question has claimed their free Google Places page so that they are easy to find. For restaurants, and any bricks-and-mortar businesses, a Google Places page will impact any local search. If they don't have a site, maybe they have taken advantage of a directory site such as Yelp or Urbanspoon in order to have some web presence.

I hope you are updating all your profile information regularly as that is how your clients find you. When you are active on your social platforms, commenting on and sharing those interesting posts, you become easier to find. When you take advantage of social platforms directly linked to Google, Google+ and YouTube, you are really loading the search in your favour. The advent of Google's semantic search makes your efforts in social have an important impact on your ability to be found in search.

Besides making great friends and discovering cool stuff online, building your online scrapbook of interests is part of building your presence as an interesting person that your potential clients can come to know, like and trust.

Chapter conclusions

The search engines and social networks are constantly updating their modus operandi. To design relevant content one must develop a process for identifying what users are looking for; helping you to create, curate, format and distribute such content into the search and social sphere, whilst ensuring it contributes to your agenda in some way. The rules are that there are no hard and fast rules, just an essential, ongoing cycle of analysis, testing and optimization. What is true, however, is that there is a critical relationship between search and social. They work hand in hand and need to be understood in context of one another.

CASE STUDY   Young and Well Co-operative Research Centre/Zuni

The client

Young and Well Co-operative Research Centre (CRC) – an Australian government-funded body.

The agency

Zuni.

Campaign

The Safe and Well online project.

The challenge

Treating mental health issues in children and young adults currently costs the Australian government AUS $98.3 million each year. Mental health issues are brought on by many factors, but research conducted by Zuni and the Young and Well CRC identified that body image in particular was a key trigger for mental health issues in young adults. It affected self-esteem, general well-being and could lead to more serious issues such as social isolation and depression. The cultural ideal of body image – in large communicated through the media – has a huge impact on the well-being of all people but in particular adolescents, who are voracious users of mobile and social media channels that are largely unmonitored by parents, teachers and authority figures.

A cynical, hard-to-influence target audience

Our target audience was 12- to 17-year-olds. Focus groups conducted with young adults in 2013 by Zuni and Young and Well CRC told us that as an audience this age group had 'heard it all before'. They were resistant to authoritative messaging from adults. These digital natives were highly media savvy and could be cynical and tough to please. They didn't want to be patronized and had a nose for sniffing out the inauthentic.

These formative years are the time when even the most robust youth struggles with insecurity regarding their image, as their body undergoes huge change. A sudden growth spurt, the appearance of breasts, bad skin or a breaking voice can create unwanted attention and great upset. At this life stage acceptance from their peers is craved, so anything that makes them stand out for the wrong reasons is hugely problematic. Social media and associated cyber bullying can add to self-doubt and dislike, and create the feeling that these problems are both insurmountable and inescapable.

The viral nature of social media was exacerbating the issue

While providing young adults with increased connectivity, social media had also added a new pressure point on their self-image. Young and Well CRC set themselves the challenge of building young people's resilience to negative body image pressures.

As an example, in 2013 the mainstream media reported on, and largely criticized, a trend that swept through social media – that of the 'thigh gap', a seemingly unattainable physical ideal that was driving teen girls to diet to unhealthy levels.

This trend was all the more worrying as it was proliferated through the social web, from peer to peer. Research done by Young and Well CRC taught us that for young adults, despite the hype and noise surrounding them, their best friends – or the boyfriend/girlfriend or person they had a crush on – still remained a key influence on their body image.

A topic young adults are reluctant to discuss seriously

The perception of body image as a problem leads to a reticence to discuss it. Young adults viewed it as something they could distance themselves from. It is an issue you cannot see or hear, or – in the traditional (advertising) sense – measure; one that young adults did not really want to discuss in the open, and especially not with a government body.

A government organization attempting to influence young adults

To shift young people's attitudes and perspective on their own body image in a genuine way, we needed to change their behaviour. Thinking around behavioural marketing suggested that behaviour change was more likely to occur when:

- people witness other people taking part in that changed behaviour;
- people view the changed behaviour as rewarding;
- people view the changed behaviour as socially valuable.

How to effect that change when the campaign was coming from the exact authority figure that young adults distrusted, without being rejected by them for appearing too contrived, was not going to be easy.

Tackling mental health with technology

The increased role of technology and the internet in the lives of young adults prompted Young and Well CRC, a government-funded body, to launch the Safe and Well online project.

The remit of the project was to examine the role of technology in the lives of 12- to 25-year-olds and work out ways that technology can be used to improve the mental health and well-being of young people. The primary objective of the campaign was to make young adults feel better about themselves. More specifically, we wanted to see at least a 35 per cent uplift of young adults claiming a positive emotion after campaign use. In order to achieve this we would need:

- 36,000 unique visitors (which represents a 25 per cent increase on the previous campaign);
- average dwell time with the campaign of more than one minute;
- for people to recommend the campaign to friends: 40 per cent;
- for visitors to the site to share content from it: 10 per cent;
- for them to return to the campaign site: 10 per cent.

Target audience

Our target audience was 12- to 17-year-olds.

Action – individual concerns, universal desires

Young and Well CRC's focus groups and workshops with teens helped us to gain a better insight into what concerned and motivated young adults to take action online. The results were vital in shaping our strategy.

While individually young adults worried about a myriad issues – growth spurts, spots, being too tall, being too small, nose too big, chin too small, too thin, too fat, no boobs, boobs that are too big – they were united by very similar desires, namely:

- 'I want to feel more confident about who I am.'

- 'I want to feel accepted.'

- 'I want to be inspired.'

- 'I want to help my friends feel good about themselves.'

While they were each struggling with self-confidence, they also wanted to help the people they cared about to feel better about themselves.

The insight

The teenage years are characterized by monumental physical changes that often result in teenagers focusing on the negative. They have a tendency to dwell on what they believe is wrong with them. However, their true close friends can brighten their day by simply pointing out their positives and helping them to see themselves with fresh eyes. Interestingly, social media could help them to help their friends feel better about themselves because it gave them a window into the highs and lows and minutiae of their daily lives (through the content they shared in social).

Our strategy

To influence and change young people's attitude to body image by giving them a means by which to get involved and celebrate their unique features and differences. We believed that offering young adults a fresh perspective on their positive traits would help them to rise above their doubts and fears. Spinning a perceived negative into a positive led us to our central thought: 'Everybody has a feature worth celebrating'.

Our tone: focus on involvement not preaching

Talking about the issue in a new way was not going to be enough. Young people do not like being told what to do or think. Preaching is ineffective at creating behaviour change.

The solution

Appreciate a Mate: an online tool that enables young people to generate compliments for and about their peers. Authenticity was key. We knew our young adults didn't want to be preached to, especially by an authority figure.

Our idea was to create a tool that young adults felt they owned. A platform they could use to help their friends spread positivity and acceptance. We developed a digital platform called Appreciate a Mate – a mobile-optimized website and iPhone app whose functionality was simple:

- Step 1: find a compliment that you would like to share with a mate.

- Step 2: customize it.

- Step 3: share it with your social networks and tag the mate you are appreciating.

We approached the campaign in three core phases:

- Phase 1: co-design and development.

- Phase 2: promoting it.

- Phase 3: testing, optimization and extension.

Phase 1: co-design and development

We didn't want to tell young adults what to say – rather, we wanted to give them a tool to help them express themselves and the positive things they saw in their friends. We held R&D sessions with schoolchildren to create a pool of positive quotes that would form the backbone of our digital platform (app and website). This pool of quotes was written and selected by our test group and, as such, captured compliments in an authentic way that addressed the confidence issues plaguing young adults.

Given we were asking young adults to share these messages with friends across social networks, they needed to be aesthetically pleasing and true in style to the types of content that were already being shared across social networks such as Tumblr, We Heart It, Facebook and Instagram. We needed the content to have the 'cool' factor if we wanted it to have the necessary cred in order for it to be shared.

We reached out to the design community and asked designers to create a beautiful piece of typography that would go into the app. The response was immense and our first iteration of the mobile site featured designs from 33 designers across the world.

The platform

In order to ensure accessibility for as many young adults as possible we created a mobile site (that was also accessible via desktop). For those with smartphones, the site featured a prompt to add a home tile to their screen. Once that was done it could be accessed like a regular app.

Phase 2: promoting Appreciate a Mate

Knowing our audience suggested it was important that the tool be something they discovered and therefore 'owned' themselves. As such, launching it from Young and Well CRC's digital channels was not an option. So, we created @ppreciateamate accounts across the platforms we knew young adults were using (We Heart It, Facebook, Instagram and Tumblr) and began to populate them with our appreciate tiles. We then followed key influencers and encouraged them to share the positive images with their friends and networks. Shareability was a central function of the app and site. It encouraged users to create and design their own quotes then share them across a number of social networks. This further increased the reach of @ppreciate and its positive messages.

We created a media strategy that ensured the application was put in the hands of our target audience. Within our target audience of young adults, young men were identified as a priority. We brought on board an ambassador, Glen Thurston, a pro-bodyboarder and youth advocate with a huge following of young male adults who looked up to him – who he could speak directly to and engage that audience.

Glen promoted the app to his 26,000 Facebook fans and 4,000 Instagram followers. We also got support from *Riptide Bodyboarding Magazine* on their owned social channels, where they posted to their 72,000 followers and 14,000 Instagram followers four times over the course of two weeks.

Alongside support on social platforms, we secured two editorial spots in *Riptide Bodyboarding Magazine* and ran a competition with the publication, inviting their readers to submit their own positive compliment. Display media also ran across Riptide's online publication inviting young adults to try the Appreciate a Mate platform, serving 65,471 impressions.

Phase 3: testing, optimization and extension

Our mobile site was only step one for Appreciate a Mate. We went back to our test group of young adults, working with them to develop additional quotes that were used to refresh the existing stack of quotes we had. We also went back to our designers for them to add their magic to the quotes and bring them to life in a way that would appeal to our young adults. Recently we took this opportunity to adapt our mobile site into an app, which launched into the app store in January 2014. This allowed us to incorporate additional functionality, promote Appreciate a Mate in the app store, and run additional display media on mobile, encouraging young adults to discover and download our new mobile application.

Links to campaign

http://www.appreciateamate.com/

About the creator

The Young and Well CRC is an Australia-based, international research centre that unites young people with researchers, practitioners and policymakers from over 75 partner organizations across the non-profit, academic, government and corporate sectors.

CASE STUDY Crabtree & Evelyn/Über

Client

Crabtree & Evelyn.

Agency

Über.

Brief

Campaign for hand therapy hand cream.

The challenge

Handy Tips Handed Down was an integrated campaign with all the online and social elements designed and developed by Über to help promote Crabtree & Evelyn's bestselling hand therapy hand cream. The luxury beauty and body-care brand approached Über to develop a six-week social-led digital campaign to engage its Facebook and Twitter followers to share their best-loved beauty tips in exchange for a £5 voucher to put towards any hand therapy product online or in-store. Social was chosen to help improve the brand's presence and visibility amongst a younger target audience, and the online beauty community. The campaign was also extended to include a dedicated microsite for users without social media profiles.

As part of the campaign Über created a fully fledged social media content campaign comprising partnerships with beauty bloggers and key influencers in the online beauty community, as well as competitions and viral videos.

Tips were uploaded by social media users to the dedicated microsite and Facebook application. Social media users were also able to share tips with one another via Facebook and Twitter, and the hashtag #crabtreehandytips was also launched to further the campaign's viral reach.

Über also commissioned two prominent beauty bloggers to help widen the campaign's reach to its target audience. Crabtree & Evelyn's in-house marketing team chose to extend the campaign beyond online and social to include in-store marketing collateral comprised of live window displays and in-store events.

Target audience

Crabtree & Evelyn is already an established brand for female customers in the 40+ ABC1 customer profile. However, as part of the Handy Tips Handed Down campaign, Crabtree & Evelyn wanted to extend the appeal of its hand therapy hand cream to a younger audience without alienating its core customer.

With this in mind, the Handy Tips Handed Down campaign was developed to focus on the universal appeal of hand care products, and the cross-generational ritual of sharing and passing on beauty tips.

With Crabtree & Evelyn's core audience in mind, Über extended the campaign to include a dedicated microsite. This allowed customers without social media profiles to participate in the campaign and upload their tips.

In addition to appealing to a younger customer, the brand also wanted to promote its website and e-commerce platforms and make customers aware of its stores nationwide.

Action

Über developed a dedicated microsite and social media application to allow customers to upload their tips and receive a £5 voucher to put towards any hand therapy product online or in-store. The initial idea was to have tips uploaded to a tree inspired by Crabtree & Evelyn's own branding and this design was applied across the microsite. The Facebook application was also developed with a like gate to encourage customers to like the brand's Facebook page and increase its brand following on Facebook.

The tree included six separate sections to help organize tips into categories. Upon uploading a tip to the tree, users were immediately rewarded with a message and call to action to share the campaign with friends. Users were able to share these tips across various social media platforms and also vote for their favourite tips within the application.

Every participant received a special voucher via e-mail to thank them for taking part in the campaign.

Over the course of the campaign over 1,300 tips were added by unique users to the online tree, creating an entirely crowdsourced bank of knowledge curated by Crabtree & Evelyn customers. To support the application, Über developed a six-week content schedule across Facebook and Twitter. Content included products, competitions and selected tips from the tree. The hashtag #crabtreehandytips was also launched to further the campaign's viral reach.

In addition to image-led content, Über produced a series of viral videos featuring members of the Crabtree & Evelyn marketing team to serve as inspiration for potential tip posters. The videos were used across the microsite, Facebook, Twitter and YouTube and were seen by thousands of participants.

Über also approached members of the online beauty blogging community to take part in the campaign, commissioning YouTube bloggers Miss Budget Beauty and Hollie from Give Me More to film short videos of them discussing their favourite beauty tips with friends and family, and produce sponsored content for the brand.

Results

What they achieved – statistics, graphs, revenue etc:

- 22 per cent increase in Facebook followers;
- 1,259 comments, shares and likes on Facebook;

- 584 per cent increase in Facebook page reach in the first week alone;

- 1,562 tweets relating to the social media campaign and hashtag #crabtreehandytips;

- 13 per cent increase in Twitter followers and increased reach of over 180,000 Twitter users thanks to tweets;

- 30 per cent increase in traffic to **www.crabtree-evelyn.co.uk**;

- a significant increase in sign-ups to the Crabtree & Evelyn loyalty scheme.

Links to campaign

http://crabtreehandytips.co.uk

CASE STUDY   James McCabe/Hit Social

Client

James McCabe.

Agency

Hit Social.

Brief

Content and promotion on Facebook page.

Overview

Hit Social were asked to provide a couple of months' content and run a promotion on the James McCabe Facebook page. The prize was one of the brand's own watches; the brief to obtain as many page likes as possible. We decided to use the free Easypromos app for this.

James McCabe Watches
2,822 likes · 656 talking about this

Jewelry/Watches
In celebration of the late great watchmaker James McCabe our timepieces honour his life and times and bring to life his history for all watch enthusiasts.

About – Suggest an Edit

2,822   WIN!

Photos   Likes   Win A Victory Watch   Browse our Watches

SOURCE: Image used with permission from Dartmouth Brands Ltd.

Approach

The competition was pushed out to Facebook and other social media channels. When the competition ended, we had taken the page from 11 likes to over 2,800 likes, just in a couple of months.

Outcome

If you want to attract more followers to your social networks, a competition or promotion is an excellent way of doing so. Just follow each network's guidelines and push the competition to all relevant sources.

How to budget for social media activities

03

OUR CHAPTER PLEDGE TO YOU

When you reach the end of this chapter you will have the answers to the following questions:

- What is the difference between owned, earned, shared and paid media?

- What KPIs should I use to monitor performance and ROI?

- How should I structure my social media team to get the best return?

- How can I improve the performance of all our actions?

- How can I plan my spend across brand seasons?

- What activities should I outsource and what is most cost-efficient to keep in-house?

- What tools are worth paying for?

- How can I split out the costs of my social media activity to clarify value to my chief financial officer (CFO)?

So where is the spend really going to get us?

Maybe it has a lot to do with the word 'social' itself. I can almost hear a CFO I know mumbling under his breath, 'Work is called work for a reason. If it was a social activity we'd call it fun.' Planning your social media budget can be far from entertaining and getting it signed off by your CFO can prove an even harder task. It's easy to see why. Many marketers will still confess, if only in private, to being unclear as to the true fiscal value of their social media spend. Embedding the personality of your brand with your customers through social engagement may have been a primary KPI a year ago, but now finance officers are seeking more concrete financial returns for their ever-increasing investment in the space. And with that comes more planning of where the money is going out to and how it is coming back in. This requires the development of robust, seasonal pro-grammes that are budgeted and line-itemized. It makes sense that marketers who are most in control of their spend are the same ones who can readily prove its value in return.

The social landscape is changing as fast as I write this down. The 'free' communication arena where companies could channel their communications direct to their 'freely available' users has rapidly grown up and taken on the capitalist attributes of its creators. Social media is by no means a free space any longer. Where there used to be ample opportunities for creative content producers to grab a free win on a viral campaign, now there is a gamut of advertising options and super-smart free and paid-for tools to support your channel activities and analyse their effect. Trina Albus, president of the Magenta Agency, rightly ascertains in her contribution to this chapter that, as social media grows even more crowded, brands will no longer be able to survive on social media with an organic-only strategy. Marketers have to put their hands in their pockets and amplify their social engagement using big data and hard cash. The problem is that speed of change in the social media landscape is so rapid that there is no time to wait for the paint to dry before people plan their next spend.

So how *can* you decide where to spend your budget in this climate of constant reinvention? Start by being very clear about your business objectives and KPIs, and develop a channel programme of activities over the short and medium term. And always highlight within your budget's line items where you can still attain free activity to appease your CFO, as Laurent François, founder and digital strategist from Re-Up agency suggests in this chapter!

Developing a clearly defined team around that social media plan will define further the overall budget you will need to activate it. Deciding what stays in-house and what you can farm out will help you to align and manage budget constraints transparently. In the past year design, technology and copywriting have been key components of social media spend that have been most commonly outsourced, and this trend looks to continue as the need grows for authentic content and focused engagement.

Planning your social media activity and associated costs will largely depend upon the scale and complexity of your operation. Small businesses have different needs to larger ones. As Ema Linaker of Leo Burnett/Holler affirms in her contribution to the chapter, it is imperative that you continue to listen and pay attention to what your social community is telling you once the investment has been made. You will learn more from them about the effectiveness of your spend than you will from any other source available to you.

Laurent François, executive creative strategist and co-founder, Re-Up

Budgeting is one of the most difficult tasks when it comes to marketing, and it is even more complicated when it comes to social media. From a CFO's perspective, there are a lot of 'irrational' layers. Their concerns might sound boring at first sight for any social media enthusiast, but in fact raise a lot of opportunities to better sell social strategies, therefore improving the performance of our actions.

Splitting the different lines of tasks

Budgeting is all about structuring costs and defining objectives. There is a need to set up basic costs, explain to CFOs what is crucial and what is simply nice to have. Products and services do not immediately generate value per se but help in achieving results. It is possible, of course, to do everything with *free* tools but you will quickly come across limits. CFOs are here to generate ROI. Justifying which services achieve which goals is a way to demonstrate how profitable spend can be. And showing to CFOs that you have included 'free' services is a way to prove you are budget-savvy.

Here are a few suggested budget lines for you to work with:

- Community management tools:
  - 'free' tools such as Tweetdeck;
  - 'paid' tools such as solutions to find influencers in the quickest way.

- Social listening tools:
  - 'free' tools such as the basic features of Twitter counter to analyse the growth of a community, Facebook insights etc;
  - 'paid' tools such as SocialBakers to better know your audience;
  - monitoring tools such as Radian6 or Synthesio to better understand consumers' expectations.

When it comes to social media, we often forget tools that are not dedicated only to social media specialists. Nonetheless, your team will require a lot of other tools to make the strange chemistry happen:

- Photo editor:
  - 'free' tools such as apps that you can get on Play;
  - 'paid' tools such as Adobe Creative Cloud.

- Video material:
  - 'free' tools such as Google Hangouts;
  - 'paid' solutions to better edit interviews such as Premiere or Final Cut.

- Presentation, text editor etc.

It is not because social media is perceived as 'digital' that other costs don't occur: good social media specialists tend to write a lot on sticky notes, walls – and good old paper.

Team

Once you have created this very first list of costs, it is now time to justify which team members you need and which sorts of profiles you require. These talents are fairly expensive (junior social media specialists start at £16,000 while top managers can earn more than £120,000).

Again, it is important to split between talents who will be necessary every month to implement the strategies, and digital specialists who will be important because of specific needs and specific actions.

That is why you need to align the presentation of your budget depending on your social activities. Not everything can be planned, however you definitely need to create your own 'brand seasons' with key momentums. Oreo is a good example: their ability to react in the *now* and to really understand real-time marketing is actually very prepared, designed and mastered. In social media as in any other practice, most of the work is actually invisible for the end users.

Team pillars: there are key skills that need to be spread among the organization. Depending on your structure, these can sometimes be allocated to other collaborators as part of their activities, or directly outsourced:

- *Digital strategist*: depending on the size of your business, you might require few of them. These people are responsible for the global coherence of the projects; they must be very digital-savvy but, most importantly, understand what your brand is about. They must lead the process and provide insights, while developing state-of-the-art ideas.

- *Content strategist*: once you have the global strategy, it must come to life. Content strategists will create editorial pillars and tone of voice, and will adjust the social brand with the digital strategist and the brand team leaders. They will also diffuse the brand culture to all the other components of the social media team.

- *Creative team (copywriters and designers)*: this team will play an important role to create executions; a simple action such as a Facebook contest actually requires the right user experience, the right words and the right appealing visuals.

- *Social media analyst*: they will crawl the web, analyse social media presence and measure impact. They are as important as the strategists because they are the ones who will actually justify ROI (or not).

- *Co-ordinator*: making sure that everyone is aligned, calling for quick catch-up and supporting social media team ideas to the other departments, which are key tasks.

- Most of the time, organizations are not aware of what the 'geeks' are doing. Ten years after the very first social media activities, this crucial part of the business – *internal communication* – is still an issue.

Each of these functions can be outsourced to agencies, freelancers, or allocated to other business functions. There are many examples of good 'hybridization' of talents, as in the long term every collaborator will have a role to play in 'social'. Nonetheless, it still requires co-ordinators to make sure that virtuous loops are happening. The worst scenario is to outsource all the social media tasks to an agency, as the loss of control and the lack of reactivity will lead to two mistakes – a lack of 'change' within the organization, and less synergies between the brand ideas and what external experts can bring to the table.

For word-of mouth accelerators, among the diverse social media activities that a team must do on a daily basis there are activities that require specific talents:

- Developers: developing an app for a contest can be either bought from an agency (ie there are many companies that specialize in Facebook apps) or developed in a more bespoke way, either internally or with freelancers. It is important to anticipate your key momentums: do you want to arrange a contest for Christmas? Then what will you require?

- Database of customers: some companies already own strong databases of existing customers or prospects, others don't. In order to accelerate word-of-mouth, you might need at some point to hire a customer relationship management (CRM) specialist.

Advertising

If something has tremendously changed in the last couple of years, it is the link between advertising and social media. Before this, some activities could have a chance to go viral because it was new, out-standing, inspiring. And because social networks were running after critical masses of users, they were offering a lot of tools to marketers for free. Times have changed, however, and it is now key to forecast the boosters that you will need in order to foster your campaigns.

Splitting the different lines of activities

Once this first work is done, a tremendously efficient way to prepare your budget is to split your costs directly on the social media editorial plan and explain which goals are then expected:

- *Permanent costs*: it is important to explain that a core team will not be able to create magic every day but will be able to complete growth in diverse areas: fans, followers, leads, e-mail addresses, drive to e-commerce etc. It's great because it is also a way to justify the fact that CFOs also need to invest in accelerators at some point in order to generate peaks:
  - A bit like the 'listening' task is always 'on', your core team will be permanently working on your organization's storyline.
  - Licences will then be plugged to this 'support' line.
- *Additional costs for specific events*: you can now explain how to generate peaks, accelerators to acquire new sorts of publics etc:
  - Might you need social media correspondents to cover specific events?
  - Might you need more budget to buy an app for Christmas?

CFOs will then have a full understanding of what you want to achieve and why you require specific manpower and tools. With this split by tasks and activities, CFOs can, in an easier way, discover if the organization can become a profit centre – and how.

Trina Albus, president, Magenta

Over the past few years, social media has changed drastically for brands. Getting results used to be easy; all a brand needed was a strong identity and a consistent posting schedule to rack up follows, shares and retweets. Today, however, the social media space is crowded with brands, making it challenging to stand out from the noise. Nevertheless, with a strong team, the right tools and a clear paid strategy, you can harness social media to produce better results for your brand than ever before.

Building a strong team

Social media is an extension of your brand identity, so it is important that you entrust your brand with competent professionals. Whether you are hiring in-house staff or an external agency, you will need people with the right skill sets to manage both organic and paid social media activities.

For organic social media activities, the following skills are needed:

- social strategy;
- graphic design;
- copywriting;
- posting;
- community engagement;
- data analysis and reporting.

For paid social media activities, the following skills are needed:

- advertising strategy;
- advertising budget and bidding;
- graphic design;
- direct response copywriting;
- data analysis and reporting.

As you can see, there is some overlap between organic and paid activity skill sets. It is possible for smaller firms to hire a social media manager with all the above skills. As you build out your team, however, it is essential that they can work closely together – organic and paid social media activities are most effective when they are co-ordinated.

If you hire an external agency, expect to be charged a monthly retainer fee. If you staff in-house, then you will need to hire for different skills across organic and paid activities.

Choosing the right tools

If you are spending money to hire skilled staff and to advertise on social media channels, you will need the right tools in order to maximize efforts, measure goals and get the highest ROI. Most businesses use a mix of free and paid tools to address their diverse goals and needs. Here is a breakdown of the various tools you are likely to need:

- 'Native' analytics built into the platform: Facebook, Twitter, Pinterest, LinkedIn and Google+ all offer free built-in analytics that can be used to monitor post-performance and track demographic data.

- Third-party analytics: Google Analytics is the most popular web analytics tool used to monitor social referral traffic, tracking link performance and more. Many businesses use monthly fee-based tools such as Piqora or Tailwind to supplement native Pinterest analytics. Iconosquare is the leading analytics tool for Instagram, and it is currently available for free.

- Dashboard and monitoring: to measure performance across social channels (such as total post impressions across all social channels for a particular month), use a paid dashboard tool such as Sprout Social or Brandwatch.

- Scheduling and team collaboration: tools including Buffer and Hootsuite allow scheduling of posts in advance, team member collaboration, community engagement monitoring, and access to data and reporting. Both of these tools offer free and paid plans.

- Promotions, contests and giveaways: to foster community engagement, increase fans and followers, or capture lead generation information, many brands regularly run contests and giveaways on social channels. If you decide to use a third-party platform such as Agora Pulse or OfferPop, you will either pay as you go, or pay a monthly fee.

- Link shortening and tracking: generally, shorter is better on social, so you will need a link-shortening tool. Free tools such as Bitly offer link shortening and basic analytics. You can upgrade to the enterprise version if you need more robust analytics. Awe.sm (acquired by Unified Social) is also a popular paid tool if you need more complex analytics such as social funnel optimization data.

How much should I spend on tools?

Many tools offer a free trial. Some tools offer both free and paid versions. Some tools offer only paid versions. Do your research and find the right combination of tools that works to support your social media efforts and helps your business to meet its goals. Start with free tools and work your way up to paid tools as your business grows.

Creating a clear paid strategy

Facebook was the first social channel to roll out paid advertising for businesses, and Twitter quickly followed suit. Both of these platforms now offer sophisticated conversion tracking pixels so that advertisers can closely monitor success and measure ROI. LinkedIn also offers advertising best suited for business to business (B2B) brands. Pinterest, Instagram and Google+ have rolled out beta advertising products to select brands, with a wide-scale launch on the horizon.

As social media grows even more crowded, brands will no longer be able to survive on social media with an organic-only strategy. All brands will eventually need to incorporate social advertising on multiple channels into their paid media strategy.

How much should you spend on paid social? If you are not sure, start small and carefully measure your ROI, and then spend more where you are seeing the best results.

Here is a case study from one of Magenta's beauty clients. We started with a social ad budget of US $10,000 per month. At first, we split the ad spend equally across Facebook and Twitter ($5,000 each channel per month). Consulting the native analytics on Facebook and Twitter, we found that Facebook ads performed better than Twitter ads, showing more total sales converted and a lower average cost per sale. Therefore, we shifted 70 per cent of the total budget towards Facebook and continued testing and optimizing on both platforms to refine our strategy.

Before running an ad campaign on social for your business, you should first determine the campaign goal:

- to drive website traffic;
- to drive website sales;
- to drive brand awareness;
- to drive donations;
- to drive mobile app downloads;
- to get more likes or followers.

Based on your goal, you will set up the corresponding ad campaigns, measure success and determine your ROI. The social channel with the highest ROI is where you will want to spend most of your remaining ad budget.

One of the great features of social media is that you do not have to spend a lot to gain valuable insight on what is working. So as you incrementally increase your budget, you can predict results with greater accuracy than ever before. With the right team, the right tools, and the right paid campaign, success can be yours for the taking.

@magentaagency | www.magentaagency.com

Ema Linaker, head of Social Centre of Excellence (MENA), Leo Burnett/Holler

First, let's make one thing really clear: social is not about Facebook, Twitter, LinkedIn or any of the other million platforms there are out there today where people are congregating. Communications and consumers have changed irrevocably over the past decade. Indeed the world of advertising has literally been turned on its head, because people who are supposed to be listening, watching and reading traditional advertising have stopped listening and paying attention. Why?

Because the way that advertising communicates to people is plain *rude*. It interrupts you, it shouts at you, it doesn't even consider you to be an individual. What does it mean to be social? It means you must have *people* as the medium of your message.

There are six easy steps to becoming a social brand without breaking the budget:

- have purpose;
- be human;
- pass the 'why care, why share?' test;
- make the experience social;
- integration;
- pay attention.

Each of these six steps is explored below.

Have purpose

When your brand takes a position, not just a positioning, you become something worth talking about. For example, Dove believes the world would be a better place if women realized they were more beautiful than they thought. This allowed them to create a platform that literally changed the way women saw themselves in the mirror – through Dove Real Beauty Sketches. Nike believes the world would be a better place if we all found our own greatness – this led to a product invention that has created a whole new category and industry through Nike Fuel Band and Nike Plus – wearable tech is now such a force that it is becoming an exciting area of innovation for brands and technology companies alike.

So ask yourself some really basic questions:

- *Why* are we on social?
- What do we stand for?
- How will we achieve this through content and engagement?
- What is the role for platforms, and how do they all fit together?

This will help you to arrive at defining your *purpose* on social.

Be human

There is nothing worse than seeing bland, blah social media content on Facebook or Vine that has no personality and sounds like a robot on Prozac. The key to great social is in the name. It's social and it's about communicating with people by people. This means there is no room for corporate speak or jargon. Great brands on social take this one step further and spend a lot of time and energy in creating detailed social brand personas, producing real social brand characters that the audience wants to connect with. They typically fall into three types – a person, a persona or a mascot. Whichever you choose for your company, you really need to stick to it and commit to it. People buy from *people* – and showing personality through this technique is very powerful, just ask the likes of Marmite, whose acerbic and witty persona on Facebook has created a real cult following of over 1 million passionate fans who adore their pithy updates.

Pass the 'why care, why share?' test

People do not follow passively, as if infected by a virus. Instead, people spread deliberately, propelled by a range of social needs or existing behaviours. Social is about people, not product. You can only make people care if you really understand them, what motivates them, what challenges they face, what triggers matter to them. You must invest time and energy into creating true social insights based on facts and data that you have gleaned from social community analysis and listening.

Make the experience social

What this means is to facilitate participation and sharing. Social platforms are a reflection of social and human interactions. So you should not be afraid of inviting participation and giving your audience an experience worth talking about and sharing with their friends, family and network.

Integration

This is often harder to do well because of the structure of your client or organization, but when done well it really pays off. This is because you are creating a seamless experience that the user doesn't see but understands its power because they have continuity of experience and message – and consistency is so important when dealing with people. As Wendy Clark, senior vice president of integrated marketing communications and capabilities at Coca-Cola says: 'None of our plans are simply social, or TV, or mobile or experiential. On the contrary, it's the combination of owned, earned, shared and paid media connections – with social playing a crucial role at the heart of our activation – that creates marketplace impact, consumer engagement, brand love and brand value.'

Pay attention

The art of being a good friend is based around the ability to really listen to what your friends or others are saying. This is a skill much underrated but is a core foundation on what makes good *great* and takes you beyond the norm. With all the social tools now available to marketers to listen, analyse behaviour and measure impact of content by individual stories, we know a lot about people and how they behave – and what they want and when they want it. It is imperative that a brand or company wanting to do social media understands that, once you make all the investment, you need to continue to listen – to pay attention to what the community is telling you. You will learn more from them than you will from any other source available to you.

Chapter conclusions

In this chapter our contributors have placed their focus on the balance between achieving a robust programme that is both flexible and scalable, with budgets that can be realigned as activity proves its value, or not. With a strong team, the right tools and a clear paid strategy you should be able to justify spend to your CFO or client. The key to winning their commitment is conviction, clarity and a true understanding of the value of each budget line. Qualify spend where you need it by recommending the use of key *free* analytics and content tools where relevant. As the social media industry grows up, *paid* is becoming a crucial aspect of your media spend, so make sure that you budget for it wisely.

CASE STUDY Expedia/[a•mo•bee]

Client
Expedia.

Agency
[a•mo•bee].

Project
Valentine's Day 3D campaign: Find Yours.

Overview
In preparation for Valentine's Day, Expedia wanted to capture the excitement surrounding vacation travel with a disruptive and captivating mobile advertising campaign to catch consumers on the go. The four-day burst campaign allowed potential holiday travellers to imagine themselves in key Valentine's Day destinations: New York City and Las Vegas. The campaign encouraged users not only to book their holiday travel through Expedia, but also to download the Expedia mobile app in order to expand Expedia's brand presence and promote repeat travel bookings.

Execution and use of media
- Engage target audiences through 3D mobile advertisements.
- Drive downloads of the Expedia mobile app.
- Demonstrate the myriad of travel destinations and benefits of the Expedia mobile app.
- Portray Expedia as a progressive, early adopter of cutting-edge mobile marketing technologies.

Using proprietary [a•mo•bee] 3D mobile ad technology, Expedia created stunning virtual landscapes of two of the most visited Valentine's Day travel destinations: Las Vegas and New York City. Once a user clicked the ad, the image expanded to a full-screen, accelerometer-driven cityscape that allowed the user to navigate across each landscape, and enticed engagement in ways not possible with traditional rich media ad units. User participation was maximized with clear and concise messaging that highlighted the advantages of booking with Expedia, and prompted the user to 'Find Yours' by downloading the Expedia mobile app.

Results

Intrigued by the ability to interact with the landscapes, mobile users' time-in-ad averaged 70+ seconds, more than double the industry benchmark. Additionally, the 'Find Yours' campaign saw an average engagement rate of over 21 per cent, nearly 1.5 times the industry benchmark, resulting in both app downloads and hotel bookings.

Links to campaign

Download our mobile app: view fully functional examples of our award-winning creative work, including 3D mobile ads, only from [a•mo•bee]:

amobee.com/adshowcase

CASE STUDY HomeServe/Reevoo

Client

HomeServe.

Agency

Reevoo.

The challenge

- To give our customers a voice, a way to talk about their experiences of using our services on a platform they could trust without being moderated by us.

- We wanted to *learn* from our customers and have two way conversations; essentially we wanted to use Reevoo as a communications channel with our customers.

- We use Reevoo in a product-specific way. This allows us to drill down and really understand what does and doesn't work for us across our products and update/improve them based on feedback from our customers.

- We also chose to use Reevoo to help improve our online reputation.

- In social media specifically, we wanted to use genuine customer reviews to try to address the balance of positive versus negative conversations that are taking place about our brand.

Target audience

Existing and prospective HomeServe customers.

Action

- Our product scores are integrated into HomeServe.com and updated dynamically, meaning we're always displaying real-time customer feedback and accurate scores.
- Reevoo has been fully implemented into our marketing strategy. We've used Reevoo in the following ways:
  - We created the very first Facebook app. This allowed us to showcase our products and real customer feedback via one of our main social channels to an audience of over 16 thousand followers. A new way to share our information socially with our customers.
  - As part of our social content strategy. For example, on our Facebook page we've used Reevoo wordles and what-our-customers-say templates to share customer-specific content.
  - Customer magazines – showcased the customer journey.
  - Billboard – proudly displayed across the road from our Walsall HQ.

Results

- Implemented Reevoo across our four core product categories – Combined, Plumbing, Electrical and Boiler. As of 18 February 2015 we've collected over 8.5 thousand customer reviews relating to these products and our services.
- As a result of using Reevoo as a communications channel we've helped over 900 people.
- Mailings using the Reevoo badge and score have been sent out to millions of our customers. For example, our recent door-to-door mailing was sent out to 4.5 million people.

Links to campaign

Our Facebook app featured in Reevoo's blog:

https://www.reevoo.com/blog/business-thinking-social-media/

Setting KPIs and measuring success

OUR CHAPTER PLEDGE TO YOU

When you reach the end of this chapter you will have the answers to the following questions:

- What are the key performance indicators I should be monitoring?
- Which tools should I use to analyse the data I accumulate?
- What values should I place against digital listening?
- What do I learn from likes, shares, follows and comments?
- What is the difference between applause and engagement?
- What is the difference between a conversation and a conversion?
- How do I monitor user journeys and drop-off points?

Making it all count!

No longer satisfied with thousands of likes on your company's Facebook page or hundreds of followers on Twitter? Had enough of people telling you how important social is to your business but still not truthfully sure what impact it is having on your bottom line? Getting your KPIs in order will help you to straighten out the maze that is social media and give you methods for analysing how effectively you are employing it to help your business grow.

Before you even begin to define what those KPIs are, step back and consider where your target audiences get together online:

- What do they talk about and what are they interested in once they get there?
- How long do they hang out for?
- What actions do they take and how are they incentivized by one another to do so?
- Who do they listen to and what do they do with the information they receive?

Once you have a good grasp of their habits and trends, it will be far easier to work out how your brand fits into their interests and networks and, by association, what your KPIs should be in order to ensure you are getting right your communications to them.

Follower-growth is an essential KPI. Over time you should watch your audience grow. It may be a slow, organic growth, or one that is fuelled by paid media campaigns and extensive online activity. Your following should not stagnate. Brand building requires amplification through social engagement, and followers give you a direct benchmark for growth. Understand the difference between applause and engagement, as chapter contributor Adolfo Aladro García from ADTZ, Madrid, explains.

Competitor analysis is also a critical gauge. Employ a tool such as Rivaliq.com to find out what is effective for them. Building loyalty and increasing footfall are essential KPIs and this should help you to work out what your expectations, realistically, should be.

Frequency is another key. How often are you posting content or tweeting and what uplift is that producing for you? No two brands are quite the same, so don't follow convention, test it out for yourself and adapt constantly until you get the balance right.

Budget planning, as we heard in Chapter 3, relies on a clear understanding of your KPIs – ensure you are gathering the correct data to understand the effectiveness of your social media activity. As our first contributor to this chapter, Magnus Jern, from agency Golden Gekko explains, be clear about your objectives. Is your focus on brand building, increasing loyalty, raising footfall, transactions or improving the perception of your customer service? All of these may be pertinent, but define your KPIs according to their importance in order to help you understand the resulting analytics.

Magnus Jern, Golden Gekko

Should any mobile strategy be treated separately from overall social media objectives? Here Magnus Jern of Golden Gekko discusses:

Mobile is an amazing social media marketing tool as it can convert advertising dollars directly into sales like no other channel and it can be measured with great accuracy. Therefore, every mobile and social media marketing initiative should start by:

1 Establishing the KPIs of the service.

2 Specifying how to measure them (tools and methods).

3 Agreeing how to use analytics to improve the service further.

These are all key elements of budgeting for, and building your stats and insights in, mobile. In this chapter we consider these three steps in more detail, including examples.

Setting KPIs

Before setting your KPIs you need to agree clearly on the objectives of the service. The objectives are usually one or a multiple of the following:

- Brand building: create awareness among new target segments and remind existing customers about your brand, products and services, including sign-up to Facebook pages and other opt-in engagement programmes.

- Loyalty: engage with existing customers to buy more of your services and/or more frequently.

- Driving footfall: get people to your store (or other venue), whether it is online or in a retail store.

- Transactional: generate purchases from the target audience of the service online or in a store (or a combination thereof).

- Customer service perception: improve the customer satisfaction and propensity to buy through enhancing the interaction with the brand.

Each objective can be translated into measurable KPIs:

- Brand building: audience reach measured through, for example, ad displays, unique site visits, app downloads, video views and Facebook likes.

- Loyalty: engagement through, for example, sessions per user, time spent, return rate, sharing of content, liking content, sign-ups to opt-in programmes, time spent with a specific product or service.

- Driving footfall: visits to store, such as the number of customers who went to the online or physical store/venue.

- Transactional: for example, customers who purchase a product or service can be measured by voucher redemption rate, payments made, conversions achieved.

- Customer satisfaction: customer feedback of the service, such as app store ratings and reviews, customer survey results.

Finally, there are also some non-functional KPIs such as average loading time, service uptime, page/app errors and so on.

Tools to measure success

Once the KPIs have been agreed upon, the next step is to agree how they should be measured. Some of the tools are tailored for a specific purpose, such as tracking usage behaviour, attribution, conversion rates, download benchmarking versus other similar apps, etc. There are usually two ways to collect the data and do the analytics: 1) online analytics tools; 2) custom log files and analytic tools.

Online analytics tools

Google Analytics, Flurry, Adobe Marketing Cloud, Yahoo Web Analytics and other online tools are fairly easy to implement in a mobile site or app. Set up the account and project with the online tool and put the tags in the website code or application. These tools provide an easy-to-use interface with lots of great data (dependent on how well you tag your site or app). These tools provide limited customization, which is enough for most services and purposes.

Custom log files and analytic tools

Another alternative is to implement a custom analytics solution of which there are hundreds of commercial, shareware and open source options. In this case all you need is to define the attributes to log from the site or app, where a raw log file or database will be created. If you define too many this may create major overheads for the analysis, so make sure that you define only the attributes you really need. The advantage of these may be that they give a bit more control in terms of customizing reports, managing the data and creating custom reports, and that they provide better data privacy and security.

Some organizations have existing business intelligence tools such as SAS or Qlikview and want to aggregate all information in one place. The advantage of this approach is that you could potentially merge this with other data such as purchases or redemptions from other systems.

Using analytics data to further improve the service and ROI

Unfortunately, most organizations only use a small fraction of the available data after the service has been launched. This is usually due to a combination of lack of clear KPIs and post-launch plans. The best-performing services plan dedicated time, budget and resources to monitor performance versus KPIs, ongoing analysis, improvements, minor tweaks and major updates based on customer feedback.

So how can you use the data to improve the service? Here are just a few examples:

- Analyse which parts of an app or website gets the most visits and optimize the service accordingly.
- Understand the drop-off in each step of a redemption or purchase process.

- Understand the demographics of your audience and tweak the targeting accordingly, or analyse further if the target audience is right – but different from what you expected.

- Use the data to personalize and increase targeting of your service (such as products offered, rates, packages and so on).

- Read ratings and reviews to understand what customers like and don't like – and improve the service accordingly.

Agree on the objectives and KPIs for your mobile service, find and implement the right tools to measure your KPIs and plan to use the data for ongoing improvements and performance benchmarking!

Adolfo Aladro García, chief operating officer, ADTZ, Madrid

Nowadays it is crucial to measure the impact of social media on a brand. All businesses need to understand how social marketing helps the business. Setting the business KPIs is the best way to understand the business goals and define the metrics that are important to your organization.

Depending on your business goals and objectives there are metrics that make sense to be considered and others that do not. But before going deeper on this, there is a previous step that consists in understanding that social metrics usually measure two things: applause and engagement.

Applause and engagement

The applause metric shows that people are watching and enjoying. That is, your business is getting awareness and generating attention.

The engagement metric is a bit more complex and can be measured in many different ways. For example, if you are sharing links or photos, engagement means how many people actually look at them. Are there many people following your links or watching your pictures? Another component of engagement is measured by considering the number of people who share what you are doing. If someone shares what you are doing, it means that they find it interesting. That means a step beyond the applause metrics, since it demands an additional effort: people are not just viewing, they are sharing with their contacts what you do. Finally, comments are a great way to measure engagement – and can be useful to start a conversation with your audience.

Social metrics

The metrics shown below are the ones you should consider in your master KPI list. All of them should be monitored on a daily basis in order to be able to measure success. Depending on your business goals, some metrics will be more important than others in your KPI list. But in order to get a big picture of your success, all of them must be considered.

Followers

The number of your followers is probably one of the first things people see when they visit your Twitter or Facebook. Followers show credibility and brand recognition. Of course we are talking about real followers, which means people who are really interested in what you are doing. In the last few years, some businesses have tried to increase the number of followers in an artificial way. But it doesn't make any sense. Those who don't interact with you (by watching, sharing, following, giving comments, etc) are not likely to buy your products. You need to create your community with real people who are interested in you.

Followers are usually considered as part of the brand equity. They indicate too the potential number of people you are reaching. Of course, having many followers is just the first step. You have to be capable of making them engage with what you are doing.

Social shares

If people share the content you produce then it indicates that the content is good – interesting in a way that means they are willing to do the additional effort of sharing.

The key to sharing is promoting quality over quantity. Producing a lot of content does not make any sense. You have to produce the *right* content, that which your audience really likes – not only to see it but also to share it. The periodicity is also something to be considered. You must publish new content with a frequency that suits your audience likes. If you publish a lot of contents in a short time, you will tire and confuse them. If you publish too few things, they will forget you.

Applause

Applause (such as likes, favourites and so on) helps to boost your vanity. It is a fairly passive and undemanding form of recognition. Your audience is just saying that they are watching, and so you are catching their attention. Applause can even influence how your content shows up on Facebook or Twitter, for example. The more applause you get, the more these social platforms treat your content in terms of organic distribution. So it is important to get a lot of favourites and likes and then to measure these in order to know what is important for your audience – and aim to get more people sharing the content.

Comments

It is vital to analyse and distinguish between new commenters (people who just leave one comment) and repeating commenters (people who are continually returning to comment). By counting and monitoring these two metrics you can understand how your audience interacts with your content, and therefore if your content is suitable for your brand. For this, there are two concepts that must be part of your master KPIs list: brand mentions and brand conversations. Classifying and reacting is as important as counting comments.

Brand mentions (with sentiment analysis)

Your followers will likely be talking about your brand, so be sure to listen and know what your audience is saying about you. There are several tools that can help to monitor brand mention across all sources, such as Hootsuite, TweetDeck, IceRocket, HowSociable.

It is a very good practice to count how many times your brand is mentioned over a period of time. You should then classify all these mentions as positive, negative or neutral. This allows you to get a wide view of what people are saying about you, what they think about your brand.

Your KPI must be to minimize the negative mentions and maximize the positive mentions on a daily basis. What can you do to achieve this goal? The next metric is the answer.

Brand conversations

You cannot measure in a passive way – join the conversation and contribute. If there is a positive mention, answer with a 'thanks'. If there is a negative mention, find out what the problem is and try to solve it. If you limit yourself to just viewing what is happening, you won't be improving anything. Positive mentions boost brand recognition. Negative mentions that are treated in the right way can help too. People like to know that they have been heard.

Conor Lynch and Ivan Adriel, Connector

Listen carefully: your consumers are talking about you online

When it comes to social media, consumers are responsible for doing most of the talking. They evaluate, praise, criticize and share their opinions about your brand. Word of mouth has a major influence on sales whether businesses like it or not. Nevertheless, your company should not feel powerless but should instead act and harness the power of social media.

A great starting point would be to monitor online content and conversations. Social media monitoring, or digital listening, is the name for the activity whereby you take advantage of the numerous clues that people leave lying around for your business every day. We strongly advise carefully monitoring or listening online to customers, potential customers, competitors, your competitors' customers and influencers who impact greatly on your market.

Social media monitoring reports can have a powerful transformative impact on your business, empowering more than just your communication strategies but also providing insights for many departments beyond marketing.

10 benefits of social media monitoring

Here are 10 ways in which listening to social media may be an invaluable resource for your business.

1. Market research

Understand a specific behaviour of a particular subject or theme. For this type of research, you must be very careful that the analysis is statistically valid and the sample actually provides valid answers to your questions.

2. Audience segmentation

Map conversations in social media that are related to the brand target audience using personas. This helps further segmentation and makes the brand positioning more accurate.

3. Influencer mapping

Identify people with influence in a given market segment or subject area who are relevant for your brand. This type of mapping seeks to find brand ambassadors with power to influence, which can increase the effectiveness of marketing campaigns.

4. Campaign measurement

Monitor the buzz around certain activations or campaigns, which can be very useful for product launches or new marketing activity.

5. Brand exposure

Understand where consumers spend their time online talking about specific products and services. Brand exposure metrics are used to determine if media investments of a campaign are performing as expected or if amendments are required.

6. Lead generation

Find online conversations featuring your target audience so that you can engage them to offer them the opportunities to learn more about your products and services. If you get your timing right, they may even want to make a purchase.

7. Reputation management

Monitor the consumer perception of a certain brand, or a campaign or specific product. Reputation management is the most popular application of digital listening and its value is in the insights that can be unearthed from this research.

You will also want to manage a brand's activity online, which may serve to protect it from threats such as fake accounts and people selling counterfeit versions of your products.

8. Customer service

Monitor consumer conversations in order to offer quick answers to questions and solutions to problems. This type of monitoring has become an essential support for brands in social media and must be used continuously. In some companies, you may have staff working full-time every day of the week for fulfilling such tasks, while other companies outsource to marketing and PR agencies.

9. Competitor research

Monitor the online activities of competitors or brands that are within your market. It is possible to map the activity of various brands and create a matrix positioning of each, thus showing how a brand is positioned relative to the competition.

10. Innovation

Find insights from research that can be directed towards the improvement and innovation of products, services, processes and communications.

Social media monitoring process

Deciding what information you would like to find out about your business is a good starting point. This will help you to identify what data about your business you would like to find using social media monitoring.

Set goals

After discovering all the possibilities of digital research, it is time to decide your goals and start your project. Your goal may be to find data to help you solve a problem or unearth a hidden opportunity.

Here is how you structure it:

- map keywords;
- test and optimize your keywords;
- classify your content;
- report and refine.

Map keywords

At first, it is best to map as many words and word combinations on the subject to be researched in social media, as follows:

- the name of the brand and its products and services;
- name of products, services, technical terms of products;
- words related to campaigns and events;
- abbreviations and 'aliases' that people use to refer to brands and issues around them;
- competitors' brands and aliases;
- misspelt words.

We suggest you use tools such as Google Insights for Search and Google AdWords Keyword Tool to find keywords.

Test and optimize keywords

For each research project, it is important to find pre-assessment results to identify posts that are not related to the subject and think of ways to combat this. You can refine searches by exclusion and combining words.

Classify your content

To facilitate the analysis of the data, it is necessary to go beyond sentiment and build a framework of categories to classify posts. By rating categories, posts with similar characteristics are grouped into smaller groups. This allows the comparison between categories and for conducting cross-checks, which helps with the identification of patterns in what is being said online. This assists in generating insights. For comparison with competitors and the market, it is best to use the same research structure whenever possible.

Before beginning the actual classification of posts, it is important to test the classification by category and sentiment analysis in real and random posts to ensure you develop a correct method. Without such care, the data may become inconsistent. Sentiment analysis shows how words may have different interpretations. The sharing of content published by a brand can be identified as positive or neutral depending on the objective of the project, or on the context of the words used.

Report and refine

The final stage is to complete the report and modify further research based on the findings and the process undertaken. A good report will have comprehensive sections for data audit, analysis and an action plan with key recommendations.

The metrics for monitoring social networks

According to your goal you can compile reports on sentiment analysis, brand exposure and consumer perceptions. To generate these reports, you must use well-defined metrics.

The metrics vary with each tool, and social platforms change over time. However, there are certain metrics that do not vary much. These references come from traditional marketing and can help your company to see which points are most important to monitor. We can separate these important indicators into three areas: reach metrics, conversion metrics and affinity metrics.

Reach metrics

These are the most popular and important metrics and are measured by those who manage a profile on a social network.

For example:

- How many people like a particular business Facebook page?
- How many people are followers of a page on Twitter?
- Was there an increase/decrease over the previous month?
- Was there an increase/decrease in the number of people reached by your content?

Using reach metrics as a digital strategy is not always the most appropriate. Reach is important – after all, you always want more people to see your marketing. However, you must work within your budget.

Conversion metrics

An institution can bet on social media to stimulate business and new connections. In such cases, we recommend that you track performance of your digital strategy.

Key questions include things like: how many people visit your website? What is the percentage of users accessing your website who are asking for more information?

Affinity metrics

The metrics that usually give the most impressive results for managers who have never used monitoring are affinity metrics. Here you may find insights into consumer perceptions of your brand.

Key questions include:

- In what context is your business mentioned?
- How often is it mentioned?
- In which areas did users take the time to talk about your brand?

- What terms were used?
- Can you classify the comments into clusters of negative, positive or neutral?
- How many people endorsed your brand?
- How many criticized it?

Choosing digital listening tools

The monitoring of social networks requires specific tools, the choice of which depends on your goals, your chosen metrics and your budget.

There are several tools that offer this monitoring service, some of which are free. If you are getting into digital marketing now and your marketing budget is still small, it is certainly worth opting for one of the free alternatives. However, if you are a larger business and have a large volume of users interacting with your brand on social networks, websites and blogs, it is often worth paying for a premium tool.

The two main types of social media monitoring are: partial monitoring and full monitoring.

Partial monitoring

This uses software that does not allow adding information and advanced treatment of the collected data. For example, the use of Google Alerts, Social Mention, Google Insights, Socialbakers, Crowdbooster, Simply Measured, Iconosquare, Klout and segmented search tools (Topsy, IceRocket etc). In general, these are free tools that can be perfectly adequate for beginners if you can learn how to use them.

Full monitoring

This enables and aggregates research in a single software platform. The different stages of monitoring of brands and conversations include: data capture and classification; generating comprehensive reports, sometimes including automated sentiment analysis from big data. These features are generally from paid tools such as Brandwatch, Socialmetrix and Radian6.

Conclusion

As we said at the offset, you should listen carefully as your consumers are talking to you. By adopting digital listening, these once distant consumers can become a very important part of your team.

As a note of caution, there are certain subjects that people are not comfortable talking about online. As a result, the amount of data you can expect to find is dependent on whether consumers are actively talking about your keywords in sufficient numbers to make monitoring a viable activity. This is especially the case if you are using the more expensive tools and professional support.

In general, however, by implementing social media monitoring in your business you should be able to turn online conversations into valuable insights that can transform, empower and grow your business.

Alpesh Doshi, CEO, Fintricity

In a relatively short period of time, digital and social media has become a mainstream marketing channel for brands. However, the data that is generated by these social media activities and other data categories such as transaction data, mobile data and other 'big data' sources is largely being underused by brands and agencies. Data is key to building one-to-one engagement with your audience and to delivering more compelling, personalized customer interactions. Being able to link data together, and perform relevant, scaled, data analytics to understand audiences better will increasingly drive marketing in the future. At the moment, marketing complex execution strategies without hard data relies upon gut instinct and 'doing what we have always done'. To compete for audience and engagement – such as Facebook, Google and other media channels driven by data – involves a different way of working. Data must become the fuel that drives a new digital marketing age.

Digital marketing

To drive digital marketing, data must become central to the marketing process and, further, to the whole business. Data must be applied across the value chain for creative media planning and buying, execution, feedback and measurement, and personalization. Data should be considered holistically and in a timely way, rather than using outdated or disjointed reports from agencies and their 'data' tools, or not using data at all.

The digital market today demands intimacy across channels, providing integrated customer experiences at a time, place, device and method that the customer chooses. Customers also demand a more personal and holistic relationship, from initial acquisition to customer service – a continuous engagement approach. There are a number of areas where data could be used more effectively:

- *Profiling users*. Marketing teams can accumulate data about individuals from their public profiles, activities, web analytics, purchasing behaviour and so on. With Facebook alone providing over 300 data points to access for each user, being able to profile each customer is a marketing imperative. A 360-degree customer view has been the marketing holy grail and with big data and analytics is now achievable.

- *Making better decisions*. You can take guesswork and gut instinct out of the marketing process. This can work throughout the whole process, from knowing where your audience has their conversations, analysing and planning the best content on the best channel, to creating customized experiences and navigation for each customer derived from predictive analytics. As an example, Capital One conducts more than 30,000 experiments per year with different interest rates, incentives and direct mail. It uses data and analytics to find their best customers.

- *Analyse customer–product fit*. Teams can analyse purchasing behaviour to correlate to the right products and services that a customer wants. This helps sales conversion rates, and helps to navigate the customer to what they are looking for.

Zara combines data from fashion houses together with their internal data to determine which products to make next. They have about 11,000 distinct items of clothing, far more than their competitors.

- *Targeted advertising.* Digital campaigns can now take fact-based approaches and use data to make sure that the channel, time and type of advertising will be most effective to reach an audience. The available data can then be reused to understand whether a campaign worked – in order to plan for the next campaign. As an example, Quantcast provide real-time integrated access to web data that enables targeting and retargeting of customers navigating across the web, using their own big data platform.

Data, central to the new marketing model

In a brand, traditionally, each department collects their data independently. This can make it difficult to see a complete picture. Combining data from across different landscapes provides more opportunity to build better relationships with customers. Sourcing data externally (from the public web and social data sources), from trusted third-party sources and enterprise data can be aggregated into a 'data lake'. The data lake then enables data to be used across the brand.

Once data is combined into a single logical data lake it becomes possible to build out a continuous engagement model (a model where the customer is *always on*) to supply data to analytics and insight tools and applications. This would include sales, marketing, customer service, operations and IT to digitally serve the customer. Some of the ways this data could be used are as follows:

- Customer relationship management (CRM): the drive to personalized, one-to-one relationships requires continuous capture of interactions between the brand and the customer. According to an article in *Harvard Business Review* (Unlock the mysteries of your customer relationships, July–August 2014, by J Avery, S Fournier and J Wittenbraker), there are 29 types of customer relationship, and breaking down the relationships with data to support that segmentation enables a more targeted relationship model.

- Business analytics and insights teams: as data is aggregated the capability to serve marketing and other business areas across departmental boundaries becomes possible. The whole business can then use the same version of the data and becomes central to fact-based and analytical decision making. Data becomes a key input into all decisions. This is not to remove creativity, but to enhance it.

- Product and service development: traditionally, businesses use very little data as input into product development. With the combined data available, brands can use data as significant input to develop new products and services, quickly test them, and modify them to suit the customer need. This significantly reduces the risk of failure and, more importantly, delivers the products and services a customer wants.

- Real-time marketing decisioning: no longer is it necessary to wait for month-end reports from your agencies to find the success or failure of your marketing activities. Building a real-time data-driven analytics service enables the design, creation, modification and execution of your strategy to ensure financial and marketing success. Feeding from your unique combination of data can provide significant competitive advantage over your competitors and enable you to adjust your strategy as success (or failure) is seen through real-time analytics.

Leaders in using data

Viewing data as central to the decision-making process can lead to success. Some examples of real applications of big data include:

- *Amazon*: a pioneer in serving customers better by combing all their data to provide recommendations based on usage. They combine data from your web navigation; web analytics data on clicks, pages, timings, etc. Amazon produce a 'graph' of that data, which represents the relationship between you, the products they sell and your activity. This enables them to recommend the right products for you at the right time.

- *Netflix*: collects every click, every view, every movie viewing and has enriched almost every second of content that you watch in order to customize and recommend the content you may like. The data is used to enhance their personalization algorithm, which recommends what other shows to watch. The driver here is to make sure that a Netflix subscriber remains one.

- *Facebook*: has more information about users (more than 300 data points each) than any other site (apart from Google!). Facebook maintains one of the largest 'graphs' in the world, which connects people, objects, activities, places, brands etc. This enables Facebook to then ask questions such as 'show me all my friends who like X'. Together with all interactions they enable personalized targeted advertising on their site or customizing of what you see on your activity feed.

These few examples clearly demonstrate where data is disrupting how a business works. Data is truly the lifeblood of a brand.

Chapter conclusions

If your brand wants to serve customers better, then building a comprehensive data strategy and embedding data in every stage of your marketing and business activity is an imperative. If you don't figure out how to do this, your competitors will. Combining all sorts of data from within and outside your business requires significant effort and collaboration within your business, and the change required must not be underestimated. Embrace data with both hands and become a data-driven business!

The best-performing services dedicate time, budget and resources to monitoring performance against defined KPIs. They include ongoing analysis, improvements, minor tweaks and major updates, based on customer feedback. Unfortunately, most organizations use only a small fraction of the available data and tools to measure the success of their activities. This is usually due to a combination of lack of clear KPIs and post-launch plans. Understanding your KPIs at the outset of a project or campaign, and ensuring you have a persistent programme of analysis against key factors while it is active and once it is complete, will help you to monitor, manage and constantly improve your performance.

CASE STUDY   Goody Good Stuff/Shoutlet

Client

Goody Good Stuff, a UK subsidiary of leading European confectionery company Coletta.

Agency

Shoutlet.

Brief

Market research through a social promotion.

Overview

Goody Good Stuff offers consumers a healthy alternative to typical sweets. With a variety of all natural meat-free, gluten-free, dairy-free, soy-free sweets, and so on, the brand attracts a target audience largely comprised of vegetarians, those with allergen intolerances, and other health-conscious consumers. To better understand its fans and why they purchase Goody Good Stuff, the company conducted market research through a social promotion.

The campaign

In an effort to gain deeper, more vital insights into its consumer base, Goody Good Stuff ran a promotion on Facebook recruiting fans to be part of an exclusive taste-testing team. Built in Shoutlet Canvas™, the Facebook app featured an application requesting basic demographic information and a strategic question to uncover what drives fans to purchase Goody Good Stuff. After the promotion, the company chose 250 winners to be part of the taste-test team, creating a customer-centric product and supporting future product development.

How Shoutlet helped

Shoutlet empowered Goody Good Stuff to create the Koalaty Taste Team app entirely in-house, avoiding the services of a designer. Working strategically with their account manager and Tech Therapy, the Goody Good Stuff team built the app in Shoutlet Social Canvas™, tailoring the promotion to their unique audience. This allowed them to automatically gather customer data as fans entered to build their Shoutlet profiles.

To monitor the success of the promotion, the company used Shoutlet Reports weekly to correct and define its marketing strategies throughout the promotion period.

With seamless data acquisition and customized apps, Shoutlet made it possible for Goody Good Stuff to reach their target demographic, uncover a key insight, and tailor their future marketing message to impact sales.

Results

After the six-week promotion, the team analysed data collected through the contest and discovered a high volume of fans purchased because of the brand's 'all natural' element. Based on this key insight, Goody Good Stuff aims to shift a portion of its marketing strategy to promote a more natural theme to increase sales with its target demographic.

In addition, Goody Good Stuff acquired nearly 5,000 new Shoutlet Profiles for its database, a 64 per cent increase in new customer data. Growing Shoutlet Profiles with customer data empowers Goody Good Stuff to understand their fans on a deeper level and to provide a tailored customer care experience.

Client testimonial

'In a digital world of data overload, Shoutlet is a fantastic tool to help define and understand a brand's digital presence. Shoutlet's capabilities aid brands in their quest to discover consumer insights digitally.'

Charlie Jenkins, marketing manager, Goody Good Stuff

CASE STUDY Facebook Audience Insights for
MENA/Red Blue Blur Ideas

Project

Facebook audience insights for the Middle East and North Africa (MENA).

Agency

Red Blue Blur Ideas.

Authors

Harvey Bennett, Mark Brown, Hani Anabtawi and Holly Richardson.

Overview

Once a brand has set up their Facebook page and started publishing content, the next step is to grow the number of connections. A brand's desire for more connections should not be focused on the prestige of having a large number associated to the page, but rather their ability to communicate to a loyal audience who have shown an interest in that brand.

The mechanism of a user 'liking' a Facebook page essentially gives the brand permission to appear within the user's newsfeed. Therefore, the more connections a page has, the more users they will be reaching and engaging with. There are over 30 sources of likes to a page. Each of these sources can be categorized into organic, viral and paid. Let's distinguish these categories below:

- Organic likes: when a user visits a page directly or through a recommendation generated by Facebook's algorithm.

- Viral likes: when a user sees an activity from the page as a result of a friend interacting with the page, such as a page like, post like, comment, share or RSVP.

- Paid likes: likes resulting from paid 'like' advertisements, such as amplified page posts and sponsored stories (desktop and mobile).

Our analysis demonstrates that over 50 per cent of total likes come from paid sources. The fact that so many likes are attributed to paid-for advertising suggests that advertisers are finding this paid medium to be effective. In an attempt to avoid paying for ads, brands often try to create organic likes through offering contests and other utilities to users (such as games and offers) to encourage users to like the page.

They rely on the virality of the contest to carry the message to their target audience. However, it is critical to understand that a contest that is not supported by advertising will not have the reach it needs in order to generate substantial volumes of likes. This is due to Facebook's newsfeed algorithm (often called 'Edgerank' by social marketers) that typically restricts the reach of a page to between 10–20 per cent of its fans. Despite containing more than 100,000 ranking factors to determine whether or not a user sees a post, the initial Edgerank framework of affinity, weight and time decay still play a major factor according to Facebook. These three factors contribute heavily to what content fans actually see in their news feed.

Peculiarly, during our study we noticed a decline in the number of likes coming from mobile devices, despite Facebook reporting an increase in its mobile revenue. The decline in likes suggests that device targeting is not yet applied as best practice in the MENA region as it is in other parts of the world. As a result, the competition is lower and the estimated cost per fan is also lower. This discrepancy points to an opportunity for brands in the region to exploit device targeting.

Our data indicates that 54 per cent of all likes came from paid advertising. This points to the effectiveness of advertising for generating new fans for brands. We believe there are two fundamental reasons for the success of 'like' advertising: reach and targeting.

Reach

Upon releasing the 'reach generator' product, Facebook revealed that on average only 16 per cent of a page's fans (or person's Facebook friends) would see that post organically. If a page relies just on organic reach to generate likes, it restricts the number of friends of fans who will see that their friend had liked a page. The low reach results in less likes coming from viral sources, such as the ticker and newsfeed. This all goes back to the key message that if a brand wishes to extend the reach of their page's content beyond their existing fan base, they can amplify the voice of their fans' actions very effectively through paid media.

In 2011, Facebook launched 'voice of friend like ads' (at the time they were simply called Sponsored Stories). These Sponsored Stories enable brands to extend the duration and reach of a viral like by pinning these stories to the right-hand side of their target audience's Facebook browser.

Users began to see what pages their friends were liking, and this led to the introduction of social context within advertising. As the popularity and success of this format grew, these messages were introduced into newsfeed and eventually mobile. Having these messages in the newsfeed and mobile is much more effective than being located on the right-hand side, as users generally have advertising blindness with content in this location.

Targeting

Facebook targeting methods are increasingly sophisticated and Facebook is dedicated to continuously enhancing them. In 2013 Facebook established relationships with data partners that provide advertisers with enhanced targeting options. For example, in some markets Datalogix and Bluekai can provide purchase-based targeting with data gathered from e-commerce. Epsilon offers enhanced lifestyle targeting. Acxiom can provide advertisers with clusters based on target audience income.

By being able to segment the audience into specific common characteristics, brands can target specifically which segments are relevant for them to target – and position content appropriately to these audiences. This results in campaigns that are much more effective than organic activities at capturing the type of audience that is relevant to your brand. Our research confirms that Facebook ads (such as the ad unit designed to get more page likes) are significantly more effective than running incentives and contests. If you must run a contest, we recommend supplementing it with an equal investment in page like ads for exponential effectiveness.

We have often asked Facebook for input on the best day of the week to post. In most cases, brands are operating under the assumption that there is a specific day of the week when Facebook usage increases. That may be true. However, it does not mean that this specific day is the most effective for you to capture likes.

For example, financial services are less successful on the weekend than fun-loving fast-moving consumer goods (FMCG), and there are only a finite amount of eyeballs (and time) for advertisers to vie for. Our approach and recommendation is to analyse your brand's Facebook insights data. In the meantime, we have provided a normalized view of like acquisition by day of the week, based on our data.

We identified the number of likes generated per day, and used the number of posts for each day to ascertain that the natural days on which users tend to like a page are Friday and Saturday (the weekend in the United Arab Emirates (UAE) is on Friday and Saturday, and the working week commences on Sunday); the least effective day is Wednesday.

Like seasonality

Generally, there is an absence of 'always on' fan acquisition strategies in the MENA region. However, there are specific industries that invest throughout the year. FMCG, apparel and automotive are the verticals most likely to invest in an 'always on' strategy. Despite the tendency of specific verticals to invest continuously throughout the year, there is a very clear trend that occurs through the Christmas period. During our study, we saw a steady increase in the number of likes leading towards Christmas, followed by a huge drop in the week between Christmas Day and New Year's Day. It could be argued that the reason for this dip is that less people are on Facebook or less likely to like a page during this period. We would argue that less paid campaigns are being run. This is valuable to advertisers because less competition in the auction will reduce the cost-per-click (CPC) price. On another note, we were interested to understand the impact that the new mobile ad formats had on like acquisition. We already understood that there was a decline in total mobile likes from October to February, but how did that stack up as a change in distribution of device likes?

Mobile likes versus desktop likes

Facebook reported growth in ad revenue through mobile at a global level. Regionally, our data showed a decrease in the share of mobile likes. This offers an opportunity for advertisers who are sophisticated enough to target by device by entering into a less busy auction place.

Paid likes by industry vertical

Naturally, some industries attach greater importance to acquiring likes than others. The industries most commonly paying for likes are travel, financial services and automotive. By understanding the share of likes coming from paid/organic, we can estimate the relative competition in CPC by industry. For example, knowing that travel, leisure and events is competitive, we can deduce that the cost-per-like will be expensive. This is useful for forecasting and planning your Facebook campaigns.

Impact of organic page recommendations

Historically, Facebook made it relatively easy for a page to spread organically. Stories like 'unmilon de voces contra las FARC', whereby a simple page created in someone's bedroom had spread overnight without paid advertising are becoming increasingly less common. This is because Facebook draws its primary revenue source from advertising, so they therefore make it difficult for a page to spread virally without paid media to springboard it.

We examined the share of likes being generated through Facebook's 'recommended pages' unit and extracted the pages based on size. Recommended pages give users a list of pages they might be interested in. Perhaps unsurprisingly, we discovered that the larger the page, the larger the share of a recommended page's likes. Once again, the key takeaway here is that unless your page has a large number of likes, the likelihood of your page to grow organically is limited.

Facebook went public before the time period of which the sample was taken for this analysis. However, we found that the share of these organic recommended likes had declined while the share of paid likes had increased. Interestingly, the drop in recommended pages occurs shortly before Facebook posted an increase in revenue in their fourth quarter of 2012 earnings.

Paid versus recommended like share over time

When comparing the relationship between paid like ads and recommended page likes, we found a negative correlation. In other words, the number of recommended page likes is lower when there is a heavy investment in paid advertising. Facebook appears to be subsidizing like acquisition when advertising budgets are low. These subsidized likes represent a greater proportion of total new likes when a page has reached a substantial size (>99,999 likes).

We can deduce that, for a brand to generate any meaningful volume of organic visibility through Facebook, they must grow to a minimum size of 100,000 likes. However, when a brand is advertising it is less likely to generate organic likes.

Market behaviour

With over 1 billion users of Facebook worldwide, reaching your target audience can be challenging. Your brand may desire to acquire likes from particular markets or geographic locations. Our analysis shows that the majority of brands in the MENA region are competing for likes in Egypt, Jordan, Saudi Arabia and the UK.

Be sure you are reaching the correct markets when you run your advertising. It is no surprise to see Egypt, with the largest population in MENA, so far ahead of all other markets. However, be careful not to fall into a trap and accidentally reach an audience that will never help you to achieve your business goals.

Who likes your pages?

Reaching the right audience is difficult. Knowing that your communications are being delivered to the people most likely to respond to your brand in a meaningful business manner is almost impossible, even with digital and all its 'bells and whistles' targeting methods.

We reviewed the demographic data of our 40 brands and found that nearly 61 per cent of the audience doing the liking was female. This means one of two things. Either women in MENA are more inspired by brands than men, or content being posted by brands is resonating louder with MENA's female audience. The key takeaway here is that it is important to understand the audience with which you are communicating, and the audience most likely to amplify your message by liking you.

Understanding that males and females behave differently on Facebook is as important as communicating across generations. If your brand is seeking to conquer Facebook, our data suggests going directly for an audience aged 18–24. However, depending on the vertical you occupy, this may change. For example, travel and leisure get more likes from men than women, and the most popular age bracket is 25–34. Although financial services are reaching an audience very similar to travel and leisure, this vertical typically concentrates its fanning on UAE. On the other hand, sportswear is most popular with much younger age groups. We initially felt this was likely because of the popularity of the brands within this vertical. However, the FMCG vertical includes some of the most recognizable and longest-living brands in history, yet it generally attracts likes from an older audience.

Average size of a page

As a benchmark, we found that over a five-month period the average page size was 103,000 likes.

Conclusions

- Paid advertising is by far the most successful method to acquire fans.

- Mobile is a growing part of the fan acquisition arsenal.

- There is an opportunity in the MENA region to capitalize on mobile as a source of cheap likes.

- More likes come from paid advertising than organic.

- Post on the weekend if your objective is to acquire viral likes triggered by your existing fans.

- Facebook is generating more and more likes. However, there seems to be a break in liking immediately after Christmas. This could be an opportunity for brands to take advantage of lower CPCs.

- Travel and leisure is generating the most paid likes across the MENA region.

- Pages with more than 99,999 likes will benefit more from Facebook's organic like units (page recommendations).

- Egypt is the source of most page likes in the region.

- Women are more likely to like brand pages more than men.
- The 18–24 age group is most likely to like a brand, but this varies by industry.
- Average page size varies by industry.

CASE STUDY   Positive Power Sp. z o.o./MusclePro

The client

Positive Power Sp. z o.o.

The agency

8a.

The project

MusclePro.

The challenge

- To reach new potential clients interested in outdoor sports.
- To strengthen customer loyalty.
- To increase brand awareness.
- To present 8a.pl offer.
- Sales boost.

Target audience

Active young people, open to innovative solutions and new technologies; people who positively react to all solutions facilitating the shopping process. The campaign should be original in form, catch attention and be untypical. It is also important to give the target audience a clear benefit.

Action

The beginning of the campaign included creative work, particularly the development of a new, fictitious product to market. The basis of the campaign was an 'innovative system MusclePro', sports clothes made of fabric supporting bodybuilding. A humorous presentation included a detailed product description, such as material equipped with Wi-Fi access.

The humorous character of the campaign was visible in the name of the product 'MusclePro', referring to body shaping and the suffix 'Pro' characteristic for the names of innovative technologies in the outdoor market. The main motto of the campaign was transformed from a phrase well-known in Poland 'first mass, then sculpture' to 'first sculpture, then sculpture'.

The comedic nature of the promotional campaign could be seen, above all, in an unusual description of the 'unique global solution coming from Finland'. Besides slimming and bodybuilding properties, it can also be used to wean the user away from snoring, and also discourages reptiles, night insects and gooseflesh.

Main strategic guidelines of the campaign

- To carry out humorous promotional action to go viral and reach the clients of the e-shop.

- To maintain a characteristic way of communication with the clients, using interactive, multichannel transmission.

- To present different marketing activities in a characterful way, giving clients a clear benefit – a concession coupon.

The campaign was based on the surprise effect and eye-catching comic overtones. The main point of reference of e-marketing activities was implemented for the needs of the campaign landing page: **www.8a.pl/musclepro**.

The campaign was also carried out in:

- additional promotional activities on the website;

- an e-mail marketing campaign;

- social media activities.

Results

Thanks to the creative approach, the campaign excited interest from the public. It caused surprise with fans of the store who were not sure whether the implemented product was real or not. Only after a careful analysis of the description of the product did they guess that it was fictitious. The idea for the campaign MusclePro spread fast in social media and has been taken over by another fan page, including those belonging to the competition.

Facts

- Brand awareness increased.

- 11.2 per cent increase of the average basket value.

- 8.7 per cent increase of the number of e-mail addresses in the mailing base.

- Threefold increase of the traffic on the website, which resulted in an increased level of interest in the offer.

Links to campaign

http://www.8a.pl/musclepro/
https://www.facebook.com/sklep8apl?fref=ts (fan page)

Understanding social media ROI – what matters and what doesn't

05

OUR CHAPTER PLEDGE TO YOU

When you reach the end of this chapter you will have the answers to the following questions:

- How can I calculate the value of social media activity?

- What is the difference between impact and sales generation?

- How can I put a monetary value on share of voice or share of conversation?

- How can I avoid vanity metrics?

- What are the different views on how to set up metrics and what to use as benchmarks?

- Which tools will help me to manage metrics most effectively?

Please give me clarity!

We would all like complete clarity over the meaning of ROI when it comes to social media spend, but as Ema Linaker is right to point out in her contribution to this chapter, 'meaningful ROI in social media is a work in progress'. We are all engaged in a digital, social experiment and each iteration requires a recalibration of the metrics we employ to ascertain the value of our social engagement. There is, however, a critical business need for metrics that calculate the *financial* impact of our social activity at every iteration. Your social media campaign will be deemed to have failed if it does not achieve the fiscal business objectives that you or your stakeholders set for it, however many likes, shares or conversations a campaign may have generated. Clarification around fuzzy social media activity is therefore essential if you are going to prove and manage value. Ana Jesus makes a pertinent point in her contribution to this chapter when she advises that a key metric is 'to refer to the number of conversations about your brand versus your competitors' brands, so you can understand how yours stands in the market versus competition'.

Employ the right metrics and you will be able to keep the business objectives on track and prove positive impact to your stakeholders. Set your conversion criteria according to your business goals at the outset; for example: online purchases made, contact form filled-in and lead achieved, online quotation request submitted, newsletter sign-up created, e-mail details captured, information PDF downloaded, and so on. Monitor key metrics such as reach, traffic, leads, customers and conversion rate in order to understand how effective you have been at achieving returns. Add a monetary value to each metric, either by using historical data as a benchmark or by producing guesstimates that get signed off by your CFO or stakeholders. Measure the total benefits by channel and qualify their value based on the amount of spend required to achieve them. Once you have calculated the actual cost you will be able to measure impact through analysis and shape the next stage of your strategy for improved returns.

Ana Jesus, EMEA marketing manager, Shoutlet

The question of what social media ROI means is still being asked. Some call it 'return on engagement' or 'return on influence'. These describe a few of the ways in which companies are getting value from social media, but technically they do not describe real ROI. Social media ROI is a measure of financial impact.

That is not to say that the ways social media is beneficial to your company are not important – they are critical (and they also contribute to the company's bottom line, albeit indirectly). The interactions and engagement your social media programme generates are not always linked to a sale, but they are important components in achieving business objectives.

Under this topic, we will be looking at the metrics that drive most tangible social media ROI results, whether directly related with sales or engagement, and at those that will not be accurate indicators of success.

What matters

- URL tracking: if your campaign goal is to drive people to a particular page on your website, by adding a tracking code on all links you can monitor through your analytics tool such as Google Analytics the number of unique page views, time on page and total pages viewed. By defining conversion goals based on the action that you want visitors to take, such as making a purchase, you can analyse direct campaign success.

- Unique landing pages or voucher codes: when a campaign leads people to a unique landing page or incentivizes purchase using a voucher code, its success can easily be measured by analysing the number of people who purchased coming from that landing page or using that specific voucher code.

- Share of voice (SOV): this refers to the number of conversations about your brand compared to your competitors' brands, so you can understand how yours stands in the market versus competition. Are customers talking more positively about your brand? Has a specific social media campaign helped to increase the company's SOV?

To identify the total number of conversations, you can use a free tool such as socialmention.com, or for more advanced listening capabilities you can use technology such as Shoutlet.com.

- Share of conversation (SOC): this is defined by the topics and conversations that your customers care about. They may not be brand related but market related. For example, what people say on 'comfortable footwear' can be relevant for a shoemaker. So, by listening to what is being discussed around that topic with a tool such as Shoutlet, the shoemaker could drive a campaign to focus on what they find that is important for customers in regard to comfortable footwear.

- Community insight data: when a campaign drives additional social profile data – such as contact information and other likes and interests – this feeds your marketing and customer support team with very useful insights. These can typically help you to segment your customer base to drive more targeted marketing and support that will, eventually, lead to more sales.

What does not matter

- Amount of friends, fans and followers: to measure the success of your campaigns based on your number of followers is a commonly established misconception of digital success measurement. The reason is that, just the fact that you have many people following or liking your brand on social channels does not actually mean they are engaged with what is being published and it certainly does not reflect your bottom-line revenue. For example, it may be that a specific campaign, such as an enticing competition, drives a large number of people to follow or like your brand page in order to enter the competition, but it does not reflect any future engagement or purchases.

- Amount of retweets and comments: these 'vanity metrics' give a false sense of hope that your content is generating leads. Just as for the number of fans and followers, these might have been generated due to a particular campaign or topic that interested them, but do not reflect their purchase intention.

- Sentiment: the sentiment measure refers to the amount of positive or negative comments across the web about your brand. Several tools can provide this measurement by using automated analytics that tag specific words, usually referred as negative or positive presenting their total representation. These, however, are not 100 per cent accurate – because if, for example, a tool tags a comment as negative for having the word 'hate' in the same sentence as the brand name, it is not considering sentences such as 'I hate that I just missed out on the brand's promotion'. So, the best way to monitor sentiment accurately would actually be to go through each mention manually. However, will brands actually get results that affect their social ROI based on that analysis? Not necessarily. For example, Ryanair is probably one of the airlines with the highest negativity sentiment across the web, but it still remains Europe's largest discount airline with over €1.5 billion in revenue.

- Klout score: this is a number in the range 1–100 that represents the level of influence of a social account, where the highest scores represent the most influential accounts. Although this score is meant to measure your authority on a topic, it is not truly accurate. For once, it mainly focuses on quantity rather than quality, meaning that if a person or brand communicates frequently about subjects with meaningless importance, they will still score higher than someone who sends really insightful communications on the same topic but that is not as regular in publishing.

The available measurement methods for social media success are varied and identifying what works best for your team does take time based on your social media goals. However, there are certainly metrics that can provide more tangible results towards your bottom line ROI than others. You should focus your efforts in measuring these metrics so you can prove the importance that your daily work has on the organization and, ultimately, justify to the executive team the need for further investment into social.

Ema Linaker, Holler/Leo Burnett

When social media first arrived on the scene, it was a numbers game: the person with the most Myspace friends was king. It is unlikely that this idea will ever entirely go away. Since time immemorial people have sought to surround themselves with worshippers. Brand pages with communities in the double digits will always look sort of sad, and the thrill of thousands of Twitter followers presumably hanging on your every word will always be intoxicating.

That is simply human nature. No one denies that a social media presence is now a crucial fabric of a brand itself, yet social media marketers are still finding their way through some murky waters; they are still trying to measure properly how many people they are reaching and how much engagement they are generating – and what constitutes value in this environment. Meaningful social metrics are still a work in progress.

For example, a winner at the Cannes Lions creativity awards in June 2014 – the Volvo Trucks' 'Epic Split' commercial – drew 74 million views by the end of the year. But what exactly did the brand get out of that? Was it a success from a messaging perspective? That is debatable. After all, when asked about the commercial later, many people were unable to recall the brand that staged it.

As marketers, we struggle with how best to sell these newfangled products to our clients, and because some of us were new to them ourselves, we handle the concept of social media ROI pretty clumsily at best. We equate inflated numbers with social media success, assuring our clients that if they hit wildly arbitrary number-based milestones, they have won. We soon learned, however, that these wins were tiny compared to what we would later learn were the most important benchmarks of all.

But just as social media's initial users grew up (sort of), our thinking around the true value of social media matured as well. We started to realize that you could have 500 Facebook friends, but only share a personal connection with a fraction of them, if you were lucky. You could have 50 likes on a single Instagram photo, but not a single word of real conversation – it is odd how things often stay the same.

Follower numbers will always impress clients. Inarguably that is the easiest metric to understand. Everyone knows that 5,000 is more than 4,000, but not everyone can see why a Facebook comment is more valuable than a Facebook page like.

And there is nothing wrong with hitting big numbers. Numbers hold value, but savvy marketers know they are not the *only* thing that holds value, especially when you consider the click farms and spam accounts that drive those numbers sky-high. Even worse, the more followers you have, the lower your engagement metrics will be, unless every single member of your community is engaged, which is rare to the point of being virtually impossible.

From social media metrics to social media engagement

Consider this:

- In 2013, Twitter was forced to admit that at least 5 per cent of user accounts were fake or spam.

- Facebook is currently battling claims that the majority of page likes come from 'click farms', ie users who are paid to click the like button.

- Instagram received so many comments about fake accounts that in 2012 they had to issue a formal statement addressing the issue.

So marketing has changed forever. Social media metrics that worked when we started do not work any more, and measurement must evolve and adapt to the new era of social media engagement.

We must think no longer of marketing in siloed channels but rather as a constant connection with consumers. This allows us to have 'real time' dialogue and to drive instant impact on sales through that approach. Long planning cycles have been relegated to the history books. Marketers must think of how they can drive forward continuous 'social media engagement'.

Even today, people will chuckle cynically 'Who wants to engage with a soft drink?' or 'Why do I want to have a conversation with a tube of toothpaste?' (although some tubes of toothpaste are wittier than the average marketing professional). Sadly, they have missed the point of social media. They are missing the fact that we no longer care about reach – we care about impact and how we can help to create 'data-driven creative'. So what can we do as social media marketers to prove our value to the organizations we serve? Frankly, we need to use data to optimize business results not (just) activity. In this new age of measuring social media ROI, we have been forced to reshape our definition of desired online behaviours. It is not enough for a user to simply click 'like' on our client's brand page. There is a whole slew of actions we are hoping they will take that we now realize are far more powerful en route to the holy 'path to purchase'.

Social media accounts are run by human beings. Smart people who run social media accounts on behalf of brands know that those accounts should behave like human beings, and the KPIs that we put a premium on should reflect the things we value as part of the human experience, namely:

- experiencing emotions;
- having conversations;
- sharing information.

So what should we be measuring and why? All campaigns should focus on the following metrics to gauge whether the right emotional connections have been achieved:

- audience profile;
- share of voice;
- nature of conversations triggered;
- influencer engagement;
- conversions;
- tribal/community reaction;
- geography.

Questions to ask yourself are:

- What is the size of the audience exposed to the message? (This gives you the reach of your campaign; see community metrics below.)

- What is the exposed audience's awareness, preference and/or perception of the brand? (This will enable you to find out the attitude/sentiment.)

- Finally, you need to measure action: what bottom line actions did the exposed audience take, eg purchase?

Here is a recommended checklist of everything we think a basic measurement programme would track:

- Brand and campaign performance through social listening:
  - Sentiment. (Tracked over time, has our campaign created a shift towards positivity?)
  - Share of voice tracked against competitors and general industry conversation. (Has our campaign earned a bigger share of online mentions for the client?)
  - Conversation themes. (What types of conversations has our campaign generated? How have they affected consumer perception and opinion of the brand?)
  - Influential commentators. (Has the campaign generated involvement from influential voices and how have they influenced the conversation?)

- Community and content:
  - Community growth: as a direct result of campaign messaging and engagement.
  - Content impressions: indicator of traditional ad metrics eyeball-on-branding.
  - Engaged users: how many people have chosen to interact with our messaging, an image view, video play, a link click.
  - Engagement rate (engaged users/impressions).

- Engagement analysis (eg likes versus comments, depending on their relevance to the content message).
- Commercial impact metrics:
  - Traffic and conversions (tracking links across channels that drive traffic to a point of sale, and their conversion rate).
  - CRM integration (aligning sales and purchase databases with the social audience and consumer profile, ie is our social audience actually buying our products and can we track it?).

If we live in a new world that is centred around the premise of data-driven creativity, we need to skill the organization accordingly. Talent needs to have different kinds of skill sets and attitudes to deliver that new vision. You need to work with individuals who thrive on experimentation, who relentlessly drive for insights that inform creative thinking:

- They focus on connecting the data they collect through social media listening and analysis tools to their client's business.
- They are highly collaborative and break down all siloes both within the agency and the client organization.
- They are a new breed of individual that works based on facts not opinion.

James Eder, founder and head of new business, The Beans Group

Since founding Student Beans back in 2005 the world has changed. We are now more connected and have access to more information than ever before. The lessons that we have learned from marketing to the 16–24 age range do not have to apply to the youth demographic in isolation – as marketers we have needed to be smarter in how we approach the way we work in order to succeed, both in terms of how we market ourselves as a brand and how we deliver success for our partners we work with. Growing the business to establish ourselves as a leading youth media brand, and working with some of the world's biggest brands, I want to share three key messages that have helped us get to where we are today: know your audience; be authentic; be social by design.

Know your audience

It is really important to identify who your core audience is and what they want. Since starting Student Beans, there has always been an intent and focus on young people. Our mission is to produce content that makes life a little more awesome for students. Whether that is through our discounts, our digital student lifestyle magazine or our jobs board – everything we do has our users at the forefront. It is also important to stay connected to your audience. Under the wider umbrella of The Beans Group, we also run youth insights consultancy Voxburner, which gives us a platform to help our partners really understand the youth market, giving them the edge on the new generation via daily insights, research and industry events. Young people constantly change and new trends emerge – and brands need up-to-date information, ideas and inspiration in order to stay connected.

Be authentic

With today's consumer being more savvy than ever, marketing messages that lack depth and are seen as a plaster or a quick fix will not be received well. Whilst there may be some quick wins in the short term, in the long term it won't work. Gone are the days when a brand can say one thing that we all believe; it is what a brand *does* that we all see. In *Who Cares Wins: Why Good Business is Better Business* by David Jones (2011), he acknowledges that there was a wave when corporate social responsibility was an add-on by companies to make them look good. This simply doesn't work any more; it is no longer what we say but what we do. Consumers can see through this – and the real winners will shine through. Can you speak confidently and genuinely about your company and what you do?

Be social by design

Do you have a product or service that people want to talk about? If not, I would suggest to stop marketing, go back to the board or product team and question your purpose. If you were with a group of friends would you talk about your product or company? If so, what would you say? Too often marketers are tasked with running campaigns for products or services that people just don't want. One of the ways we grew Student Beans to reach millions of visitors every month was to start with the user in mind. What do people want and what will people naturally share? Whilst we have worked with lots of brands in the past, from pizza companies to cinema chains, theme parks to fashion retailers, the common theme is that people will share their experiences with each other. Student Beans is at the heart of the conversation. We help students on their journey, whether that be saving money, discovering something new or getting a job. Social media is just a new tool to share things people want to talk about (albeit a much easier platform that reaches many more people). If what you are saying is not of interest or relevant, you are likely to have a lot of false starts. How can you be at the heart of people's conversations?

Jenna Hanington and Molly Hoffmeister, Salesforce

If you are like many marketers, you spend a generous portion of your time monitoring your social channels, often with little idea of how they are performing for you. But as increasingly sophisticated reporting tools emerge on a seemingly daily basis, it should come as no surprise when your boss finally approaches you to ask for concrete proof of the value of your social efforts.

After all, you probably knew this day was coming. Across the board, technologies such as marketing automation and other reporting platforms have brought the art of marketing closer and closer to a measurable science – it was only a matter of time before goals such as 'having a presence' and 'building relationships' were no longer enough to justify spending large chunks of time on Facebook and Twitter. While these are very real and very valuable goals of social media marketing, the C-level will likely need some hard metrics to prove that time (and money) spent on social media is worthwhile.

So how do you get started? How do you quantify social media success, and what metrics does your boss really want to see? Gauging your social media ROI – the right way – requires going back to the basics: goal setting. Without deciding on some specific goals, it is difficult to determine which factors need to be measured in order to show success. Let's take a look at some common social media goals, as well as the appropriate metrics that can be used to measure them and how you can obtain these metrics yourself.

Goal 1: increase follower engagement

Metrics to measure: growth in follower counts, interactions and more
Tracking follower and engagement numbers is the simplest and most logical first step towards proving that your efforts are yielding results – and something you should be doing even if you are just maintaining a very basic presence on social media. Start by creating a spreadsheet to keep track of how your social following is growing over time. Keeping an eye on these numbers will allow you to pinpoint trends and jumps in your follower numbers, helping you to gauge the impact of your efforts and share progress with your manager.

While your boss likely doesn't care how many retweets you received this week, overall engagement levels *are* important – after all, listening to and engaging with your customers is what having a presence on social media is all about. Take time to aggregate your social interactions (likes, comments, shares, retweets, replies etc) and keep track of these numbers over time. Having these records to compare month-on-month gives you metrics that you can point to in order to demonstrate growth: growth in your follower counts, growth in engagement (retweets, social interactions) and more. As a result, you can go to your boss and say, 'This month, we acquired 650 new fans and followers across our social channels and increased engagement levels by 15 per cent', instead of giving a vague response about how well you *think* your active campaigns are doing.

Goal 2: increase brand awareness

Metrics to measure: impressions, clicks and traffic

While engaging with your current fans and followers is certainly an important goal of social media, so is reaching people who may not be aware of your brand but could potentially end up being valuable prospective buyers. One of the most effective ways to use social media to this purpose is through paid social advertising.

Facebook, Twitter and LinkedIn all offer self-service advertising options for businesses of any size. With a little budget, you can experiment with boosting your social postings for increased engagement, or promoting your page or offering to reach new users. Furthermore, social ad targeting options allow you to narrow your focus to your exact target audience, based on both demographical information and interests. However, with added budget involved, your boss will likely require even more metrics as proof of campaign success.

An advanced reporting platform such as social.com can provide thorough insight into the success of your social ads and can help you to organize your campaigns by objective. But if you are just getting started with paid social and are not ready for the investment, tracking impressions and clicks is a good place to start. These numbers indicate how much exposure you are getting from your campaigns, and can prove that your social efforts are helping to gain visibility for your company and generate brand awareness. Even if your social campaigns are not exactly driving the revenue results that you had hoped for right away (remember that developing successful social ads is a process; you will get a better idea of the content and messaging that works on each channel over time), being able to report that a post had 10,000 impressions and drove 400 visitors to your site can show that your campaigns are still contributing value.

If you are investing in paid social advertising, all three platforms (Facebook, Twitter and LinkedIn) provide easy access to these metrics. When you pull reporting stats on your advertisements, you have the option to download them as a data file (CSV format) and quickly grab sums from whatever metrics you prefer (clicks, click-throughs, engagements, impressions, etc). But even if you are not yet investing in paid social advertising and do not have access to these reports, using bit.ly links and website analytics can provide insight into clicks and traffic, and give you some basic metrics for brand awareness.

Goal 3: prove social media ROI

Metrics to measure: leads generated, revenue generated

The ability to prove social media ROI is the ultimate goal of social media marketing – and, if you are planning to invest a large amount of time and resources into social advertising, proving the impact of social on your bottom line will likely be crucial to demonstrating the importance of your efforts, especially to upper management.

Even without advanced social media reporting tools, you can take your reporting to the next level and start calculating social media ROI using a marketing automation platform. Create tracked links for your social media campaigns, tie these links to a campaign you create within your platform, and start keeping track of how many prospects your social media campaigns are creating. Interactions with your campaign will be pulled into the prospect's profile, and as these prospects move from lead to opportunity to closed deal, you can start to see how your social media campaigns are contributing to the bottom line of your business.

Whether you are just getting started with social media or ready to invest a large amount of budget in paid social advertising, tracking metrics has become an important part of social media marketing success. Knowing which of your social campaigns is bringing in the dough can help you to prioritize budget and time allocations so that your resources are going towards the initiatives with guaranteed success. So work on aligning your goals with the metrics that make sense – then get measuring!

Mark Walker, content marketing and social media manager, Eventbrite

Social media is ubiquitous in our lives these days. To tweet, like and pin have become verbs that everyone understands, and yet so much remains misunderstood about social media, and particularly the role it plays in business.

For many businesses, social media is often looked at from two extremes. On the one hand, many executives see it as an exercise in time-wasting, full of vanity metrics and dubious ROI; to others it is seen as a free and easy way to connect with eager fans who are just waiting to buy their products.

The truth, of course, is more nuanced. To really understand social media ROI, we first need to start with and define the 'return' in ROI. What do we hope to get from using social media? There are many returns we could look for – followers, retweets, mentions, likes, fans, engagement, pins, shares, feedback, impressions, cheaper customer service and, yes, even sales. I suggest grouping them into three kinds of return: distribution, engagement and sales.

Which of these you should aim for depends entirely on your business goals and strategy. The return has to align with your existing strategy, otherwise you cannot compare apples with apples, and the likelihood is that the outcome of your social media dalliance will not be satisfactory to senior management.

Let's look at each in turn.

Distribution

You might focus your efforts on distribution if you are a media company wanting to reach a wider audience, or a new company looking to build awareness of your brand and aiming to establish a thought leadership position in the market.

The kinds of metrics you can measure to judge the return will be things such as retweets, shares, pins, site visits, subscriptions and impressions. These can be further grouped into two types of metric: direct and indirect.

Direct metrics such as retweets and shares are impressions that can be measured directly in the social media channel using tools such as Hootsuite; indirect metrics such as site visits and subscriptions are best measured using tools such as Google Analytics to tell you the sources of your traffic. You can then look at the conversion from traffic source to subscriber using goals and funnels.

Engagement

You might focus your efforts on engagement if you are a community business such as an events company, but it equally applies to media companies who want a two-way dialogue with their audience, and commerce companies looking to get user feedback, increase their net promoter score (NPS) or improve their customer service.

Depending on which of these goals you are aiming for, you can track metrics such as followers, mentions, likes, fans, conversations, NPS or customer-service response times. Again, some will be directly trackable in each social channel, while others will require additional tools to understand which channels have directly fed into improving results such as NPS and customer service.

One hard to measure, but potentially large benefit I would put into 'engagement' is feedback and research for future product or service developments. Sites such as Twitter, Quora and Facebook can be goldmines of information for the diligent company looking for new features to develop or gaps in the market.

I would argue that finding quantifiable market needs that your company could fill is definitely a return that is worth a little invest-ment in research and social listening.

Sales

You might argue that every business should be focused on this particular return. And you would be right. However, most businesses are sophisticated enough to know that other strategies ultimately support sales. Market share, brand positioning, customer awareness, high NPS, loyalty and all manner of other goals should lead to an increase in sales, and these can all be positively impacted by social media activity. So let's break sales into two: direct and indirect.

Direct sales via social media might involve a company that puts out a time-bound offer each day for one of its products through a particular social channel. You can then measure how many people that click on this offer convert into a sale. Simple!

Indirect sales can be more complex to measure. For example, you may share a lot of tips and useful content with your audience, who are then driven to your site, and from there they purchase your hot deal of the day. Do you credit your social strategy for that sale (at least partially)? Do you even know where the customer journey originated?

Even more difficult is if someone begins to follow you, pins an item or two on their Pinterest account, likes your Facebook page but has no immediate need for your product. However, 60 days later they do, and so they use Google to search for you, and ultimately make a purchase. Will you credit the sale to the awareness driven by that early social engagement, or to search engine optimization (SEO)? There is not enough space here to discuss the 'how' of setting up multitouch attribution models that can track a user's journey across channels and devices, from discovery through research and eventually to decision. The point is that you will need to set it up in order to understand social media ROI.

Investment

Once your return has been decided on (bear in mind that you may have more than one goal), it is time to decide on your investment. How? Well, you should benchmark against your other promotional activities. For example, if retargeting typically provides you with a 150 per cent ROI, then you should probably aim to see similar results from social media (after a reasonable period of time). Now you can work backwards.

Let's say you want to see uplift in unique visitors per month because you know there is a direct correlation between visitors and sales. Your conversion rate is 5 per cent per month, with an average sale of £50. Retargeting delivers you 50,000 monthly uniques at a cost of £50,000, typically leading to 2,500 sales and therefore £125,000 in revenue. You want your social media activity to increase uniques by 10 per cent, a 5,000 increase. This means you should look to invest £5,000 in your social media activity.

As another example, Eventbrite found in their Social Commerce Report that every time someone shares an Eventbrite event through social media, that share drives an average of 16 visits back to the original event page, and generates approximately £2.41 in incremental revenue for the event organizer. Armed with this kind of information, it means you know that every £1 spent on getting a share on social media (or hour – whatever form your investment takes) should result in an average £2.41, an ROI of 141 per cent. Quickly you can start to understand the ROI of social media.

Conclusion

The key to really understanding social media ROI – what matters and what doesn't – is to implement this model:

1 Define your return to align with existing strategy.

2 Set up your tracking.

3 Benchmark your investment against other marketing activities.

4 Measure the results.

With this model in place, you can clearly understand the ROI of your social media activities – and forget about everything else that doesn't feed into your overall strategy, it is just a distraction.

Kieran Kent, managing director, Propeller PR

Business to business (B2B) communications as a whole has undergone a dramatic shift over the last decade. For one thing it is increasingly fragmented. Blogs, tweets, peer-organized events and other forms of social media now work alongside mainstream media to meet the continuing appetite for real-time insight, analysis and debate. Most B2B businesses now have a social media footprint, but the fact remains that only a minority of B2B brands are getting their social strategies right. They have a strong focus on ROI, but that should not negate an integrated social media strategy that supports it.

In part this is because the advent of social media upset the traditional B2B media apple cart. For years, media activity sat neatly in a silo of either 'paid' or 'earned' media with in-house marketing teams collaborating with PR, creative and media agency partners to devise effective strategies around those channels. The rise of 'owned media' has made it necessary for companies to rethink these traditional siloes. Social media forces businesses to act like publishers and manage their own communications channels – and whilst social media presents fantastic opportunities to engage with key influencers, clients and stakeholders, it also presents a number of challenges:

- Which tools should companies use? Twitter, LinkedIn, Google+, YouTube, Facebook and Pinterest, to name just a few, all provide different benefits and present different challenges.

- Who takes ownership? Should the in-house marketing and communications teams be responsible for social activity or should it be outsourced to partner agencies?

- What is the right tone of voice for a B2B brand? Authoritative? Controversial? Conversational? Witty? How much personality do you really want to convey through your brand's social channels?

It is no surprise that most of the great social media case studies we tend to see are from business to consumer (B2C) brands, which are all desperate to achieve the next 'Oreo Moment', when a clever real-time tweet during Super Bowl XLVII's now infamous blackout went viral. Consumer brands are quick to develop social campaigns around major events, as witnessed at the 2014 football World Cup, where brands such as Snickers wasted no time piggybacking conversations about Luis Suárez's notorious bite.

For B2B brands, these sorts of impactful, attention-grabbing social campaigns are harder to achieve – but that does not mean that all B2B social media should be dismissed as 'Boring2Boring'. So what is the right approach for a B2B brand to social media?

Setting social media goals

At Propeller PR, we specialize in working with B2B marketing, advertising, media and technology businesses, helping them to implement multichannel comms campaigns. We recommend that all B2B brands should have three common goals that drive their social media activities: extending reach, developing brand awareness and engaging with influencers.

Extending reach

By building a strong social media presence, B2B brands can use social channels to communicate good news and information about their company to a much wider audience than they would normally be able to reach. What is more, this sort of activity remains firmly in the control of the messenger, from the frequency and the timing of communication – you can react to conversation threads in real-time, making adjustments to content on the fly if you need to, something that is not easy to do outside of the social media realm.

Developing brand awareness

Thought leadership is a major strand of B2B PR, most often centred on a cause or specific hot topic in the industry. Done well, and done credibly, thought leadership creates a brand around an individual, which extends the ideology of the business they represent. Social media – Twitter, in particular – makes it easy to connect with others interested in similar themes, communities and people, and to build a network of advocates.

Engaging with influencers

Influencer engagement is still an area where many B2B brands fall short, yet it is probably the most critical step. If you are going to invest time and energy in social media then don't just go through the motions. Setting arbitrary targets for how many tweets you do each week and adopting a one-way-broadcast only social approach will get you nowhere. Social media should be used to engage with your audience, and a quality over quantity approach should be the order of the day. Focus on interacting with key influencers and stakeholders and on building a community of followers who will value the content that comes from your brand.

B2B success stories

Despite the fact that B2C social media campaigns usually grab the headlines and accolades, there are an increasing number of B2B social media success stories. Take a look at HubSpot's blog for a great example of a company that updates content frequently, utilizes thought-provoking contributors and promotes its content through every available channel.

SAP's Better Run World social media campaign is also an excellent example of a campaign that helped to alter perceptions of a brand. Traditionally seen as an enterprise resource planning (ERP) provider, the campaign helped to position SAP as a business innovation partner and led to an increase of 42,995 followers on Twitter and 30,000 visits to the campaign landing page.

Virgin Media's Pioneers campaign is another success story, bringing together an online community of enterprising people who use videos and blogging to share their ideas and experiences, network and collaborate with each other.

Without doubt, each of these examples are of businesses that have greater depth of resource than many B2B brands, and some companies simply do not have the capacity to devise and implement large-scale, highly creative social campaigns. But that doesn't mean your social media strategy won't deliver results. Irrespective of your size of business, there are a number of best-practice principles that you must adhere to in order to see a strong ROI.

Bake social into the rhythm of your business

B2B brands often start social media with the best of intentions, only to stop because it is not properly integrated into existing operations. Given the decision has been made about what the objectives are, it is important to look at the balance of the existing team, what the skill sets of any retained agencies are, and decide where the responsibility for social channels should sit.

Also remember that sustained engagement, growing an audience and interacting with the right influencers takes time and investment. Like a media company, a brand has to earn attention by being timely, entertaining and informative to its target audience and getting the balance right across social channels.

In these cases, running social channels can become time-consuming if added to an existing person's remit; and the strategy can become disjointed and incoherent if spread across too many people. Make sure you have the right resources, skills and expertise to achieve the objectives that you have set.

Put in place an editorial strategy that makes sense for your brand

A B2B brand's approach to communications should reflect and reinforce its own values, and its approach to social media should be no different.

Traditionally, smaller 'challenger' brands have greater latitude to be more playful or spiky in their approach to advertising, and many brands play to that strength. Other brands are far more conservative and closed: the classic example is Apple – who tend not to focus on social media and believe it doesn't need to. But with three decades of history, a loyal following that predates the web itself and a unique, iconic brand, its ambassadors, followers and advocates do the opinion-shaping work on social media, irrespective of what media have to say. The company is large enough and successful enough to play by its own rules and operate a 'closed' culture: most businesses without those luxuries have to work harder to earn attention.

Crucially, the approach to social media must reflect a company's own culture and values:

- follow and retweet third parties that reflect those values;
- repost blog pieces on LinkedIn from leaders within the business;
- develop infographics that illustrate a specific point.

In addition to corporate news, whether it is executive hires, new partnerships or expansions – blog posts that reflect the day-to-day operations of the company can also be effective in communicating the values of the business. Openness and transparency implicitly communicate confidence and inspire trust.

Develop a different approach for each platform

If engagement and growing a company network is the aim, it is important to work within the style and context of the platform. The overwhelming majority of people on Twitter will also have LinkedIn and

Facebook profiles – not to mention Google+, Instagram and a myriad of other accounts, but engagement works differently in each network.

Brands frequently get burned for taking the wrong approach with new platforms: whether that is being overly corporate and stilted in the wrong context (eg posting an organization chart on Pinterest), or overly personal or familiar (as some brands have been criticized for doing on Facebook).

LinkedIn, once seen as a website for job seekers, has become the de facto network for professionals. Features such as news feeds and the ability to follow thought leaders have helped the company to refine its position between the simple but sticky Twitter and Facebook – for many professionals connecting on LinkedIn has become as second nature as swapping business cards – in effect, it is a cloud-based, open address book that has hit scale but is focused on growing the interaction between its users.

While LinkedIn may be better suited for direct engagement, Twitter remains the platform of focus for B2B marketing. Unlike Facebook, which has introduced its own algorithms to influence which posts you see in your feed, Twitter has not been selective. The upshot is that it has got harder to find relevant content unless you are actively searching or 'always on', 24 hours a day, seven days a week.

As such, much of the art of good B2B social media is in understanding the optimal times that your audience use the platform – sending tweets early in the morning, during lunchtimes or post-work commute times, tied to market time zones – and gives the best opportunity to catch your audience.

Whichever social channels you use, make sure you set targets and measure your results. This will mean that you can refine your approach based on what proves successful, and make iterative changes to your social strategy as you go.

Conclusion

Done well, social media is now a business-critical communications channel for switched-on B2B brands. There is an enormous opportunity to build communities of engaged, fully informed, identifiable individuals who are kept up to date with your brand's latest activities, thoughts, commentary, media coverage or commercial successes – and this is financially valuable.

But the question still remains as to how to build this community. Remember that social media success is just like success in a physical meeting or networking event. The more you say that is of interest, of value and on-topic, the more likely you are to make a connection. Social media is not a one-way street. It is not a soap box for you to proclaim your views to a captive audience, or like a 'bad first date' where the other person spends the whole time talking about themselves. When it comes to social media for B2B companies, it is far better to listen to others, actively contribute to conversations – and do all you can not to be boring!

Chapter conclusions

To understand social media ROI properly, we first need to start with and define the 'return'. Gauging your social media ROI – the right way – requires going back to the basics: goal setting. Without deciding on some specific goals, it is difficult to determine which factors need to be measured in order to show success. Meaningful social metrics are still a work in progress but there are some key business needs that you will need to meet. Define your return to align with existing strategy, set up your tracking, benchmark your investment against other marketing activities and then you will be able to measure the results.

CASE STUDY   Quantcast/Tweeting to the right audience

Client

Quantcast.

Brief

Tweeting to the right audience.

The challenge

There is an active community on Twitter amongst media and marketing professionals, making it an ideal channel for Quantcast to reach new customers and re-engage existing site visitors. Quantcast used Twitter to achieve two campaign objectives: the first was to increase European traffic to the Quantcast website; the second was to drive lead generation through white paper downloads and survey completions. Quantcast were keen to test Twitter against a benchmark cost per action (CPA).

Target audience

The campaign was intended to generate sales leads for Quantcast's Advertise service. Quantcast Advertise allows marketers to reach audiences using programmatic (real-time automated) advertising, so the primary audience for the campaign was a highly targeted niche B2B audience of brand side (in-house) marketers and media agencies.

Twitter-tailored audiences in action

Quantcast implemented tags on their website to create target segments for Twitter to match to its users. Quantcast's advertising technology sent this data to Twitter in order for them to find matches within their user base. The segments included prospecting and retargeting data.

The retargeting data identified Quantcast website visitors who were also Twitter users. The prospecting data was derived from Quantcast's custom audience profile, which identified Quantcast's most likely customers from across the internet. Quantcast informed Twitter of other internet users who matched the audience profile of its most engaged website visitors. Quantcast's comprehensive and instantaneous map of web activity was used to identify ideal prospects. Once again, Twitter then matched the segment with their user base. These Twitter users had the most data points in common with current customers and engaged website visitors.

With the segments available in the Twitter interface, targeting options were then set in Twitter and tweets were created to promote Quantcast's latest white paper and research survey. Quantcast then leveraged the power of real-time advertising to reach only the new prospects and existing website visitors to influence their journey and drive them to conversion. When a Quantcast ad was shown and clicked on, it linked through to a landing page. This enabled them to capture contact information. The leads were then nurtured and qualified for the Quantcast sales team.

Results

Record-breaking audience engagement.

Quantcast's Twitter ads campaign using tailored audience targeting drove their highest yet engagement rate on Twitter: 9.55 per cent. This was almost four times higher than the average engagement rate and was more than two times higher than previous Twitter campaigns, which used standard targeting. The organic and viral nature of Twitter also worked to Quantcast's advantage by driving down the CPA – because advertisers only pay per first engagement, any further engagement was of no extra cost. Ultimately, Quantcast's Twitter-tailored audience campaign succeeded in outperforming the previous best-performing paid marketing channel.

Links to campaign

https://www.quantcast.com/

http://www.brandrepublicinsight.com/DynamicList/Session

http://www.thedrum.com/knowledge-bank/2014/06/17/twitter-s-new-
targeting-options-make-tailored-real-time-advertising-0

https://www.quantcast.com/twitter.com

About the creator

- *Quantcast*: a technology company specializing in real-time advertising and audience measurement. As the pioneer of direct audience measurement in 2006, Quantcast now has the most in-depth understanding of digital audiences across the web, allowing marketers and publishers to make the smartest choices as they buy and sell the most effective targeted advertising on the market. More than 1,000 brands rely on Quantcast for real-time advertising. As the leader in big data for the digital advertising industry, Quantcast directly measures more than 100 million web destinations, incorporates over 1 trillion new data records every month and continuously processes as much as 30 petabytes of data every day. Quantcast is headquartered in San Francisco and backed by Founders Fund, Polaris Venture Partners and Cisco Systems.

- *Konrad Feldman, co-founder and CEO*: Konrad Feldman and Paul Sutter launched Quantcast in 2006, its aim to transform the effectiveness of online advertising through the use of science and scalable computing. Prior to co-founding Quantcast, Feldman co-founded Searchspace (now Fortent), the leading provider of terrorist-financing detection and anti-money-laundering software for the world's financial services industry. As CEO of Searchspace's North American business, he established the business in the US and directed its rapid growth to become a market leader. Prior to Searchspace, Feldman was a research fellow in the Intelligent Systems Laboratory at University College London. He holds a BSc in Computer Science from University College London.

CASE STUDY   Remington SE/Shoutlet

Client

Remington SE.

Agency

Shoutlet.

Brief

Grow product awareness and generate sales.

Overview

In an effort to increase brand awareness and social exposure across Scandinavian countries, Remington Sweden leveraged blogger relations to demonstrate the Silk product line through Facebook. By involving bloggers, Remington ensured brand-engagement with these influencers whilst they advocated product credibility.

SOURCE: Image used with permission from Spectrum Brands, Inc.

Approach

Shoutlet Social Canvas enabled Remington to design a completely customizable, branded Facebook app with six embedded blogger videos connected to a voting poll. Shoutlet's tech therapy and account management teams ensured Remington had both the technical and strategic support to build the application, with ease-of-use in mind in order to enable a seamless experience for fans to participate and share the campaign with others. The voting submission included data capture and newsletter opt-in fields that fed directly into Remington's Shoutlet Profiles, allowing the brand to get further insight into their customers.

The campaign: Get Ready to Turn Heads

Using a Facebook page app, Remington listed a selection of blogger tutorial videos providing tips on hair styling using the Remington Silk curling wand. Fans were then invited to vote on their favourite tip in order to be in with a chance to win their own set of Silk styling appliances. By submitting their vote and a sentence explaining the reason for their choice, Remington ensured that entrants had seen the videos, therefore gaining more exposure to the product and what it can do.

The competition generated 517 votes over a three-month period, having successfully reached a wider audience beyond Remington's Facebook fans, through shares and general Facebook promotion.

Results

- 52.7 per cent year-on-year sales growth during the period that the app was live.

- 34 per cent increase in Facebook fans.

- 49 per cent increase in engagement.

- 283 new contacts added to mailing list.

Client testimonial

'Our Swedish Facebook page was very new and had a small number of fans before the campaign launch but the level of awareness our page received from this campaign made a significant difference both in terms of fan numbers and localized social engagement. We are really pleased with the results and with the support we received from Shoutlet to make this happen so quickly.'

Amy Roberts, Remington, Spectrum Brands

About the creator

Shoutlet is an enterprise-class, cloud-based social relationship platform that empowers brands to build meaningful customer relationships by harnessing the power of social marketing. More than 600 brands and agencies in 50 countries use Shoutlet to publish, engage and measure social marketing campaigns that gather consumer data to drive measurable business impact. Headquartered in Madison in the United States, Shoutlet has additional offices in New York, San Francisco and London. Current customers include 3M, Regus, Corinthia Hotels, Best Buy, NASCAR, Canon, Shutterfly, Norwegian Cruise Line and Cloetta.

Why social media is central to customer experience

OUR CHAPTER PLEDGE TO YOU

When you reach the end of this chapter you will have the answers to the following questions:

- How does social media help to shape customer experience?
- What does 'think customer' mean?
- Where do social and customer experiences cross?
- How can I better segment my social audiences?
- How can I make the communications consistent across all channels?
- How can I use data monitoring to create success?
- Where do my communities and their conversations happen?
- Why is 'advocacy' marketing gold dust?
- How can viral campaigns destroy a brand?
- Why do real-owner stories help to shape outbound content?
- Do I still need to engage with customers via e-mail?
- Should I create a social media strategy or a social media policy for our workforce to use?
- Why do connected customers thrive in an omnichannel world?

The customer is always right, right?

In the early years of the world wide web, online shopping was a lonely experience. Gone were the days of observing the buying habits of other customers in a store before making our own purchase decisions, or of asking a sales person for expert advice. Gone were the days of haggling in the marketplace for the best product at the best price and sharing banter with other shoppers along the way. Gone were the days of overhearing conversations between other consumers about their preferences before making a choice. And gone were the days of shopping with a friend or partner and making shared purchase decisions.

Then along came social media and the digital aisles became crowded with voices, the marketplace bustling with conversations. People were talking to each other as they travelled across the super-highway, just as they had in the good old days down the high street. They were comparing experiences, sharing product reviews and making recommendations. But unlike in their former, physical environment, now their views, opinions and purchase habits were being shared virally, digitally and through data mining. Those with the loudest voices found themselves being heard far and wide. Their tastes and recommendations were not only being picked up by their friends, but also by other, previously lonely shoppers, relieved to hear a review before making their own purchase, albeit a review by a complete stranger. The reason? Because they were a fellow consumer and their views instilled an instinctive feeling of *trust*.

That emotional feeling of trust is key to why social is now at the heart of customer experience. Trust is what we as marketers must instil in the customers we want to attract if we want to engender loyalty and long-term commitment to our services and brands.

Trust requires authenticity in the message. Consumers are far more likely to trust a peer-to-peer conversation than they are an impolite interjection or automated marketing message from a marketer. They are cynical of misplaced or clunky sales techniques. They are too intelligent to fall for cheap ploys to capture their attention.

What they want is to get the right product message, offer or infor-mation, at the right time, in the right place. They do not want to be marketed toothpaste when they are in the middle of a conversation about their daughter's birthday celebrations. They will be as annoyed by an inappropriate approach as they were when a cold caller came knocking at their front door.

This provides marketers with a challenge and an opportunity. Using the best social channels and accurate consumer profiling, accurate data supported by quality content and authentic brand advocates, we can attract the attention of our customers like never before. Get it wrong, however, and that opportunity can all too easily become a catastrophe. Offending one consumer no longer remains an isolated incident. We upset one, we upset many.

Social journeys are fluid and consumers are fickle. We need to go where they go and speak their language. We need to embed our social messaging around their experience. We constantly need to create and innovate with fresh ideas and novel approaches to keep their interest alive. We can no longer rely on short-term campaigns. Persistent engagement requires long-term, personalized communications, peppered with brilliant ideas and offers to make the consumer experience feel real and enriching.

Given the title of this chapter and what has been said so far, it should come as no surprise that this is the central and longest chapter in the book: customer experience is central to social media. In the old days, word of mouth – supported by great advertising campaigns on TV and billboards – spread brand advocacy for us. Now the digital space accelerates and amplifies every message and word that our customers say about us. But one thing hasn't changed. We all know that bad news travels fastest.

Marc Duke, consultant specializing in B2B marketing

Social media presents marketing with a real challenge. We can reach millions but we have to be prepared for one-to-one dialogue. So when we look at social media and the customer experience, this is an area that has to be handled with care, about as much care as you (should) show your customers.

The theory is simple. Facebook, Twitter, LinkedIn, Google+, WhatsApp, Instagram, Vimeo, Vine and so on are tools that give marketing a way to communicate with existing and potential customers like never before. If Kim Kardashian can have the Twitter following of a mid-sized European country, the opportunities are just huge for marketing – and with every metric from likes, favourites, shares and plus ones being easy to obtain, it is a marketer's dream.

Let's take a step back and think about the customer and his or her experience. So much is written about user-friendly websites, responsive designs for mobile apps, a smooth user experience. All that means is, if I can't get what I want or need quickly, I won't bother. The B2B situation is a little different, but when we say 'think customer' that means consider what it is like for the customer to be in your shop, on your site, on the help line, trying to fill in a form.

When it comes to social you also have to think of something else. How do they use social? Here is a clue: the word social; it is linked to sharing, connecting to others. Chances are, the readers of this book will be 'socially' literate, ie you know how to use Twitter, Facebook, Snapchat, WhatsApp, and you are unlikely to use them for transactions but rather to share content, information, views; basically, to function socially with all of your friends and colleagues. With this in mind, let's consider the customer experience and social.

There are likely to be three scenarios where social and customer experience cross:

- A poor customer experience: a customer takes to social media to express their frustration.

- A great customer experience: a customer uses social to tell everyone they know about a great experience.

- A promotion on social: an ad of some description that gets consumers' attention that takes them off social and onto a website or landing page.

If you are a consumer-facing brand and you ignore social, you are ignoring your customers. I have worked with a provider of social media insight, monitoring and engagement, called Sentiment. Its entire premise is that social is a layer across a business, not simply a communications channel. They espouse that marketing, customer care and sales all have to listen and respond appropriately to customers on social. The business as a whole has to take a 'unified social communications' approach. When a retail customer releases a promotion on Facebook and Twitter announcing cut-price products, if the customers are left disappointed when stock runs out, they will vent their frustration on Twitter and Facebook. In order to overt such a negative customer experience, everyone in the business needs to be involved in the planning and implementation. If only the marketing department and store managers had spoken before the campaign was launched, this social disaster would have been prevented.

While marketing understands the power of social, it also has to understand how customers use it. As a consumer, if I contact a brand on Twitter I don't want to be told by the brand that I should e-mail or call someone. If I had wanted to do that in the first place I would not have taken to social! As a communications media, social operates very differently to e-mail or voice. Twitter is limited to 140 characters – while chat on Facebook tends to be that, chat. So we have to understand what customers are doing/saying on social and respond to it accordingly.

This is not theory. Here are a couple of case studies. The telecommunications company O2 is often used as an example of great social customer service. When its network went down it responded to each and every tweet in a human way, while when an Argos customer tweeted in bling-speak asking when new headphones would be available in its Moss Side store, getting a response in bling-speak meant the tweet went viral. As marketers we cannot forget that a tweet or a post is written by a human being who has likes and dislikes and feelings, or that some feel more comfortable in sharing electronically than over the phone.

As a marketer you have to start with a clear understanding of exactly who is your customer. How do you segment them? Do they use social at all? Before even starting on social you have to get these things straight and then look at how you are going to respond on social. Twitter does not have opening hours so you have to have the resources to respond. The phrase 'you snooze you lose' applies to social – as social customers are always online.

The words multichannel or omnichannel are often spoken about in relation to how customers have multiple ways to interact with a brand or business. There is e-mail, Twitter, Facebook, a website and, dare we say, over the phone or in person. The problem for a business is that a consumer might use all of these 'channels' or 'touchpoints' but the experience has to be consistent and relevant. You would not use 140 characters to reply to a question posed by a customer at a till! So while social is crucial to the customer experience, others things are too.

Often I hear B2B marketers struggle with social; they don't see it as relevant. I beg to differ. The decision-making unit is made up of people who all use social, and nurturing leads and generating social leads is built around the fact that people will share their business needs and wants as much as personal ones. But again, there is a need to understand who your customers are, and how they behave.

With all of the above in mind, it is clear to see why social media is central to the customer experience, but care must be taken to ensure that the experience is as good as possible so that the power of social can be utilized to build your brand and help you to excel as a great (social) marketer.

Isabelle Quevilly, independent digital strategy director

Most briefs I receive are still asking for social media to be another layer of an integrated campaign. It is our role to advise brands that there is another way forward, one that builds growth over time – slowly but surely setting the ground for a successful digital transformation of your business.

I am a true believer in this idea: 'Your brand is the sum of its interactions' (Big Spaceship). It says a lot about how our job is changing. We are now in charge of structuring complex systems of conversations in relation to a brand, a business and its customers. The latter is key, of course, when designing a valuable customer experience. Is anything really social if not shared? You might not want to say that walking into your client's board room. However, our industry has been working with skeuomorphic concepts that are not sustainable any more.

With the rise of smart devices and unlimited data plans, the customer experience has become an always-on and fluid journey that is literally in the hands of consumers. The way that brands communicate should be agile and constantly evolving in order to keep up with the incredible pace set by the market. It should not be an on–off voice dictated by the company's need to sell its latest products.

Instead of hoping for some happy accident of high engagement rates, brands should proactively embed social platforms around their customer experience. How? By diving into data monitoring and highlighting the multiple layers of conversations happening at each stage of the experience. I'm talking about all the one-to-one conversations people have together.

Instead of designing our efforts around the brand, we need to build a strategic narrative from the people. The objective is to scale these into the many-to-many conversations that the digital space is unique at delivering. This will not only generate more value for the business, it will also position your brand as being more respectful and open to the reality of people. This is what Zappos has done with the #OOTD Fans on Instagram, for example: instead of trying to create new behaviours, they have identified an existing one-to-one conversation and embedded the brand within it. This is the way to create meaningful and valuable customer experiences. The content is purposeful, entertaining and relevant. Therefore the engagement is high and the impact on the customer journey is more significant. Our job, as thought leaders for a new generation of work, is to transform the way we, as an industry, look at the role of communications in creating value and exploring new directions. Let's review the three key components:

1 *Communications planning frameworks do not fit the complexity of social systems.*
   We have spent years working on 'social media frameworks' to help companies scale and reduce costs for social media communications. However, the reality is that we have to stop trying to simplify social systems for the sake of management efficiency, because we are damaging long-term opportunities.

Instead, we need to develop our capabilities in understanding two new levels. First, spotting the one-to-one conversations that are happening organically in your world. Second, we need to learn how to convert these native conversations into a beneficial asset for the business that can be leveraged as a many-to-many conversation. There is very little need to advertise and buy media when you have set up the right tools to earn advocacy and fuel your customer journey on a larger scale.

2 *The culture of campaigns is making it worse for everyone.* Most briefs are still focused on supporting campaign efforts imposing constraints of time and scale that are not relevant to the social space. How disappointing this is for customers to see their experience broken into campaigns, especially if they love a brand and do want to get involved. When it comes to scale, this question of scaling to get a broader reach is also a 'broadcasting-led' idea that is not relevant in this context.

It is probably better to invest in many pilot projects to find the real nuggets than trying to be the next 'viral' hit, which can be meaningless as a performance indicator. The Old Spice campaign is a great example of this situation, which is often created by agencies. I would love to see how much of that 'noise' has converted into valuable long-term assets for the brand. As expressed in the *New York Times*: 'Getting your content shared is just the beginning'.

3 *Facebook, Twitter, Pinterest are not social media.* They are technical platforms where communities of like-minded people live and communicate. Each of these smaller communities of people facilitates an actual social media, where information is shared between people. The platform hosting it doesn't really matter. People are social, technologies are not. Our role is to dig out these communities and to understand their rules as mini societies, to find which ones are relevant to the growth of your business. The business can then adapt and create communications that are relevant to those groups.

What are the new principles to consider?

- Design a customer experience that everyone in the business understands and that integrates into their work.

- Encourage a digital mindset throughout the organization.

- Build on reality; identify existing interactions that the people you want to engage with are already having.

- Set relevant indicators of success; focus on areas where your effort will grow value for both the customer and the business.

- Immerse your team in the world of customers.

- Generate a continuous stream of pilots and transform through learning.

- Understand the needs and wants of customers from their one-to-one conversations.

- Proactively transform the customer experience based on the data you gather.

We all want to be a thumb stopper – to create conditions for the unexpected and to put forward purposeful activities for customers. In this, we have the obligation to remember that they are on their mobiles, getting on with their busy lives and the last thing they want is an interruption from some awful content from a brand they barely know. Quality will come from the brands that truly design a customer-centric system of communications.

Neil Witten, chief technology officer, founder and product owner, StoryStream

There is a new world where people are choosing to spend increasing numbers of hours. To find this world you need to look through a 'digital window', which might be a desktop computer or a tablet but more and more it is the smartphone in your pocket. The thing that keeps people dipping back into that world throughout their day is the vibrant and varied communities where conversation flows in real time. And when we use the term 'social media' it is important to remember that in this world it is the communities and the conversation that we are talking about.

A recent report from eMarketer stated that nearly one in four people used social networks in 2013, with an annual increase of 18 per cent (**http://www.emarketer.com**). So it is clear that this new world is vast, and when considering the growth rates over the last three or four years, we can be confident that it is here to stay. So social media is prolific and increasingly that is where conversations are happening. As a consequence, the way that we communicate is changing, both between individuals and, critically, with brands and businesses.

In recent years, exponential advances in technology have disrupted industry to the point that the only true differentiator is the customer experience. What this means is that for businesses to survive and to thrive they need to be relentless in pursuing the best possible customer experience. To do this social media plays a significant role – after all, that is where so many of your customers are hanging out, talking about your brand, your products and the quality of your service. They won't hold back, in this new world of social media the rules have changed.

Everyone has a voice and everyone has access to an audience that is immediate and global. What does great customer experience look like in this new world? Great customer experience in itself has not changed. Put the customer first, build a meaningful relationship with your customer, listen to them and keep them up-to-date with engaging and relevant stories.

The days of the hard sell are almost over. Today's customer is smart, and has a new level of visibility into what your brand stands for, your product range and, critically, the quality of customer service that they can expect from you. So if what your company is doing is great, then expect there to be advocates who are shouting about how great it is. They will be sharing their experience of your brand across a range of social networks with a variety of rich media. If you happen to be listening, you can be using that content to tell your story from their perspective. Because it is earned advocacy, it is real customers telling potential customers how great you are. It is marketing gold dust. Your customers are doing the hard work for you in reward for the great products and service that you have given them. Equally, if what you are doing as a brand or business isn't great, then don't expect silence. Expect the opposite, expect that everyone will know about it and, worse still, expect everyone to be talking about it.

A recent example of the role that social media can play in surfacing bad customer experience can be seen from a phone call that was recorded by Ryan Block, a vice president of product at AOL and a former tech blogger. Ryan was moving house and with the move was taking the opportunity to change his digital cable provider away from Comcast. Having spent 10 minutes on the phone trying to arrange a disconnection from the service, Ryan was feeling 'completely flustered by the oppressiveness of the rep'. Ryan says that: 'within just a few minutes the representative had become so condescending and unhelpful I felt compelled to record the speakerphone conversation on my other phone'. That recording was uploaded to SoundCloud and was tweeted by Ryan to his 83,500 followers.

If you haven't heard the conversation, it epitomizes bad customer experience: in a nutshell, Ryan is politely requesting to cancel his service, but the sales rep is following a process that won't let him proceed without having a clear reason for the customer wishing to leave. The SoundCloud recording went viral, with 5.6 million people listening to the conversation. Don't let this happen to your brand!

If 5.6 million people were to turn up outside of your office to protest about your poor customer service, you would want to make sure that you are in the office and looking out of the window – then you would probably want to go out there, understand who the key players are, and begin a dialogue with them. So it stands to reason that if your customers are existing in this new world of social media, you need to be present there too. Protests can happen virtually in this world of social media at incredible speed and scale. So don't make the mistake that Comcast did.

So what about brands and businesses getting it right? Porsche, like many luxury car brands, have historically positioned their outbound marketing activities around the strength of the brand, the technical data of the cars and the general design aesthetic. The missing component in this mix is the emotional consideration. What does it actually feel like to own this car? How would it make your kids feel? What is it like to grow up with a dream to one day own a Porsche and then for that day to come, maybe decades later? What does that day feel like, and how does it feel to be that person a year later? Is it everything you had hoped it would be, or could it be more?

Only a few years ago it was almost impossible for a brand like Porsche to surface these emotional stories of brand advocacy, especially at scale to a global audience. In today's world of social media, Porsche, like many brands, have access to a wealth of these kinds of real-owner stories that positive advocates are sharing to their social networks every minute of the day, globally. Where this really starts to impact customer experience is when brands like Porsche surface these stories alongside their more traditional outbound brand communications. It helps the audience to feel more connected, more aware of the positivity and advocacy of the brand. For owners it reinforces their purchase decision, and for potential owners it provides a view into the world of an owner who they otherwise might not have access to. For Porsche, it allows them to harness the power and immediacy of these advocates and creates a more effective, relevant and real-time way of generating meaningful outbound content. This leads to more effective marketing activities at lower cost, which can be joined up between different markets globally – examples of the rich advocacy that Porsche harnesses globally into their ever-evolving brand story.

To summarize, social media and customer experience are converging. That convergence can cause global brands to trip up in a hugely significant way, or it can act as an incredible way to simplify, amplify and build upon genuinely great customer experience, and advocacy. You want your brand in the latter category, so to do so I would suggest that you follow these rules:

- Be relentless in pursuing the best possible customer experience. Don't compromise: the customer is king, put them at the centre of every decision that you make, and treat them as you would like to be treated.

- You need to be listening. You've got all sorts of golden nuggets of advocacy scattered out there, don't ignore them, harness those positive stories! Sweep them all up and use them in your outbound marketing activities. If what you are listening to is not positive then understand the problems, show humility, then go above and beyond to fix the problems.

- Go where your audience is. Engage your audience with the right content at the right time.

- Conversations are a two-way street, speak *with* people, not at them.

- Be smart about the tools that you use to make this process manageable throughout your organization.

Ellie Mirman, director of marketing, HubSpot

Thirty terrible pieces of social media advice to ignore

1. You need to be on every single social network

Especially if you have limited time and resources, do not spread yourself too thin by trying to maintain an active presence on every single social media site. Research and learn about the make-up of the audience that populates each social network so you can figure out where you should focus. If your audience is not there, don't waste your time. And as new social networks pop up (as they do all the time), feel free to experiment with them, but be ready to let them go if they don't work for you, and let your analytics be your guide. At HubSpot, we have tried pretty much every social network that has popped up, but some have fallen by the wayside, and we have focused our efforts on the networks that continue to generate results for our marketing. Not sure where to start? LinkedIn, Facebook and Twitter are safe bets. They have huge audiences that span many demographics and industries.

2. Focus on Facebook...

Or LinkedIn... or Twitter... or social network XYZ. Yes, you *should* want to focus your social media marketing efforts but, at the same time, no single social media site is the Holy Grail. Experiment with a few sites, determine where your audience hangs out, and focus on the few that are the best fit for your company.

3. You don't need e-mail

The day that Oprah Winfrey signed up for Twitter and user registration skyrocketed, we didn't all cancel our e-mail accounts. I have been using Twitter for five years, Facebook and LinkedIn for even longer, and I live in my e-mail. Social media did not make e-mail marketing extinct: it just added another integrated channel to make e-mail even stronger. Remember: one of the first steps in signing up for a social media account is usually to provide your e-mail address. And communicating via social media, in some cases, is the same as communicating via e-mail. For example, a LinkedIn group message gets e-mailed to the group members via LinkedIn. On top of that, many people still prefer e-mail for communications, or prefer different types of content via e-mail rather than social posts.

4. Social media is the new search engine optimization (SEO)

If we're talking buzz words, then yes, social media *is* the new SEO. But social media, in terms of function and strategy, does not replace SEO. In fact, it is just another case of two marketing strategies working better when they are put together. Social media posts now show in search results, social media engagement influences search rankings, and SEO can drive more people to your social profiles and posts. Once again, social media is an *additional* channel, not one that replaces existing efforts such as SEO. Billions of searches are conducted every single day, and you don't want to miss out on that traffic.

5. You can automate all of your updates

Social media can be time-consuming, so the automation of your updates is, of course, appealing. But the tough reality of social media is that it is all about people talking with people, and people can easily see through crap. Especially automated crap. Automating all your updates (and believe me, people can tell) screams, 'I don't care about actually being here. Just come and read my content.' While it is okay to automate *some* content publishing (for example, your latest blog articles), you still need to support that with real conversations and interactions with your network.

6. Send an auto direct message (DM) to all your new followers

Whether you want to thank them, tell them to visit your website, or anything else, please, please, please don't send an auto DM to every new follower you get. Auto DMs are incredibly impersonal and are perceived as spam by most. Sending auto DMs not only seems inconsiderate, but it also makes you look like a complete newbie who does not understand social media etiquette.

7. Include popular hashtags in your tweets to get more exposure

There was a time when hashtags were used as a great way to organize tweets. In fact, it is still great for specific campaigns or events so that a group of attendees or participants can share and monitor content related to that campaign/event. But when it comes to topic-related hashtags (eg #marketing #boston), people do not really monitor those hashtags, so your organized content is not reaching a new audience. Using such general hashtags makes you look, once again, like a Twitter newbie who is trying to game the system. It is also commonly referred to as 'hashtag hijacking'. Today, hashtags have also become a way to make a comment about the rest of the tweet. For example: 'Had to wait for AN HOUR to get my iPhone 5 today. #1stworldproblems'.

8. Your prospects are not using social media, so you don't need to be there

First of all, your prospects *are* using social media. According to research, 69 per cent of adults use social media. Do you think that none of your prospects are included in that majority? If the stats are not enough to convince you, try out any social network's advertising targeting platforms (you can often go through the targeting process without launching an ad and spending money) to see how many people on each site actually fit into your target market. On top of that, there are reasons to get involved in social media aside from communicating with potential or current customers, or expanding the reach of your content. For example, you can connect with influencers and reporters who may be looking for an expert in your industry to interview for an upcoming story.

9. The more you publish, and the more sites you are on, the better

Simply having a presence on multiple sites and spraying your content as much as possible won't work. Yes, more content is better because it gives you more valuable social media fodder, but you need to make sure that all content is high quality; otherwise, people will see straight through the crap. Unfortunately, people are getting overwhelmed with more and more content. This means that the bar for remarkable content is starting to rise and, to be successful, you need to make sure your content reaches that high bar.

10. Use a tool that autopublishes your posts to all social networks at once... to save time

We have talked about how automating *all* your social media updates is never a good idea, but we also said that it is okay to automate some of your content sharing. But there is an exception to that rule, because you should never publish one message and send it out to all your different social networks at once. Yes, it will save you some time, but it is also a terrible practice. Not only does this look auto-mated, but you should also consider that different social media sites favour different types and frequencies of content. For example, images do fantastically well on Facebook. And you can post much more frequently to Twitter than to Facebook or to LinkedIn. Furthermore, you likely have people who are following you in all three of these networks. How obvious will it look that you are auto-mating your efforts if they see the same message posted to all three social networks at exactly the same time? With these key differences, you simply cannot autopublish the same post to all sites at the same time and remain effective.

11. You can outsource your social media

Social media is a way for you to communicate with your audience, which means it not only needs to be your voice, but the content of the conversations you are having need to also be based on your expertise in the industry. Not just anyone can talk about the challenges and trends that your customers face, especially if you are in a niche industry. In fact, we have seen instances of social media outsourcing (combined with automation) go terribly wrong for some businesses.

12. An intern can manage it all for you

Who is even less qualified to talk about your industry than an outsourced social media consultant? A college student with no real-world work experience. Now, that is not to say that *all* interns are unqualified for such a job. In fact, our internship programme at HubSpot has found and nurtured some amazing talent who we have brought on to the team full-time to manage our social media presence. The point we are trying to make here is that social media is not just some throwaway marketing strategy: it is a public face of the company. Would you let that same intern do an interview on behalf of your company for a TV spot?

13. Don't get personal

Social media gives you the opportunity to share a bit more personality than your website may allow. In fact, personality is often what gets you noticed in social media. After all, *'People don't fall in love with hex colours and logos, they fall in love with people'*, as branding strategist Erika Napoletano (@RedHeadWriting) shared. Show the personality behind your brand and people in order to make your social media marketing more lovable so that people naturally want to connect and engage with you.

14. Don't let your employees use social media

First of all, it is useless to try to keep your employees from using social media. Even if you block social media sites on their computers, they have got their smartphones. Move your office to a dungeon with terrible mobile reception, and your employees can still go home and get on those sites in their spare time. Forbid any use of your company name in social media, and they will just create fake profiles that don't mention you. All that does is hurt your relationship with your employees – it shows you don't trust them – and you actually give up a great asset. Your employees are your company, and they each have their own personal networks of friends and followers who can expand the reach of your content, messaging and business in general. So instead of trying to crack down on social media use, give your employees guidelines for smart use. At HubSpot, our simple policy is 'use good judgement'.

15. Don't respond to negative comments to protect your brand

If someone has said something negative about your brand, it's out there, visible to that person's network or anyone searching for information about your company. And by not responding to negative comments, a small comment can spiral out of control for lack of attention. Admit mistakes when you need to, and share how you are going to address any issues. A simple response can actually turn an angry detractor into an appreciative promoter of your business.

16. Respond to every negative comment

Respond to every negative comment and pick your battles wisely. Beware of negative comments that are simply meant to get a rise out of you. Beware of people simply trying to capitalize on your visibility by getting you to respond to their comment – or trolls who just want to cause trouble. Know when it is appropriate to step back instead of adding fuel to the fire.

17. Disable comments altogether to avoid negative comments... or delete negative comments

Disabling comments is both antisocial and unwise. People will say what they are going to say, whether you let them do it on your Facebook page or they have to use their own Facebook timeline as their platform. And by allowing people to comment on your own turf, you can manage the conversation, monitor comments and respond to people appropriately. In fact, responding can help to change people's minds and opinions about your company. Beware of deleting negative comments, too. Doing so can bring on a slew of many more negative comments about the original issue... and the fact that you deleted their comment. It will also make you look like you are not transparent (a characteristic that is central to social media success), and it may even cause people to hate your marketing.

18. If you make a mistake, you can delete the post to fix the problem

Once again, once a comment is out there, it's out there, whether it is your prospect's, your customer's, or your own. There is no stopping people from taking screenshots and sharing them with their connections, even if you delete the comment later. So think about what you say before you say it. And admit to any mistakes you make.

19. You need to have a social media policy

Social media policies waste time policing what is okay or not okay to publish in a single channel. But it is impossible to anticipate every single scenario in social media and, on top of that, you don't want to end up slowing down your publishing frequency, since speed counts on social media more than in other channels. So instead of a fully fledged social media policy, put together some guidelines that are easy for your employees to remember and keep in mind as they make their own decisions about what to publish in social media. As we mentioned in number 14, at HubSpot our policy is simply to use good judgement.

20. Social media is completely free

While, yes, there is usually no cost to sign up for a social network, you can't stop there if you want to achieve true social media marketing success. You need to actually use the site, publish content and engage with your followers. All of that takes people's time, which is not free. So to be effective in social media, you will need to invest in human resources. Furthermore, the businesses that are truly effective in social media are also paying for marketing analytics software so they can measure the ROI of their social media marketing and improve upon their strategies and tactics. To be effective in social media, you will need to invest in people resources.

21. All you need is social media

Social media does not replace other marketing strategies. Rather, social media is a new channel for your marketing efforts and works best in conjunction with other channels. (Remember when we talked about it in relation to e-mail marketing in number 3?) You cannot attract followers in social media without content, say, from your blog. You cannot convert followers into leads without landing pages and compelling offers. And those are just a couple of pieces of the marketing mix.

22. You cannot measure social media

When you approach social media, just as when you approach any channel or tactic, you should know what your goal is. Is it new leads? Is it to increase the reach of your content? Is it to reduce customer support calls? Whatever your goal, measure the progress towards that goal. Measure how many leads came from social media. Measure how many visits to your blog came from social media. Measure the number of customer support phone calls against your social media activity. Figure out your metrics, and track them.

23. Fan/follower growth is the most important metric

Sure, fans and followers are nice, but they do not actually pay you money or keep you in business. Instead, think about what matters most to your business – leads and customers – and focus on that as your top priority metric. Not to say that fans and followers *are not* important. They may be a piece in the puzzle that gets you to where you want to be. Just make sure you are focusing on the end goal.

24. Engagement is the most important metric

Engagement is not only a non-paying metric, it is also a fuzzy metric that can be interpreted in many different ways. Yes, engagement is important as it relates to understanding what content resonates with your audience, or what attracts more people to your website. But like fan/follower count, engagement is just a piece in the puzzle that leads to an actual business metric such as revenue.

25. You should only publish messages about your company

Here's the thing: if you are only publishing messages about your company, your recent awards, upcoming events, latest product releases, I really don't care to listen to you. What I do care about are my problems, my challenges and my interests, so that is what you should write about. Think how you can be valuable to give people a reason to follow and engage with you.

26. You should post X updates per day

This unfortunately comes from a misinterpretation of HubSpot's own data. HubSpot social media scientist Dan Zarrella published data around the optimum frequency and number of posts for each social media site, and some readers took that to mean they had to publish 22 tweets per day. But this data shows results *in aggregate*, based on frequency and timing of posts from a large number of accounts. So test the timing and frequency of your social media updates with your own audience, because that is what you should care about – the results with your specific audience.

27. Once you get your Facebook/Twitter/blog account set up, social media is super easy!

Setting up an account is like buying the ticket to a networking event. You still have to go and talk to people to get any value out of it. You will never get results from social media marketing if you won't put in the time and effort needed to make it successful.

28. You don't need a strategy for social media

While you *do* need to be an agile social media marketer in order to be prepared for the unexpected, it is also important to go in with a strategy. More specifically, you should know your goals in regard to your social media efforts and how you are going to work to achieve them. Do you have the content you need to support publishing? Do you know who you want to engage with and how? Have a plan in mind, identify what supporting materials you need, and know how you are going to measure it on a regular basis.

29. You should have separate social media accounts for every division of your company

I'm not sure where people are getting this idea, it must be from huge brands that have multiple Facebook pages and Twitter accounts. (Did you know that, according to Altimeter, the average large company has 178 corporate-owned social media accounts? Crazy, right?) But when I get this question (if a company should have separate accounts for each of its divisions), it is always coming from a marketer at a small business with a couple of target markets and no social media presence. In this situation, you really don't want to split your efforts (and your social reach!), especially if you have limited resources and are just getting started with social media. Instead, focus your efforts on building up a single account on each chosen social network so that you get closer to seeing results faster. When it comes to addressing multiple divisions or target markets, include a mix of content, and perhaps have each division contribute to that content in order to attract all relevant audiences.

30. You cannot simply ask people to comment, follow or retweet you

It may seem too forward to come out and ask someone to take an action in social media, but it actually works. And you don't get a terrible reaction because what you are doing is taking someone who is already reading your content, tweets, blog articles, etc and saying, 'Hey, if you like this, why not share it with someone else?' A simple call-to-action such as 'please retweet' can go a long way to generate more social activity. In fact, our research has shown that including 'please retweet' actually leads to four times more retweets!

Paul Handley, CEO, Hit Social Media

Obtaining maximum page-like increase on Facebook

So, how do you run an effective promotion on Facebook for maximum page-like increase – and stay within their guidelines?

We have all seen competitions filter through to our newsfeed – 'Like and Share to win!' There is no doubt that promotions have, on the whole, been excellent ways to increase likes to a Facebook page. Everyone is doing it, but few are doing it right (those 'Like and Share' competitions are violating Facebook promotional guidelines, by the way). As of November 2014 you can no longer force users to like your page by using a 'like-gate'. This was a very successful way of bringing likes to a Facebook page, but is now no longer allowed. So, how do we run a successful promotion on Facebook?

Incentive

The prize (incentive) is key here. Ideally, there should be some relevance to your brand. Equally, the prize must be as desirable as possible to ensure maximum uptake and viral possibilities.

App

You do not have to run a promotion on an app any more, Facebook revised their guidelines on this. If you run a promotion as a post on the page there are, however, restrictions. You *cannot* ask entrants to share as a point of entry; only likes and comments are allowed (please, no more 'like and share' to win competitions, Facebook is starting to punish pages that do this). A promotion/competition run as a post can be good for increasing your edgerank (FB algorithm) by boosting the likes and comments, but we believe there is a more effective way to promote your page and bring in likes. Because shares are not permitted, we always recommend using a third-party app. These are hosted away from Facebook, so you can ask entrants to share without upsetting the Facebook police. This type of sharing is vital for success.

There are some great apps out there that are easy to populate and install on your Facebook page. Easypromos is a good option to get started with for boosting likes to a page. You should also look at Rafflecopter and its better-looking rival, Gleam. Rafflecopter and Gleam offer additional, optional entry points, such as follows on Twitter, asking users to tweet a pre-written tweet, refer friends and more. Gleam is especially good at transforming your current Facebook fans to followers on your other social networks.

At Hit Social (at the time of writing), we are testing a new promotions app that has been designed around the like-gate ban and will offer marketers the best possible solution for getting likes to a Facebook page without a like-fate. Look out for the Knockout app!

Tip

Most apps have a 'thank you for entering' page. We normally populate this with either an image or text, suggesting that entrants share the competition for an extra entry. It is also okay at this point to ask users to 'like' the page – they have entered, so the page like is not part of the entry process and you are still within the new guidelines regarding the non use of like-gating.

Promote

The make or break of a successful competition lies in how it is promoted. The competition itself will have a viral element to it standalone, but you can do so much more to spread the message.

First, make sure you ask your followers to share. Publish a post detailing the competition, along with a link to where the competition is taking place. Make sure you are clear in the post that the share will not count as an entry. You are just simply asking for your fans to share the news. It works: if you do not ask for a share, you will not get many! Now you need to spread the word elsewhere. Does your company have a newsletter? What about a page on your company website/blog? If your business is a store, display posters relating to the promotion, get leaflets printed and hand them out locally, and tell your visiting customers about it... all basics, but you will be surprised at the uptake.

Promote online

This is where the competition will really start to bring likes to a page. As an example, in the UK there are various free online resources where you can post details about your competition. The Money Saving Expert Competition Forum and Hot UK Deals are two such sites that yield a high like count. Other sites such as competitions-uk.com and theprizefinder.com are also useful. If you have budget available, Magic Freebies will post your promotion for a fee. Generally, this offers a good return on investment in bringing extra likes to a page. There are Facebook pages that will share your competition with their own followers. We operate FB Competitions UK at Hit Social, but there are many more pages out there too. On Facebook, search competitions and contact the relevant page admins.

> **Tip**
>
> For your promotional competitions, use hashtags #Win and #Competition in your updates for Facebook, Twitter and Google+. They all have value.

Some words of caution...

- Do not spam your message. If you want pages to share your promotion, ask via a direct message. In most cases, it is bad practice to post directly onto pages. It is also fairly ineffective, as these posts do not go into the followers' newsfeeds, so unless a user is viewing the section 'Recent Posts By Others' on the page in question, it will not be seen.

- Do not spam your existing followers. Try to limit your competition posts to once at launch, and if run for a month, two further times. The day before the competition ends, publish a post with an urgent call to action (#Competition ending tomorrow! Have you entered yet? Enter here!!!).

- *Never* buy likes. *Ever!* These damage your Facebook page edgerank and will affect your overall reach. Always review the official Facebook guidelines, as these are always subject to change.

Omaid Hiwaizi, chief strategy officer (UK) and Adrian Nicholls, head of digital (UK), Geometry Global

Since time immemorial, the journey taken by shoppers have incorporated three different contexts: home, on the go and in-store. In each of those steps there are opportunities for social interaction, and therefore influence through word of mouth – whether chatting over the garden fence, seeking out an expert or bumping into a friend and asking what they think about a need, product or category.

The rise of ubiquitous digital touchpoints means that today's shopper is changing: 20 per cent of British 18- to 24-year-olds enjoy sharing photos of purchases on social networks (HighCo/Ipsos UK; 90 per cent of online shoppers trust peer recommendations (Besedo Mars 2012); 93 per cent of Americans research online before making an in-store purchase (Socialnomics); 68 per cent of tablet owners have made at least one purchase via their tablet (eMarketer); 67 per cent of UK shoppers have used their mobile device whilst making an in-store purchase (Group M Research); 4 out of 10 social media users have purchased an item in-store after sharing or liking it on Facebook, Twitter or Pinterest (Vision Critical: From Social to Sale).

So what does this mean for the power of word of mouth? Today's connected shopper uses social media to get opinions from their peers and ask friends for recommendations like never before. They do not opt in and out of social, they are constantly connected with their social networks at their fingertips.

Connected shoppers thrive in our omnichannel world where the merging of physical, digital and social means that they browse, share, compare and buy – anytime, anywhere. As we know, shoppers have always shared advice with each other, listened to recommendations, and warned friends about the little corner cafe with bad service – and they always will. What is different is that digital has transformed the scale, strength and how long its effect endures.

Embracing the power of social influence on purchase

With the journeys taken by shoppers being neither linear nor simple, the onus is on brand owners and agencies to understand this complexity and maximize the opportunities to use social to influence shoppers on the path to purchase. At Geometry Global we do this by mapping the behavioural journey that people undertake (we call it the purchase decision journey – PDJ) and analysing this to identify which steps in the journey offer the greatest opportunity to create behaviour change, usually to increase purchase rates. The key to successful communication strategies is therefore to understand consumers and shoppers:

- the way they make decisions;
- the touchpoints that influence them the most;
- the messages they respond to;
- the role that the brand should play at those touchpoints.

To understand these journeys fully, new forms of research have to be used in order to investigate behaviour and to understand what triggers the shopper to buy. Here social listening is an important tool. Using our unique insights tool Pathfinder™ we are able to map, segment and prioritize people's PDJs, identifying the steps taken before, during and after the selection of a brand for purchase. With the PDJ mapped out we add an extra level of research by listening to the actual conversations that the shopper is having on the exact occasions that influence their behaviour. For an electronic beauty product, for example, research shows that the shopper is highly influenced by the messaging in-store – and that this point in the PDJ is crucial so we can adjust messaging to trigger purchase. Likewise, we might discover in the same PDJ that consumers have doubts about the quality of the product because of reviews and opinions discovered in discussion forums and Twitter, and so are just as influenced by their peers' statements in social media. This highlights another barrier in their journey that we need to address. One way to solve this could be to communicate a two-year warranty both in-store and via online retailers in order to mitigate any doubt that the connected shopper might have at the point of purchase.

Brands are already embracing opportunities to drive sales through social influence

Integration of social media into marketing campaigns to drive more reach and engagement is now an expected approach when developing communication strategies. Few are going beyond this by integrating social to support the consumer in their PDJ in order to drive sales. The following are great examples of integrated shopper marketing that embrace social tactics – including social promotions, social sampling, experiential social amplification, and social commerce.

Carlsberg – CrowdIt – social promotions

http://www.happybeerti.me/

A brilliant example of a brand that is embracing the social shopper is Carlsberg. They have previously demonstrated their ability to connect purchase behaviour and social media marketing through their non-branded app: CrowdIt (**http://www.youtube.com/watch?v=pAhAO61h7ng**). Through geolocation marketing the app supports the beverage brand on-trade and at the same time gives the social shopper direct deals according to location and social network. Recently they launched #HappyBeerTime, another on-trade activation using marketing innovation to provide a promotional activation to pub owners and bars by distributing a USB key that by a simple plug-in creates a gamification mechanism for the consumer right at the point of purchase. By using the hashtag #HappyBeerTime on Instagram consumers extend happy hour through content creation and social sharing and thereby create a 'social echo' of the promotional campaign. Check out the case movie (**https://www.youtube.com/watch?v=2Sp_fNqCcvQ**) and search Instagram for #happybeertime moments.

Stockholm County aids prevention programme – The Sex Profile – social sampling

http://www.youtube.com/watch?v=wcR_GESc6Lw

The core of this campaign starts with a traditional shopper marketing tactic – *sampling*. But this is the only traditional element in this innovative and social campaign. People are encouraged to scan a QR code on the back of a condom pack, which they receive through traditional sampling. From there they are taken on a journey by downloading a smartphone app that measures sound and movement at the moment when they are actually using the condom. Users thereafter upload this information to a campaign site through the app and fill out their 'sex profile' with different key features: male or female, cat owner or dog owner, blond or brunette, geolocation, occupation etc. As a result, users are then able to browse different sex profiles and compare and share these graphs with their social networks, such as who is loudest, blondes or brunettes.

These graphs form the foundation for above-the-line activities such as outdoor advertising and are thus a great example of how a campaign can be formed and activated from below-the-line activities as key starting point. Likewise it is interesting to see how something so traditional as sampling can be activated through digital and social elements and thereby create a social echo that will reach and activate many more consumers than just through the sampling activity itself.

Anthon Berg – Generous Store – experiential social amplification

http://www.youtube.com/watch?v=_cNfX3tJonw

Experiential marketing often does not create enough reach or attributable impact to justify investment. Adding social to the mix can rectify this in order to reach a broader audience or to create deeper experience with the target audience. An effective example of using social to create a social echo from an experiential activation is *Generous Store* by the Danish chocolate brand Anthon Berg. They created a pop-up store in central Copenhagen where credit cards, cash or cheques were not valid tender. Only good deeds could buy the boxes of chocolate. Shoppers paid for the chocolate with a good deed. Literally. Such as washing the dishes for a week, giving compliments to a girlfriend, or driving grandma to bingo for a whole month. The transaction was made at the till as in a normal store, except the transaction was made through a Facebook plug-in to guarantee that the promises were kept. In this way the experiential campaign did not only live in central Copenhagen but spread across the Scandinavian region. It was an enhanced, live customer experience that spread goodwill and good feeling.

Only – Only The Liberation – social e-commerce

http://www.youtube.com/watch?v=kCr7ZP7KC0Q

Not many brands have been able to connect social media to the online shopping experience other than via the obligatory 'like this product' button. The clothing brand *Only*, on the other hand, has done this to perfection – by creating an online universe through interactive video, where the target audience engage with the characters and influence the storyline and additionally share, pin, tweet, post and buy every single piece of clothing directly in the video, just by the click of a button. This piece of communication is a true example of engaging with the social shopper on their terms in an engaging and interesting way, where every click can lead to actual purchase.

Bacardi/Wetherspoons – Wetherspoons Connect – on-trade social activation

http://youtu.be/6luD358fzJk?list=UU2rFE_8tOAZ1xXWCjyau8lw

A great example of a brand that is embracing social and the connected shopper is Bacardi who, in collaboration with Wetherspoons, created an on-trade promotional app to drive sales and traffic into pubs and bars across the UK. Consumers use augmented reality (AR) technology to scan Wetherspoons point-of-sale material such as coasters and posters in order to redeem deals in the bar they are in. Additionally, the app allows tagging anything in the pub such as a beer bottle with pictures and messages to friends as well as sharing these with friends and peers – allowing the promotional activation to reach beyond the pub.

Lost Animal Souls Shelter – The True Fans – activating the social footprint

http://www.youtube.com/watch?v=LONPjJX18OM

Passionate advocates can be enlisted not only to engage others but also to compel them to contribute and transact. We are all aware that organic reach of Facebook posts is on a drastic decline. Lost Animal Souls Shelter converted their Facebook fans into administrators, meaning they got people more involved in the daily management of the community. They were not mere observers any more but contributors. As a result, the community now actively participate in rescue efforts and donation drives. Additionally, the brand logo appears as an always-on tab on the left panel of their Facebook homepage, which means that a notification appears for every activity, therefore solving the problem of Facebook's organic reach. In just a week of the launch of the campaign, their average organic reach went up 15 per cent, fans went up by 6 per cent, and there was a 136.5 per cent increase in page visits, all with zero budget spent.

Conclusion and takeouts

Our audience *is* the connected shopper – it is not whether or not they are connected, it is *how* and to what extent. If we do not consider and embrace these digital opportunities, someone else is.

The ubiquity of digital touchpoints and social have exponentially increased the power of word of mouth – it is our duty as retailers, brands and agencies to make the most of these contact moments and to use social to drive sales, not just engagement.

We need to utilize the right tools to navigate and map the complexity in people's purchase decision journeys and to activate the opportunities that are highlighted.

Additional research for this chapter contribution was provided by Caroline Asmussen, lead social strategist.

Peter Simpson, CMO and strategic alliances strategist

Shopping has always been social. For centuries, shoppers have bought from marketplaces, surrounded by other people. People bought from people, and these people inevitably discussed their shopping decisions with other people, friends and family. Word would spread that certain stalls and shops had the best products and services. These businesses were rewarded with more customers.

Recommendations from friends and family about what to buy are nothing new. But when shopping activity first moved online we were expected to forget about our social selves; our online shopping journey had to be made in isolation, or not at all, as online shoppers were forced to trawl through a myriad different product listings, unsure what was best for them, or if the site they were using had the best deals, or could even be trusted at all.

Inevitably this led to many online shopping journeys ending without a purchase being made. Ask any major high-street retailer, independent shopkeeper or market stallholder – the first rule is to turn every customer who comes through your door, whether physically or online, into a paying customer. The absence of any guidance from others, friends or family, and the entire impersonalization of the online process left a gaping hole in the customer experience. Customers didn't know who to trust. People buy from people, online or off, and in order to part with their cash, customers need to feel trust.

Social media: adding trust to online shopping

This situation has now changed, of course, thanks to the explosion in social media. E-commerce has become social and there is no going back. The way that consumers buy has moved on, and forward-looking businesses have to follow suit.

So why exactly is social media central to the customer experience? The simple answer is that it instils trust. An upbeat recommendation of your product or service from a customer, shared across Facebook or Twitter, could reach thousands of potential customers; a positive review of your online shopping experience may be found by millions over the years, all of whom may be searching for a brand to trust in delivering to them what they want.

Positioning your brand for social media success

Very few of us buy anything online without a little help from our friends. Whether the conversation is with friends we already know (on Facebook or Twitter) or like-minded people who have shared their experiences by posting their product reviews, social media today is the equivalent of the medieval marketplace that existed in every village, town and city for centuries: people sharing their recommendations, likes and dislikes with other customers. Your customers – potentially.

The way you position your business on social media platforms is critical for success. A half-baked strategy can cause more harm than doing nothing at all. Remember, you are looking to become part of the conversation – and social media platforms are inextricably linked to the idea of building trust with a loyal customer base. Be open. Listen. Learn.

Ratings and reviews

Any serious marketer looking to build a 21st-century online business needs to look to independent rating and review providers too. The insights they can provide are exceptional. Unfortunately, there are more online businesses getting this critical feature wrong than there are getting it right. The majority are still fumbling around at the bottom of the learning curve instead of zooming up it. Don't believe us? The statistics speak for themselves. Those businesses not engaged with rating and review products are estimated to receive less than half the conversion rate uplift than they ought to be generating. By not engaging in these services they are failing in one of the principal rules of social media for e-commerce: they are not listening to their customers and clearly fail to trust them. It is the equivalent of a business sitting in a room with their hands over their ears in case they hear some bad news. If you are not listening, how can you change your business and grow?

According to Reevoo, the leading rating and review service for multichannel brands and retailers, the power of a review should not be underestimated. From a report that they carried out in 2012, they discovered that:

- 50 or more product reviews per product can mean a 4.6 per cent increase in conversion rates;
- customer reviews produce an average 18 per cent uplift in sales.

Both of these statistics outline the value of a strong social media presence, opening up your business to ratings and reviews – products that are shared by your loyal customers and generate a real ongoing boost to your business.

Reevoo benefits customers by concentrating on search engine optimization of reviews to increase search rankings, as well as access to Google seller ratings, recommending that all e-commerce businesses looking to improve conversions should focus on product reviews and ratings to help boost conversion rates and order volumes. The service also makes it easy for businesses to see and respond to negative customer reviews. The faster you can move on a negative review, the sooner you can turn that customer attitude around; there are many cases on social media where disappointed customers have been turned into brand champions through swift replies and the brand joining the dialogue.

Social media is here to stay

If you are not listening to what your customers are talking about – and saying about your business – then you cannot win in e-commerce today. It is that simple. Consumers now have any number of resources at their disposal to access when starting out on a purchase journey. Social media is part of it all. From pre-purchase research to sharing reviews, social media is at the heart of consumer buying online. It is not going away. Yes, social media does present challenges for online businesses. But for brave online marketers who can adapt their marketing efforts so that their businesses are more open, conversational and engaging, the opportunities are endless.

Chapter conclusions

If you are a consumer-facing brand and you ignore social, you are ignoring your customers. Setting the groundwork for the successful digital transformation of your business should fill your mid- and long-term planning, as much as scheduling your everyday social media activity. Take one step at a time to ensure you build strong foundations across key channels, which you can then iterate and evolve based on changing technologies and detailed data analysis. Social media and customer experience are converging. That convergence can trip up global brands in a hugely significant way, or it can simplify, amplify and build upon genuinely great customer experience and advocacy.

CASE STUDY   The Environment Agency/Sentiment tool,
                Dam Digital

Client

The Environment Agency.

Agency

Sentiment tool, Dam Digital.

Project

Social media evaluation tool for major incident analysis.

Overview

The Environment Agency is an executive non-departmental public body of the Department for Environment, Food and Rural Affairs. It is responsible for a wide range of work to protect and improve the environment in England. This includes flood-risk management, forecasting and communications, environmental regulation, managing waterways and fisheries, investigating waste crime and reducing the impacts of climate change. Over 10,000 people work for the Environment Agency across England.

Project

The Environment Agency uses the Sentiment tool, developed by Dam Digital, to deliver its business objectives on utilizing social channels to manage its reputation, engage with customers and empower its staff to use social media effectively. During the 2013–14 flooding, the tool was essential in helping the Environment Agency to understand the social conversation, and evaluate its impact on its reputation and resources needed for managing volumes of discussion during major incidents.

Outcome

The Environment Agency has taken a proactive approach to managing and using social media as part of its communications, customer service and incident management work. Between 2012 and 2014, the Environment Agency ran a project to embed digital engagement in its work. It was keen to use social media to ensure that it met its business objectives. In April 2013, Sentiment was brought in to provide the Environment Agency with a social media monitoring tool as part of a multi-service contract for media monitoring, management and evaluation services.

Prior to April 2013, the organization had used Radian6 for social media monitoring. The Environment Agency uses Sentiment to evaluate use of social media, understand customer perceptions and to manage its social media accounts.

The Environment Agency's approach to social media strategy and co-ordination is overseen by a social media advisory group. This group includes senior representation from all areas of the organization involved in social media policy and/or use, eg incident management, human resources, recruitment, communications, customer services and research.

Day-to-day management of the Environment Agency's corporate social media channels is overseen by the communications team and a dedicated team within Customer Services. All media officers are expected to use social and digital media as part of their work.

How it works

The Environment Agency has one nationwide social media plan, which encompasses its use across all areas of the organization and ensures that risks are managed appropriately. Social media is also included in all communications strategies as a channel for delivering messages and engaging with customers.

In order to ensure that staff and customers understand the Environment Agency's approach, both internal and external policies have been put in place:

- HR policy on how social media should be used by Environment Agency staff.

- Guidance for staff is provided on the organization's intranet to help them understand the risks and opportunities of using social media to engage stakeholders.

- An external social media policy, outlining the Environment Agency's commitment to customers via social media is available online. This explains what customers can expect from their interactions with the Environment Agency online.

Social media strategy and policies

The Environment Agency uses Sentiment to provide insight and support lead generation. Sentiment data and analytics are used as part of monthly reporting to evaluate conversation volume, sentiment, keyword analysis and channel segmentation.

Sentiment was selected after a direct comparison between Sentiment and the previous service provider. It was felt that Sentiment provided good value for money, was simple to use, would deliver the agency's requirement of e-mail summaries and keyword notifications, and provide strong analytics.

Sentiment in action

Sentiment has been used to understand and analyse:

- Conversation about the Environment Agency during incidents, eg flooding.

- The reach and impact of proactive campaigns on social media conversation.

- Online discussion around contentious issues or topics that may impact the agency's reputation.

- To identify customers who require the agency's assistance.

Sentiment has been a vital tool in understanding and evaluating the impact of social media discussion on the Environment Agency's reputation and the resource requirements for managing volumes of discussion during major incidents. It has provided management with data and insight that has helped to demonstrate the need to develop new ways of working to respond to changing ways of communication. The agency will be working with the Sentiment team to evolve its use of the tool to fit its new organizational structure.

The agency is also keen to explore how it can make best use of the new engagement functionality within the tool.

The importance of Sentiment analysis for social media monitoring for retail operations

Peter Cameron from Dam Digital explains:

> Social media has become an established, valued marketing tool for businesses all over the world, both for outbound marketing and real-time customer service. But it has its uses beyond the marketing department: the enormous amount of data made available by trawling through social media platforms can be used to help inform and improve an organization's retail operations.
>
> Social media monitoring is the act of tracking what is being said about you online. For large organizations, that involves using tools that monitor the web automatically. Marketing use this information to monitor brand awareness and sentiment, and customer service can use it to respond to complaints or negative feedback about products or services.

This is all well and good but it does not help you to understand why customer service problems occur or which areas of your business they relate to. With the technology that we have developed here at Dam Digital, you can segment and analyse the sentiment of social media content, understanding what was said positively and what was said negatively about a given service, product or experience.

This enables us, over time, to plot how specific areas of a business are being perceived through social media. In this way, we can see how sentiment specifically regarding customer service changes over time – by week, by day and, to some extent, by location.

But all this information is useless unless it can be taken in, understood and put to use by the people who have the power to initiate change. So what we do is build dashboards that allow staff to visualize the sets of this data that is useful to them. For example, a store manager may see granular information about his or her particular store, whereas an area manager may see a leaderboard of all stores in his or her area and be able to drill down into individual stores.

This allows operations teams to build a picture of their brand through the eyes of the customers they encounter on a daily basis, and encourages them to develop invaluable insights that inform the way they interact with their customers.

CASE STUDY   Mountain Hardwear/purechannelapps™

Client

Mountain Hardwear.

Provider

purechannelapps™.

Brief

Brand amplification and product messaging.

Overview

Mountain Hardwear (**http://www.mountainhardwear.com**) is a leader in innovative, premium outdoor apparel, equipment and accessories. They celebrate bold ideas, the drive to challenge the edges of their potential, and the joy, friendships and personal growth that come from that endeavour. They work with era-defining athletes to develop lightweight, easy-to-use and well-crafted outdoor clothing and equipment. Mountain Hardwear, Inc., founded in 1993 and based in Richmond, CA, is a wholly owned subsidiary of Columbia Sportswear Company and distributes its products through specialty outdoor, running and sporting goods retailers in the United States and 51 countries worldwide. In 2013, they gave their retailers the competitive edge on social media networks by deploying socialondemand® from purechannelapps™.

Approach

The online tool is specifically designed for companies that use a network of dealers, retailers, employees and other partners as a route to market, enabling centralized content curation and distribution amongst a scalable global network of brand advocates.

Outcome

Mountain Hardwear were able to reach and influence consumers in a highly competitive retail market by providing their retailer network with relevant, timely and rich content to share as their own, to their social media networks. By doing this, Mountain Hardwear were able to reach 555,000 new consumers, where it matters – at the local level. Other benefits include an average of 350 clicks and downloads per individual post created, as well as a cost-per-click (CPC) for the tool of just US $0.15, 86 per cent less than the standard CPC figure of $1.11 for search engine marketing in the retail industry.

Conclusion

'I am proud of Mountain Hardwear's success with the socialondemand tool', said Olivier Choron, CEO and founder of purechannelapps™. 'Not only have Mountain Hardwear used the tool to the maximum of its capabilities, but their partners have too. With high engagement in the tool, coupled with some impressive results, this truly shows how powerful the tool is, and a tool that can be used across the retail or FMCG verticals, as well as "traditional" channel enterprises. Socialondemand has delivered on every KPI we monitored.'

CASE STUDY   Argos/Dam Digital

Client

Argos.

Solution

Customer insight tool.

Agency

Dam Digital.

Overview

In today's ever-connected world, there are many platforms through which customers can openly discuss, comment, review, rant and commend services online. In this way, customer insight has never been more honest and available. Every opinion offered online provides precious insight into how an organization's customers are truly feeling about their brand.

Dam has been working with several clients, one of which is Argos, to develop a suite of tools that allow you to extract all of this data from its varying sources, and show it on a legible dashboard.

Challenges

With so much data coming from so many different sources, it is difficult to evaluate it all, especially in a way that makes it useful to staff. Argos spans 770 stores,

25 areas and 3 regions, and receives thousands of comments per day. These comments come from various sources including Facebook, Twitter, online and in-store surveys and customer complaints. All of this data is received and dealt with by different parts of the business, who do very little sharing of insights.

Actions

Dam quickly developed a dashboard that could extract data from different sources and display them in a way that would allow staff to understand and analyse customer feedback, making it easier for the team to respond accordingly. The dashboard was developed from a suite of tools that can be tailored specifically to requirements, and adapted and refined once implemented.

At the same time, Dam also produced tools that allowed the management team to understand how their staff were responding to the major transformation project being undertaken at the time, which helped them to work alongside each other to ensure the best possible results.

Lessons

The tools made it easy for Argos, through its staff on the ground, to know, understand and react to what their customers were saying about them online, allowing them to gather real insights straight from customers themselves. Using these insights allowed them to improve the relationship with their customers, which in turn has given a significant boost to the business.

Results

After being tested in a few concept stores, the dashboard is due to be rolled out across Argos's 770 stores country-wide. The dashboard has played a significant role in helping Argos to discover its reality with respect to being customer-focused and has helped to influence the organization's customer vision for a digital-led future.

Client testimonial

'Dam really understood the complexity of our data and the best way to visualize this to allow us to gain valuable business insights.'

Issy Linares, Argos

Links to campaign

http://www.dam-digital.com/work/argos/

Positive customer reviews are key in the business world and the link between them and an increase in sales is irrefutable.

How to build a social media team – how to pick the right suppliers

OUR CHAPTER PLEDGE TO YOU

When you reach the end of this chapter you will have the answers to the following questions:

- Are social media users natural social media marketers?

- What are the critical business attributes I should be looking for in a new employee?

- How important are passion, thirst for knowledge and a desire to grow?

- How should I structure my team?

- What roles should I keep in-house and what should I outsource?

- Is managing social media essentially a communications or a marketing role?

- Where do graphic skills sit within the role?

Hired or fired?

As an industry that in many ways is still in its infancy, finding and recruiting social media staff with the right level of direct experience and expertise can be difficult. Think of your needs as business critical and you may discover that your search will need to broaden to people who combine an understanding of social media with pertinent experience from other industries.

Authenticity is a word that keeps coming up in this book and it is as relevant here as in chapters where we have been discussing *message*. Look for social media staff who are great messengers, who can communicate your brand with integrity and clarity. Those who understand the importance of analytics, who have a keen eye for figures, who understand metrics, the importance of KPIs and how to set them, and who appreciate why ROI is so business-critical, are also skill sets that you will need.

Creativity is key to great social content, and as Mazher Abidi points out in this chapter, especially with a social media future that is ever-more dependent on great graphics and film content. Lee Wilson is also right to reason that social media employees are like any other: they need to be selected not only for their skill sets but for their cultural fit and shared vision for the future of your business. There is nothing like a bad hire to set back your business. Make sure you are clear about your needs before you go ahead and hire from a list of likely candidates.

Lee Wilson, campaign delivery manager, Red Rocket Media

Selecting talent, regardless of the industry, is always a business-critical decision. This is especially true if it involves investment of resources and capital into new areas of understanding. The focus of this contribution to the chapter has been developed on the assumption that a decision has been made to employ external expertise (notably a specialist agency) for social media, as opposed to recruiting in-house.

The main reason for this is that I feel this option will enable a wider practical application for most companies (although a lot of the logic applies to employing in-house also).

At this stage you should be thinking about the following:

- What do you (as a business) want to achieve through social media?
- How will you measure success?
- Who will be managing your social media (name, face, personality, profile, success stories)?
- What differentiates each agency from the competition?
- What do you get for your investment (tangibles)?

If you have been thinking about the questions above, you might start being able to visualize the right social media team for you. Here, my focus will be on removing the question marks over the right agency.

Why do you want social media? What are your objectives?

Before you approach anyone to provide a social media service, you need to understand fully why you need it in the first place. Taking on social media management on the basis that competitors are active on Facebook and Twitter may be a trigger event, but this should not be the driving force for a new investment. Let me qualify that statement. If you have a non-metric-based or undefined objective from the out-set, there is no clear way to say whether the campaign is delivering results, value or performance. This is simply because nothing has been put in place against which to measure the campaign.

Measurements ideally would be objective-based and fully transparent for all parties. Wanting the phone to ring more is a perfectly acceptable outcome, provided that telephone tracking is in place and that data is accessible to everyone working on the campaign.

As someone who works with data every day, I would encourage businesses to set out data-driven objectives. These can include traffic from social media (or 'x' network/platform), social conversions (last interaction, first interaction, assisted/contributed social conversions),

FIGURE 7.1   Example of Google Analytics (GA) social overview data

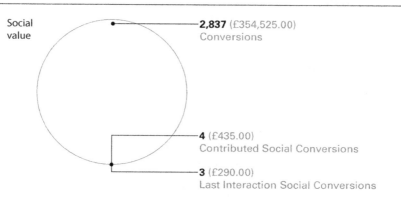

Social value

2,837 (£354,525.00) Conversions

4 (£435.00) Contributed Social Conversions

3 (£290.00) Last Interaction Social Conversions

reach and engagement metrics (Figure 7.1). If social media is a completely new venture, the first few weeks/months could focus on initial impact and setting a bar/benchmark against which future success can be measured. If the company is already active on social media, projections can be driven by previous results.

Questions to ask yourself:

- What does your social media team look like? Can you chat to them pre-sale? What have they achieved for other businesses? You should be able to answer all of these questions before taking on an agency. If you can't (or if doing so takes a monumental effort), I would suggest moving on to the next company.

- Have a look at how the business conveys itself online. Does it appear to be populated with people you could imagine working for your brand? There are likely to be times when they will need to be the first point of contact for highly public communication, so trusting them (even at this pre-sales stage) is important.

- Check out recent cases studies that your potential social media team has worked on and get a feel for its approach, as well as some expected results. When looking at case studies, try to consider how much of the success could be specifically attributed to an action (or set of actions) that is solely attributable to the social media expert/agency.

All social media agencies are the same – so it's all about price?

This could not be further from the truth. For any service selection process, once you have a narrowed-down number of potential people or agencies to work with – satisfied that they appear professional (in theory at least), have supportive results and convey themselves well online – the next stage is differentiation. What is unique about one social media proposition that you value above others? If a differentiator is not clear, it is likely that there is no differentiator at all. Social media differentiators should be based on approach, as the top agencies should all have the right expertise, experience, trust, transparencies and supportive case studies. It may seem a little subjective to judge an agency based on approach, but in reality it is the approach, culture and company values that will, in many instances, drive the success.

Update, measure, analyse and repeat: now that you have clear goals from your investment into social media, and these have been communicated (and ideally agreed upon by all involved), it is important to agree the way to measure success from these objectives.

Follower growth on Twitter may seem a logical metric for success, but perhaps a better one would be the impact that such change will cause. Here you would be looking at engagement and the impact you are having on your target audience rather than just numerical follower growth. Measurements of this could be interactions (shares etc) and supportive metrics such as traffic, which could be more useful for value measurements (and progressed with traffic quality metrics).

A starting point for social media KPIs often begins with a combination of the following:

- reach;
- engagement;
- mentions;
- comments;
- retweets/shares;
- traffic;

- responses (rates/times);
- interaction with key influencer/high-profile account holders.

Mazher Abidi, head of social media, Initiative MENA

It is well known that a business is defined by the people it employs; in an era where an increasing number of the world's most recognizable organizations employ specialists in employee satisfaction and staff retention, the make-up of the personnel within your business forms a key part of your business culture and its future success. And in the customer-focused, conversation-focused and engagement-focused world of social media, I believe that to be doubly true, especially when it comes to 'agency world'.

People from outside the agency environment often wonder as to the make-up of this 'world' that we within it refer to, but the evidence, anecdotes and day-to-day working practices confirm that the world of an advertising agency is indeed unique and, consequently, so too are the people within it.

Is it, therefore, right to infer that within 'agency world' we also have 'social media agency world'? Yes, possibly.

'Social media users are not social media marketers' – sometimes a phrase sticks with you because of its simplicity relative to its ultimate truth. This statement, which I first heard in 2009 at a talk in London delivered by Lucy Downing (@lucyjdowning; a friend and still one of the most knowledgeable social media pros I have ever met), remains as true today as it was then. We are all social media users... but that does not make us all qualified to be social media marketers.

Social media agency staff are in a unique position – owing to the still embryonic nature of this niche, employees (even at senior managerial or director level) are unlikely to have more than six years' experience within it. Those on the coal face (as with any industry, in fairness) will be fresh graduates and first jobbers, but the key difference is that they have less people within the industry with experience to learn from.

Allied to the fact that this raw talent is being entrusted with the public reputation of some of the world's biggest brands, you quickly start to see why the social media employee requires a unique skill set. They are inexperienced in business, yet are expected to be the public face of global businesses. They are inexperienced in networking, but we entrust them to network with influencers and fans numbering in the millions. They are inexperienced in business speak, yet we want them to define and deliver engagement, ROI and real business outcomes from social media (which a large percentage of social media activities by brands currently do not, and an equally large number of senior social media practitioners do not know how to when you ask them to).

And when they make a mistake, they are answerable not only to their management, but also to the client – and the audience, the social media audience, who can be cruelly unforgiving and can destroy a brand's reputation, built over centuries, in a matter of hours or minutes. And just as a reminder, we are expecting this responsibility from interns, graduates or first/second jobbers!

But you will tell me that social media teams – agency and client side – are growing faster than ever before; the industry is booming and so is the volume of work – and I will agree with you. Are we therefore all getting it wrong and hiring the wrong people, or is there in fact a right way to build a social media team?

I believe it is a bit of both, and in my current role as head of social media for the regional arm of a global media agency, I have unfortunately had experience of the former and, thankfully, learned that the latter does exist. And so my three most helpful tips in what to look for when recruiting social media talent are:

- Social media employees are still employees.
- Social media users are not social media marketers.
- Look for a balance of erudite and creative.

Let's look at each of these in more detail.

Social media employees are still employees

You may be looking for unique skills, and these may also be the first social media hires in your organization, but don't let this mean that your hiring procedures go out of the window. Assess cultural fit and client fit, and value qualifications and experience in the same way you would for other roles within the business. Don't let jargon cloud your judgement, especially if HR give hiring managers a free rein and those managers, in their desperate need to recruit staff, are happy to overlook certain key business attributes.

Flexibility, passion for the role and industry, thirst to learn, desire to grow professionally and personally – these should be a given. I can point to the time I replaced a community manager for my biggest client with a new hire with no experience but the right attributes – and saw my own productivity and output improve thanks to the simple fact that my colleagues and I trusted the new hire more, allowed him to learn on the job and let him learn from his first mistakes (which he did make, which he did learn from, and which we knew he would because he had the right personality to start with). The key point is to recruit the right person, not just the person who is in front of you at the right time... which is good business sense for any hire.

Social media users are not social media marketers

This phrase, again. If you come to me with 3,000 Twitter followers and a YouTube video with 500,000 organic views, it does not qualify you to be offered a job on my team. It qualifies you to have a conversation with me about what you did to get those numbers, what they represent, who they are made of and what you do with them – from which an offer to join my team may arise, but alone they are not enough.

And the reason is because everyone is a social media user. Your client, your brand's fans, your colleagues, your directors, your family, the man on the street... they all will have an opinion on how to market a brand on social media, but you need to be strong enough to make sense of their opinions and put them into a commercial business context. A social media employee has to take ideas on board and have an analytical mindset to query and qualify opinions. They need to be thick-skinned enough to sometimes accept the will of others even if they know it may not be right – as long as it doesn't cause harm. They need to be diplomatic enough to say no and give a reason for it. They need to be in tune with the youth and on trend, but in doing so never let that be a reason for people to call them uncommercial or immature (in a business sense).

Your social media marketer will more than likely be a social media user, but the next social media user you meet will not necessarily be your social media marketer.

Erudite and creative

Erudite

Those who have to look up the word erudite need not apply, because that suggests inadequate language skills for the job. And to be clear, this is a communications role at heart, so expert-level language and copy skills from the very start are a non-negotiable part of the role. As a social media professional, the copy you script will represent a global brand. Your communications will be seen by an audience into the millions who will not be afraid to mark out the omission of a comma, misuse of an apostrophe or (heaven forbid) a typo as a #fail, or worse an #epicfail.

And that copy has to be succinct, so the overt use of complex language is a negative. Timely. Relevant. Resonate with the brand and the fans. It is a difficult balance to achieve, but it has to be achieved nonetheless.

Creative

I include this as a unique requirement for 2014 onwards – as had this chapter contribution been written before 2014 it may not have been included. The reason is that as social media platforms move to become visual platforms, the importance of the creative becomes even more prominent than the copy. The most popular, well-received and viral pieces of content are now visual pieces: the Oreo 'Super Bowl' reactive ad, the adidas 'Wimbledone' image, memes and cat videos... we are communicating through images as much as words and if you are creating content you need to be visually creative.

Concluding remarks

Every manager will have their own opinions on how to structure a team. There is no one-size-fits-all set of characteristics for the role. But I lean on my experiences to wonder what I could have done differently to build a better team faster, and believe that if I had let my lesser-experienced self read the above, my current self would be delighted.

Chapter conclusions

Social media agency staff are in a unique position. Owing to the still embryonic nature of this niche, employees (even at senior managerial or director level) are unlikely to have more than six years' experience within it. That makes it even more critical to get right your choice of employee or supplier. A balanced team with the right levels of expertise, and a synergetic approach to delivering on your business objectives, are key to your choice of partner or new staff member.

CASE STUDY   El Armario de la Tele/ADTZ

Client

El Armario de la Tele.

Challenge

Promote APP downloads through Facebook.

Agency

ADTZ.

Overview

El Armario de la Tele is one of the most prominent fashion e-commerce brands in Spain. This is due to the quality of its products, the service offered and its digital marketing campaigns. The objective of this particular campaign was to promote their app downloads to a female target segmented by age, with very active users in social media and especially on Facebook.

Target audience

The El Armario de la Tele team and ADTZ worked to:

- reach the female target audience at the right moment with personalized communications;

- maximize the campaign click-through rate (CTR) and its creativity;

- obtain the most profitable consumer price index (installation cost).

Action

What is really important on Facebook is to attract the right audience without breaking the moment of live communication. The agency's technology enabled them to create, plan and analyse the campaign in real time to identify the most effective ways to capture audience engagement and to optimize response rates. ADTZ also created several different communication messages to two separate control groups; the first to female users aged between 18–29 and the second to female users aged between 30 and 40.

The format used for the campaign was mobile app ad, an exclusive mobile format to incentivize downloads of the application.

Outcome

The results were very positive for El Armario de la Tele in terms of branding (an indirect effect but very attractive in this type of campaign) and in terms of click-through rate, cost-per-click and app final downloads:

- Impressions – 20,000.

- Downloads – 1,700.

- Clicks – 2,600.

Links to campaign

adtz.com

Client testimonial

'Our application was created only two months ago and this action was planned in our app kick-start strategy. We wanted to motivate the downloads and without doubt it has been the action with the best benefits. The big difference with ADTZ is the technology, which allows us to test in real time, optimizing the messages and the creative approach. Additionally, it allowed us to use an age segmentation to know which was the most profitable target or most related segment. We received an almost daily campaign report.'

Rodrigo Martín, El Armario de la Tele, marketing online manager

Understanding the relationship between online PR and social media

08

OUR CHAPTER PLEDGE TO YOU

When you reach the end of this chapter you will have the answers to the following questions:

- What does B2P mean and how does it impact on PR?

- How should I use Twitter as part of a PR campaign?

- Who should I connect with on LinkedIn to amplify PR activity?

- Why does it help to be a good sharer?

- How has social media turned traditional PR on its head?

- What does a social newsroom look like?

- What is the difference between owned, paid and earned media?

How social media has turned traditional PR on its head...

Traditional PR depended on communications managed from a central control room. At the start of a campaign an agency would agree with the client on the story to break, produce the press release and send it out through the newswires, print and broadcast media. It would be delivered daily to our breakfast tables as contained content. Digital media has seen that premise turned on its head. No longer does the story start with the agency. More often than not it gets released first via a social channel such as Twitter and then its impact is managed by a PR team through a series of managed communications. The relationship between a PR agency and its journalistic contacts is now only a part of the release. At the same time as preparing the message and key messengers to take it out to market, the PR team has to introduce the idea to a whole range of channels via a range of related social media activities. Following key influencers and advocates on Twitter, sharing quality information and visual material on Facebook, purchasing paid media and building affiliate relationships to help amplify message are all part of the new PR package.

Jack Cooper from Red Rocket Media advocates the value of placing quality content across target sites as a preliminary stage in the PR process. Finding and providing content to key category websites and bloggers will set up some of the foundations for wider social media sharing. Laura Crimmons at Branded3 makes a critical point when she says that journalists more often than not now look for and pick up new stories from Twitter rather than through traditional PR channels. This makes it imperative that your hashtags are in order and that you communicate your PR message creatively and directly through the pertinent social routes in order to get a message out. Creating content on Google+ as a home PR page is also a great way to amplify a campaign and drive search engines towards your story.

Jack Cooper, Vertical Leap Digital/Red Rocket Media

The world of social media is one that keeps on diversifying and one that certainly keeps on giving. Over the years (yes years, I know!) a number of platforms have risen to popularity and others disappeared into the mist. Their success? Decided by the ability to inform, interact and engage with an audience.

Whilst for most users of social media it is a personal tool to stay up-to-date with their fast-paced lifestyle in the digital era, it was fast acknowledged that social media has a stronghold on the marketing strategies of companies across the globe. First used to reach a potentially huge audience, it was forcibly introduced as a front line for public relations and the communication of bigger business practices. Love it or hate it, social media cannot be left unnoticed.

Whilst many struggle with the basics and many get the fundamentals of social media completely wrong, one thing that cannot be underestimated is the power of social. One wrongly positioned tweet and you could turn not only the consumer perception of your brand on its head but change the views of your already loyal customers. Whilst digested content was once in the hands of the creator, the power and effectiveness is now reliant on the consumer. No longer can you rely on brand reputation and loyalty alone.

So, what type of PR is available through social media?

In taking a look behind the scenes of PR, first and foremost traditional PR has been known somewhat as a media art form that consists of know-how and tenacity. You would have to produce a portfolio of high-profile individuals with the power to promote your brand by publishing your name across a variety of platforms. The problem is they have no real obligation to do so.

> It used to be B2B and B2C but now it's B2P, with P being people. Social media cuts across channels and is all about engaging with individuals, holding conversations not relying on press releases and launches.
> (**www.thedrum.com**)

The above comment is from Nigel Ferrier, director of Optimise PR, as he explains how social media has changed the way we approach PR. Ironically, it is fair to say that PR used to be a fairly closed book when it comes to B2B promotion: face-to-face meetings, countless telephone calls and e-mails, and a sales-like pitch to promote your press release. But now, targets not only have the ability to receive content on tap, they can also carry out their own background checks to ensure it is from a reliable source – and if the source is of interest to them. Social media has made public relations, well, dare I say... public...

Social media has enabled cost-effective discovery

Find brand evangelists, reach a wider audience and impose your content on those who want it delivered directly to them. There are a number of PR-related instances that this can be applied to:

- Tweet the people you want to speak to directly, those who were previously uncontactable or uninterested. You can pitch your content without having to deal with a recorded message.

- Connect with editors and journalists on LinkedIn – they can see your background in a snapshot and register your authenticity; no more awkward on-the-spot questions, just interaction.

- Become your own content hub on Google+ and it will soon be picked up by those who are looking for it, should you share it effectively.

- As a side note, keep up-to-date with the new LinkedIn self-publishing platform!

The intricacies of search functionalities within social platforms have the ability to further enhance your targeting. You can receive instant notifications when someone posts about a topic or even specific phrase that you are digitally monitoring. You can check the frequency of posts on certain topics, where they came from, how much interaction they got and who unofficially endorsed such content. Not only can you now easily find and target those who want your content, you can find those who need your content. Did we mention that it is free? Well, practically. The range and extent of data available through social media is a PR gold mine.

There is an era of fierce competition

Many would argue that social media has devalued the integrity of PR. It has allowed even the most inexperienced communicator a chance to showcase their content. There is a level playing field as far as discovery goes, and there is an equal chance that your content will get noticed. It is all about the quality and relativity. Professionals would typically receive carefully thought about engagements, but the ease of social posting has amplified the amount of poor quality content versus well-written and relevant pieces. You can promote your content directly to the people who it would be of most interest to and it is for this reason that competition is fierce.

Not only is social media accessible, it is also a method that can take little effort for large rewards. It is unpredictable. Essentially, you can lead people to your content, but is it good enough? Let the influencers decide.

Be direct, be efficient and use the power of the hashtag

Influencer. A word that is key in anything social media. Where PR has traditionally been reliant on building a rapport and nurturing relationships, social media is a gateway to instant communication to the people who matter. There are two sides to this story...

First, this allows you to search for any mentions of your brand, product or service and to act upon it. You can answer questions, provide feedback and troubleshoot. You can dedicate as much time as financially viable to work your PR magic through social media.

Second, social media allows you to position your brand exactly where you want it to be. It allows you to talk about the things that are emotive within your audience and to be human. With social platforms updating their algorithms to serve up content to those who may be interested in it, there is always a chance you can reach new people if you are active.

Integration – using social media as a part of your PR strategy

Traditionally the end result of a successful PR campaign would be to have your editorial used on a website likely to capture the audience of your yet-to-be consumers. But what if they don't even have to look that far and it could be handed to them instantly?

As an extension of traditional PR, social media can be used to give your content legs. Where content can be fed to an influencer via social platforms, that influencer then has the choice to amplify content to its audience. Not only can you find your latest press release featured on a site, but there is a good chance that it will be posted to thousands of followers, and it will then be picked up by even more. Social amplification helps to give your content authority. The relationship between online PR and social media can be extended across many forms. Social media becomes a meeting point for your followers; it is about creating a buzz, being occasionally controversial and leading the conversation.

Social media PR can go wrong

Okay, so we have painted a pretty picture of the benefits of social media, but let's take a look at the deficiencies yet to be overcome on social media. Just as the platform has flung the doors of opportunity and discovery wide open, it can also assist in shutting them.

You can reach an audience of millions and you can target a specific band of demographic. It sounds excellent, doesn't it? Let's not forget that it also allows millions to publicly and openly vent their opinion and anger. One social media faux pas and you leave yourself open to public humiliation. Social media advocates have discovered that it is an excellent platform to gripe about a product or service after a poor experience. If this is picked up on by others and piggybacked, within minutes you could have achieved hoards of poor press.

People have tried to conquer this by avoiding social media, ignoring it and even opening separate social accounts specifically for PR responses. That way, you can ensure your response is public – this is your chance to respond. One golden rule: be passionate about your business and stand up for what you think is correct, but don't engage in a public showdown or argument.

Quality content is key

Let's not forget that quality content is now more than ever at the heart of PR, and different types of content are now essential. We can deliver information via white paper, video, infographic and so much more. The speed of discovery and delivery is excellent, but professionals are still looking for quality content, especially the big G – Google. Diversify your offering, be creative about your pitch and try not to be selfish. If you notice that someone else has written something particularly interesting or educational, then share it or comment on it. A bit of social media attention goes a long way.

Measuring the accountability of social PR

A common stumbling block is the ability to measure the ROI of social media activity. It is possible, but try not to measure it through monetary value – measure it through sentiment. If you are successful across social, you will pick up interest from the top publishers and, as a result, a much wider audience. Social Media and PR is all about initial brand awareness and the public eye. Worry about conversions once you have educated and captivated your audience.

So, do social media and PR present a fantastic opportunity for engaging with your target audience and further afield? Of course they do, but only if they can be managed properly. They require processes and they must be monitored for both opportunity and threats. As a matter of opinion, social media is most effectively used in PR efforts at the very beginning and very end of the journey. Use social media to discover your audience and share your content; nurture the relationships and use social media as your shop window to promote those relationships and the overall proposition of your business.

Jim Dowling, managing partner, Cake

Look around you during your next commute. Thirty years ago your train carriage would have been populated by mostly middle-aged men with neatly ironed newspapers and a cigarette on the go. On arrival at their city-centre destination, they would all go to their desk at the same time, every time. Look up now and probably not a single person in the train carriage is reading a paid-for newspaper. Some may be reading the news on an iPad (perhaps on a newspaper website they pay a subscription to access). Most people will be reading a free newspaper; some will be reading a book. Lots of headphones will be pumping out anything from politics to football phone-ins. There will be music from Vivaldi to The Vaccines. Some will already have started work and be checking their e-mails. Some are still off duty, looking at pictures of babies on Facebook. Someone will be drafting and redrafting a text after slinking out of the house in last night's clothes. Most will be zipping between three or four of those activities.

If you could visualize the imaginary hard drive of content currently fizzing around the average commuter train carriage it would be fairly compelling stuff. But if you are a creative or a media planner trying to sell a breakfast cereal, you've got to be good to get anyone to care. Everyone in the train carriage is doing what they want, and they couldn't care less about your product or your brand.

Herein lies the dynamic between old and new PR, and the importance of social media – it's the new relationship between the real world and the news desks of media outlets.

This used to be a very simple business. You had a product or a brand, and you had a set of journalists. During office hours, over lunch and over drinks, information passed via the PR agency to a news organization. As if by magic, newspapers would hit doormats the following morning – and lo and behold, information reaches the masses. Everything took place behind the closed doors of Soho agencies and Wapping newsrooms, perhaps meeting in the middle over a lunch table. No one saw anything, no one heard anything – it just happened. News was what large organizations (the government, business, the media) dictated it would be.

Now, real people dictate what news is. Real people read newspapers, go to websites, watch TV shows – but they are no longer passively force-fed what the organizations dictate. They are now the customer. Editors commission content that attracts them, and is consistent with their brand in the long term.

Real people also set the agenda. All news breaks, or emerges murkily, on Twitter, whether it is mundane or a front-page story. It has killed the television news flash, and has cheapened the drama of 'breaking news' on the rolling news networks. The editor doesn't call the shots – the story emerges, and if it is of interest, the audience shares, retweets and comments on it. The story inflates or deflates based on the heat that the audience places on it. So how do you navigate your way round all this?

Every PR client walks through our door with the intention of growing their business. At the heart of it are the things they want to sell, and people's perception of them. The simple aim is to use intelligence, insight and ideas to influence people's perceptions of brands.

Be intelligent

Use technology, tools and your brain. Before you start, work out what people are thinking, doing and saying about their lives. Find out what they are talking about, and what they are searching for in and around your brand. If you want them to behave differently towards your brand then you need to know where you stand at the start.

There are two new factors that PR people need to grapple with and master: data and technology. It begins with data. Today's consumer comes into contact with a brand every four seconds. You have very little time to grab their attention, understand what interests them and engage them. People are leaving clues all around the world, however, via their computer keyboards and smartphones. They tell you what they think, like, talk about and buy – and also the sort of content they are looking for, and where. In a nutshell, the online PR person is no longer operating to please the whims of a magazine or newspaper editor. They can now create and serve content and place it in channels where the consumer already is – on social media. If it captures the imagination of people, it will capture the attention of editors.

Cake has launched a social newsroom model, a creative content production unit that responds to the pace at which content is being consumed and shared by people. It is a body of people who bring all the required skills into one place, to produce content at pace. Data and social analysts supply customer information and intelligence in real time. Brand guardians and creatives carve out the brand's insight and idea. Technologists, content producers, publicists and live event producers turn the idea into output – a video, a film, a stunt, a photograph, a news story, a movement. Community managers distribute the content as it zips around the globe.

Make sure you have a great idea

Will it pull someone away from The Vaccines or Vivaldi to come and have a look at it? It doesn't matter what it is – a film, an app, a picture – but it has to be content that makes you smile, laugh, cry or scratch your head in wonder. It has to make people want to share it with others.

The opening up of social networks has led to clear channels of communication between brands and people. Whilst this presents an opportunity to brands, many operate under the misapprehension that people naturally care about what brands have to say.

People have more important things in their lives than brands and products: family and friends for one. For many, online PR and social media campaigns fail to recognize that the default position for the consumer is 'I'm not interested in you'. Hundreds of microsites, Facebook pages and YouTube channels lie dormant with failed attempts to encourage people to 'upload this' or 'submit that', doomed exercises that attempt to engage brands. Search 'Kellogg's Twitter fury' and 'McDonald's stories' and you will see examples where disinterest has turned into outright anger. In both cases, people reacted against the brands as they attempted to force a corporate agenda on an audience that didn't want to buy it, nor believe it.

Get people to see it

Find the way to get that content to people quickly and efficiently. Your content is redundant without the knowledge of how to distribute it smartly. Content needs people who understand how the component parts of media relate to one another. You need to navigate your path through social channels, search engines, RSS feeds, online platforms and publishers, in order to reach people. If you don't reach people, you can't change the way people feel about your brand.

As discussed earlier, content or campaigns rarely find their way into mainstream media unless they have built an audience in social or online first. Similarly, there is now a requirement for multifaceted types of content. Once upon a time, a press release and picture sufficed. Now online PR teams are producing video that is edited, tagged and optimized for search. Copy is provided in a variety of lengths and formats. Pictures are digital, varied and zipped around the wires. Tweets and Facebook posts are created and synched with a paid media spend to ensure eyeballs digest and share the content.

Sony wanted to share their latest model of NEX cameras to a mass but affluent audience who might consider buying a $500 camera, with a built-in Wi-Fi feature. The camera could snap a professional-quality photo, but could be uploaded to an online space within an instant. Traditional PR would have written a press release, invited journalists to a demonstration and aimed to secure editorial coverage in selected media. In a new online and social PR world, Sony's response with Cake was markedly different. Sony created content using the camera it was actually promoting – content that could be distributed and shared in social channels across Europe. People saw for themselves what the cameras could do, without reverting to a magazine article.

The Sony NEX Gallery was a real-time physical and online gallery. Three photographers were sent to three cities (London, Paris and Berlin) and were tasked with capturing images of the night. The images were then distributed and exhibited in a real gallery space in London, appearing 'live' whilst simultaneously distributed through Sony's Facebook pages across Europe. Millions viewed and shared the work of the NEX in action, and got a clear understanding of what the product was capable of.

Make sure it worked

We always make sure we measure our work. How many people have seen something? How many people have reacted positively to it? How many have promoted the brand or shared some content? How many people have subsequently bought something? There is a common-sense view (backed by countless studies and research) that word-of-mouth, and the endorsement of those you trust, is by far the most effective recommendation, more so than an advert or commercial message.

For years, PR people have grappled with proving the effectiveness of PR, and the value of editorial within traditional media. Social and online PR is providing commercial clarity. For example, IKEA wanted to increase consideration of its bedroom products. It relies heavily on its catalogue to allow people to browse products, without visiting the big out-of-town stores. The catalogue isn't always there when you need it, however, so IKEA turned to social media. It created a Facebook and YouTube app that designed a bedroom layout for you based on your living status (ie whether you were single, shared your room with your baby or a long-term love). The app played you a vision of what the user's bedroom could be, complete with photos of loved ones in picture frames by the bed. The effect was viral – people completed the task and shared their bedrooms within their channels, securing views on product.

It worked commercially. Digital and social content can pull people towards online stores. IKEA saw a clear spike in visitors inspecting their products online, leading to purchases. They had digital proof of the success, in a way that a newspaper article couldn't give them.

It's a new world for online and social PR – but the biggest lesson is the premium placed on creativity. The new judge is not the editor, it is the people themselves who act as judge and jury as to whether your message can be carried. Ask yourself two simple questions: Do you understand them? And, can you move them?

Laura Crimmons, Branded3

Online PR and social media can complement each other extremely well; it is rare nowadays that you will see an online PR campaign that does not involve a hashtag or some element of social promotion. Equally, social media campaigns that are successful will often naturally result in coverage online, ie online PR.

The key to these working well together for a campaign is understanding the KPIs for each and placing these at the heart of the strategy. For online PR the KPI is likely to be brand awareness and coverage, for social media it is likely to be increased engagement on key social channels.

To ensure online PR campaigns generate social noise and work for social teams, they need to consider social from the start. This could be as simple as having prominent sharing buttons to allow people to share the content and start conversations around it. Or it could be more integrated and pull social media noise through onto a campaign page so that the audience's tweets, Instagram photos and so on are featured on the website.

Online PR campaigns can provide social media teams with a wealth of fantastic content that they can use to engage the brand's social audience. By working together, PR and social, media teams can create campaigns that meet all objectives and truly engage the target audience.

Social media also means that businesses can find out how their customers and the public in general are talking about their brand in real time. Where previously brands may have had to commission a market research survey to find out sentiment around the brand and the talking points for customers, now there are a wealth of social media listening tools out there that allow brands to see exactly what customers are saying, where they are saying it and whether overall sentiment is positive or negative. This is fantastic for PR teams as it means they can instantly see the reaction to a current campaign and can then make smart decisions as to whether to ramp up activity or make changes to the campaign according to feedback. It also provides PR teams with valuable demographic information so that they can see whether they are hitting the demographics they were aiming for and, second, how well the campaign is resonating with different demographics, ie are males responding better than females?

Journalists' use of social media

Increasingly, journalists are using social media as their main source for news stories, which means that, from a PR point of view, if you can stimulate social conversation and noise around your campaign it is likely to get natural pick-up from the journalists you want to target anyway. Countless online journalists and writers have said that Twitter, Facebook and Reddit are their go-to places when looking at what is trending in communities and what they should be writing about. Big publications want to know what is important to their readers – and social media means that they can find out instantly.

Social media has changed the way in which stories break, and journalists have adapted to this. They know that the biggest and best stories break on social media long before they get an e-mail briefing – and they use this to their advantage. Social platforms have also adapted to this, making tweets and status updates embeddable so that journalists can embed the social media post directly into their article.

Not only does social media help journalists to reactively find stories that have already broken, but they are also using it as a source of new stories. The hashtag #journorequest is one of the most useful tools for PR nowadays as it is an instant source of coverage and allows us to see what topics journalists are currently covering.

Positioning social media in your business environment

There is often debate surrounding where social media should sit within a business. Should it sit with PR because it is about two-way communication with customers? Should it sit within customer service teams as often customers will use it as a customer service channel? Should it sit within marketing as it is a way for the brand to let customers know about latest promotions and marketing initiatives? Realistically there needs to be input from all of these teams to run a brand's social media channels effectively. Personally, in terms of ownership I feel it does sit well within PR teams, as social media is an extension of traditional PR activity.

The immediacy and two-way nature of social media means that a strong crisis-management plan is needed for businesses, especially those with high risks: for example, those dealing with people's safety. There have been many examples of brands getting this wrong and choosing to stay silent rather than address the issue, and others that have shown how social media can be a fantastic help in times of crises. This highlights the need for social media and PR teams to work together to decide on the appropriate course of action in the face of a crisis, and may at times even involve the business's legal team.

The key to the relationship between online PR and social media is communication. As long as both teams understand objectives, strategy and how each of them fit with a campaign, it is guaranteed to run smoothly. Another key element is timing; activity across all channels needs to be co-ordinated, as it does not make sense to start talking about a campaign on social media before the PR team have contacted media organizations with it. Equally it doesn't make sense for PR teams to go out with a campaign a week before the social channels start featuring content around it.

Mathew Sweezey, Salesforce

Edward Bernays (1891–1995) is a name you might not be familiar with, but hopefully you are with his uncle, Sigmund Freud. Bernays is singlehandedly responsible for changing the way that the publications industry was used by business and, in the process, created the public relations industry. PR is his creation, which he used to change the way businesses and governments reached consumers through media. In his book *Propaganda* (1928) he poignantly stated: 'Who are the men who, without our realizing it, give us our ideas, tell us whom to admire and whom to despise, what to believe... such a list would comprise several thousand persons. But it is well known that many of these leaders are themselves led, sometimes by persons whose names are known to few.' His theory was: control the source of ideas and you can control the ideas that spread.

The PR industry created a new economy of specialized marketers able to help those with ideas get them in front of people. Even in the early days of print, people responded better to the messages in articles than they did to advertisements in publications. The trade-off for PR versus paid advertising was the time to execution. For PR it might take months to get a piece into a publication, while an ad buy can be done overnight and published the next day. This has always been the major stumbling block for executing the PR strategy. The second stumbling block is, simply, great content. The 'good content' issue is not a factor of the technique, but the practitioner, and should not be considered when evaluating a technique.

Since the number of publications also limited PR, the sprawl of the internet gave this technique a new life as well. Consider that at the height of printed media newspaper and magazine titles only ran into the thousands. Now consider that there are over 152 million blogs in existence and over 1 billion people reading their social feeds via Facebook. As Bernays theorizes, PR is not about getting into print but rather allowing someone to self-discover, and in the past that was print, but now this is via social feeds.

Currently we have social publishing that carries none of the physical barriers to publishing of previous generations. We have free ways to create content, produce it, distribute it and access it, with the largest-ever readership in the history of the world. The only problem facing social publications that prevented it from taking over as the primary PR was its ability to ensure readership. When the social media algorithm was based on follower count for virility, you would buy more followers to be in more people's social feeds. Now Facebook and Twitter have both seriously slimmed down the ability for you to influence your fans and followers for free. They realized that by combining access to the targeting data they had control over, with real time in feed marketing, they could provide more value to businesses than traditional PR/marketing ever could. This is the new world of PR via social publishing. Paid social promotion, not just viral PR.

Real-time bidding

To complete the perfect storm of PR via social media, a breakthrough in advertising buying was required. It is the concept of real-time bidding (RTB) combined with ad marketplaces. An RTB is the ability for a company to buy one ad, for one person, in real time. The marketplace allows you to contract across networks, all with a single bid. So rather than pay for a static PR campaign you can buy one ad, for one person, in real time, and do it with extreme precision. The readership of the publication is no longer your limitations, but rather your budget, and targeting ability. Now you can self-publish an article, and have it distributed to the perfect custom audience, at the exact right time. This removes the lengthy timeline of traditional PR, removes the need to pitch stories, and removes the limited audience of a publications reach.

Precision content and targeting

Modern social PR hinges on the quality of the content you promote. This is still a basic fact of all PR. You need to have a good story, and it needs to be relevant to a person. This is why the concept of marketing automation has become such a huge industry. The basic lead tracking from marketing automation allows businesses to know what is relevant to a person, so they combine this information with paid social PR techniques in order to place the correct article in front of the correct people. So you can now be your own content creator (publisher), distribute via social media (PR), but do so with the precision of a surgeon, any time you want. Or use these techniques to expand the reach of your traditional PR campaign. Either way, social media and PR have forever changed due to the increase in technology, and its ability to remove all of the previous limitations PR was bound by. This new marriage is so powerful that some of the biggest brands are already using these techniques to drive over 20 per cent of their lead volume, at fractions of pay per click (PPC) advertising and traditional PR retainers.

Businesses have now found a perfect mix of content creation tool, distribution options and targeting solutions, and it has changed the way that companies look at PR, and the way content providers monetize their readership. These new innovations do not neglect the basics of marketing or the need for solid content. They only make it easier for the best ideas to rise, and put a larger importance on the relationship as a key driver of business goals. If a business uses these modern PR techniques with disregard for its potential negative effects on their relationship with their leads/consumers, it will potentially damage their brands quicker than build them. It is a fast-paced world, and it takes a lot to keep up, but for a marketer, nothing could be more exciting than this new collision of media, technology and consumer behaviour.

Ithamar Sorek, Glow Media

The latest trend to hit online advertising is a new method of target marketing called 'native advertising'. This enables advertisers to gain greater consumer interest by providing content that is linked directly to the user experience, thus removing the noise and making advertising feel less intrusive. This means that the advert becomes more desirable to a particular audience and, most importantly for the advertiser, is directed specifically at the right audience.

Classed as a step on from more traditional advertising such as advertorials, native advertising is providing brands with the opportunity to offer something that is of interest to the reader and to ensure that the brand message is clear. Advertisers are also now investing heavily in well-written, highly targeted approaches, whereas in the past, advertorial had received a bad reputation for being of poor content quality.

Platforms including Twitter and Facebook are split into two categories to form open and closed environments. For example, promoted tweets on Twitter, stories that feature on Facebook or videos on YouTube are categorized as closed platforms as the advertiser is creating profiles within a closed environment. Promoting the same advert or branded content across multiple platforms is commonly known as an open platform, due to the fact that content is advertised outside on other social channels and across multiple platforms.

How does native advertising fill the gap between brand publishing and banner advertising?

Over the years, banner advertising has been silenced due to the fact that the audience has become used to seeing published ads in this format. It is banner advertising that sits in the background of every web page, mobile app, social network and so on, but research has shown that the consumer now skips them as quickly as they are viewed.

As online advertising has evolved, so has a need and recognition that a more targeted approach is required. Native advertising either through retargeting based on your web and mobile interactions, or on behavioural capabilities, is there to make a mark on the consumer's perception in an unthreatening environment.

Think of your native environment as a busy street in the middle of New York. All the signs, sales people and stores are your banner advertising. Although they take your attention, you also skip them very quickly. Then, within this madness you suddenly see a friend who tells you there is a sale at a particular location – and you are intrigued. This is your native advertising unit. Your new-found knowledge will either make you go for it or recall everything you have been exposed to and decide if it is worth your while or not.

This is not to say, of course, that paid placement takes value away from other advertising mediums. All campaigns should form part of a wider marketing strategy, but if the advert is targeted correctly and brings relevance to the audience, then it will add more value in the long term. This is what is so cool about today's web and mobile environments, as one can better evaluate using technology where his or her audience are in order to ensure the content that they see is relevant.

The challenge, however, lies in the cross-social capabilities. Native advertising is the concept of communication and it is important to recognize that even though the campaign is heavily targeted due to the native capabilities, the advertiser must take into account that each platform is addressed independently. It is not a one-size-fits-all method of communication and it is important to remember that audiences differ between social platforms, be it Facebook or Twitter.

In terms of user experience, what other engagement tools compare to native advertising? From community management, conversational trends, to organic exposure of subject matters, the whole story of owned, paid and earned media was a focus for last year and all play a very important role in understanding the user journey and experience, whilst all native activities of a brand that are not paid for are also included.

However, the advantages of native advertising over other digital advertising channels are clear. Users are exposed to native advertising in a more natural way within their day-to-day activities, whereas traditional advertising channels are proven to be less and less effective, as users tend to just 'skip' actually or emotionally through the messages that are being delivered. To get it right – in order to target the right audience at the right time and with the right message – it is essential that the brand works with a performance advertiser that specializes in social.

Chapter conclusions

Influencer. A word that is key in anything social media. Where PR has traditionally been reliant on building a rapport and nurturing relationships, social media is a gateway to instant communication to the people who matter. Online PR campaigns can provide social media teams with a wealth of fantastic content that they can use to engage the brand's social audience. By working together, PR and social media teams can create campaigns that meet all objectives and truly engage the target audience.

CASE STUDY Proficient City/Glow Digital Media

The client

Proficient City.

The agency

Glow Digital Media.

The brief

Wartune, Proficient City: reaching the right gamers.

The challenge

Proficient City wanted to encourage gamers in English-speaking countries to play its Facebook desktop game title, Wartune. It wanted to achieve a better return on ad spend than it had managed in previous campaigns before its partnership with Glow Digital Media.

Facebook and Glow Digital Media helped Proficient City to achieve higher returns on its ad spend than previous campaigns. Its use of lookalike audiences also proved to be particularly successful. Proficient City develops and publishes mobile and web games in various languages for audiences around the world and employs over 200 people. Wartune is a multiplayer online role-playing game (MMORPG) and is Proficient City's most successful game yet in English: it was the first to gross over $10 million.

The approach

A targeted approach – Proficient City and Glow Digital Media ran desktop app ads that featured characters from the game, snappy copy and strong calls to action. These ads brought people directly to its Wartune game. Besides targeting English speakers in Australia, Canada, the United States and the UK, Proficient City used Facebook's lookalike audiences tool and its existing customer database to target people similar to existing Wartune players who have made in-game purchases. By allowing gaming companies to target people similar to existing players, Facebook helps advertisers to reach the people most likely to respond well to their ads.

Conversion tracking pixels were used to help Proficient City measure the effectiveness of its ads. Ads were run between 23 January and 12 March 2014 using Facebook's custom audiences and lookalike audiences tools. There was a higher payer conversion when lookalike audiences were used and a three times higher return-on-ad-spend than previous campaigns.

The results

The results speak for themselves:

- 25 per cent higher return per dollar on ad spend when lookalike audiences were used.

- 2.2 times higher revenue per install when lookalike audiences were used.

- 3 times higher payer when lookalike audiences were used.

- 25 per cent higher return on spend when lookalike audiences were used.

Client testimonial

'Glow Digital Media provided us with the best help with our advertising strategies on a local level while greatly improving our Facebook campaign's performance.'

Xitou Li, chief operation officer, Proficient City

CASE STUDY   Direct Blinds/Shackleton PR

Client

Direct Blinds.

Agency

Shackleton PR.

Brief

Online PR and social media.

The challenge

Huddersfield-based Direct Blinds and its product range was top of the Google rankings for generic, non-brand searches such as 'online blinds' or 'made to measure blinds' (thanks to the work of Shackleton's parent company, Epiphany). But no one searched for them online via the company name.

Shackleton was tasked with helping to build brand recognition, differentiating the company from its competition, increasing direct searches and driving sales. To address this brief, four core strategic objectives were set:

1 Build relationships with key influencers who could help us 'create' a brand.

2 Join-up online, social and traditional channels so all communication was working towards a single, coherent call-to-action.

3 Create a thriving community of customer advocates, engaged with the brand – instead of purely receiving messages.

4 Ensure PR activity complements and adds value to the great search engine optimization (SEO) work done to date. Real value could be added by ensuring that no marketing element existed in a silo.

Target audience

This was wide-ranging – homeowners and tenants looking for high-quality, made-to-measure blinds.

Action

Following thorough audience and channel research, the team developed a three-pronged strategy:

1 The implementation of an image-led campaign strategy across social, online and traditional channels. Testing showed that this was most likely to generate genuine engagement with the client, its brand and products.

2 The messaging and targeting was focused on the family market, a market that did not respond well to overly promotional or disruptive communications.

3 Content designed specifically to create a sense of 'reward' for audiences.

The PR programme was intrinsically linked with a social media campaign that consistently rewarded audiences with discounts, competitions and entertaining content. Proactively sharing news, tips and supporting PR campaigns through announcement posts, whilst ensuring that customer queries and interactions were responded to, Direct Blinds gained over 4,300 organic social fans over the space of 10 months.

Two campaign highlights

A cross-channel campaign, Room with a View, was managed via social media, reaching out to audiences and inviting them to submit images of their dismal, dreary or downright soul-destroying views. The very worst would be rewarded with a blind to cover up their eyesore. Social media came alive as people finally got a chance to vent their anger at the brick wall they stare at every day, or the old man in the flat opposite who refuses to put on any trousers. The best images were then used in traditional media, with national press coverage secured within key titles, such as the *Daily Mail*, *Metro* and *Mirror*.

This campaign alone generated 55 pieces of coverage (including nine nationally), drove 2,529 visits to the client's website, added 703 social followers and encouraged 1,200 total social engagements. In total, it reached over 11.7 million people.

Taking the learnings from Room with a View, later in the year Shackleton launched a search for the UK's naughtiest pet. Noticing a trend on social channels of a love for sharing snaps of animal antics around the home, the team decided to delve further, to discover what other mischief people's furry friends got up to around the home when backs were turned.

Armed with some great data on which animals were the worst offenders, in which towns, and how much they were costing households, gathered through a UK-wide survey, people were asked to submit images of their pets caught in the act – in a bid to find the naughtiest. Launched through the media and social channels, within just 24 hours the campaign had achieved widespread coverage.

In addition, a blogger outreach campaign was launched, sending customized boxes to 11 of the most influential within the genre, comprising treats and toys for their beloved pets (except for the diabetic dog who was on a strictly no-treat diet) in a bid to distract them from being naughty, and practical household items to remedy the damage, including scrubbing brushes and Vanish spray.

Results

Naughty pets highlights:

- Over 300 entries via social media.

- Over 20 million consumers reached, including over 7,000 social media shares.

- 47 pieces of PR coverage achieved an equivalent advertising value of over £270,000.

- Campaign featured nationally by *The Times*, *Daily Mail*, *Metro*, *Mirror*, *Daily Record*, BBC Radio 4, ITV *Loose Women* and Telegraph.co.uk.

- Lead story on the Mail Online home page for 12 hours.

- 4,900 social shares and over 750 comments.

Overall campaign results:

Media relations:

- Coverage: 168 pieces.

- Reach: 144.8 million.

- 32 online pieces with a domain authority of over 50.

- 25 pieces of national coverage (includes print and online), 44 pieces of regional print coverage, 10 pieces of magazine coverage (print) and 58 pieces of additional online coverage (excluding national media).

Social media:

- Reach: 322,876.

- Engagements: 8,123.

- Social traffic (users visiting the Direct Blinds website from social channels): 2,794.

- Conversions (sales and samples) via social: 1,009.

- Revenue that can be directly attributed from social activity: £13,113.

Website statistics (based on six-month period versus previous six months):

- 115 per cent increase in organic traffic.

- 120 per cent increase in unpaid traffic, with peak in March during the Room with a View campaign.

- 124 per cent increase in organic transactions.

- 133 per cent increase in organic revenue.

Client testimonial

'Shackleton's modern-day approach to PR is what sets this company apart. The team's knowledge and understanding stretches beyond the realms of traditional PR into social media, analytics, e-commerce and SEO. They produced a campaign that not only worked exceptionally well within the wider marketing mix, but that was fun, newsworthy, timely and, above all, effective. The results they achieved were outstanding and went far beyond our expectations.'

Nicolas Swift, joint managing director, Direct Blinds

'It's the dream marketing idea that makes the news and gets on to programmes like this one [*You and Yours*, Radio 4]. Direct Blinds has done it!'

Winifred Robinson, presenter on BBC Radio 4

Links to campaign

http://www.directblinds.co.uk/

https://www.facebook.com/directblinds

https://twitter.com/DirectBlinds

The future for social media and the vastly changing landscape

OUR CHAPTER PLEDGE TO YOU

When you reach the end of this chapter you will have our experts' visionary responses to the following questions:

- What will socialization mean in the future?

- What changes will we see in content management?

- How will the real and digital worlds further converge?

- Where will the next social explosion come from?

- How will social media further integrate into our business practices?

- What is the future for wearables and superfast mobile internet?

- How important will social listening be to the future of our activities as marketers?

The future is speeding towards us: are you ready to take the next leap?

Social media has just hit its first decade! Ten years old and early adoption has become mainstream engagement. In the West, the millennial generation has never known a life without social media, and their parents and grandparents have adopted this new way of communicating with little or no arm-twisting from their tech-savvy offspring. If we cast our eyes to the rest of the world, however, we will see that there are still billions of people yet to become social media users. The near future will see a rapid acceleration in adoption and, along with it, a shift in the social media channels adopted. China and Japan have alternative platforms to Facebook and Twitter (Tencent, Sina Weibo, Alibaba/Taobao to name a few of the giant players). The social landscape will evolve and change with even greater speed, but one thing will remain constant: social media is here to stay.

How it will look in another 10 years is a different story. No longer will channels be segmented but seamlessly integrated. Social media will not be sitting on a tablet or smart device or desktop computer. We will no longer have to log in to read the latest posts and messages. The digital and physical worlds will continue to converge. We will all be using social as an integral part of our walking, eating, working, exercising, socializing and maybe even sleeping routines. It will be with us on every step of our personal life journey.

In support, businesses and organizations will need to develop more sophisticated methods to communicate with their customers. Content curation will become ever-more honed. Quality will improve. Less mistakes will be made. More creativity will be required to capture attention, and data will be mined for its every last detail about the individual's likes and dislikes, habits and behaviours. This in turn will lead to change in human digital interaction and, essentially, in human behaviour itself. Feeling ready for the next iteration? Read on to hear how some of our visionaries see the future that we are all speeding towards!

Anil Nair, CEO and managing partner, Digital L&K/Saatchi & Saatchi

Ever since the internet was discovered, the socialization of it was an eventuality. But what people did not account for was the dizzying pace of change; a change that consumes both creators and consumers of these social ecosystems and all in between. It is unpredictable, always on, ever morphing and driven by an almost Darwinian instinct for 'survival of the best features' that can satisfy this collective 'social consciousness beast'.

As I finish my last social post for the day, I sit back and mull on the trajectory of the social media network and its future. Here are some of my observations.

Social content management: curation and social bookmarking

A beast of this magnitude needs fuel. Content and sheer volumes of it are the emerging fuel and social currency. Content management and dissemination will be key areas to look out for on the social landscape horizon.

Social bookmarking will choose the best of social content curated by this collective social intelligence. This is the era of the networking of knowledge. From knowledge by reduction (into a book or a pdf or an encyclopedia) to knowledge by inclusion (a linked network). Therefore, the game will move on from aggregation into filtering and curation.

Decentralization of power

There has been a gradual shift in the power equation: decentralization from vested interests to the people and the masses. That will continue with increased momentum. It will be a very participatory culture where the digital and the real world meet. This ecosystem is real, more transparent and very 'in the now'. Individually though, it is very 'sum of the parts'. But the whole picture is very powerful.

Behavioural shifts

The new social is changing the way that people have been doing stuff for ages. Starting with softer aspects such as communication, photography and dating, to even more lasting physiological and physical changes, erasing old behaviours and anchoring new ones.

Be guerilla

Thinking by the seat of your pants is the new name of the game. Quick reaction times worthy of the special forces, the ability to mash-up quickly and be an early adopter of a particular network or a train of social consciousness is a key ingredient for success.

Fission and fusion

Be ready to embrace rapid change, as the landscape is ever changing. Small social networks will emerge to become big, and then consolidate to become bigger only to see them break up or have new offshoots emerging. This constant fission and fusion is a reality that is here to stay and one needs to be able to navigate this minefield in order to stay ahead of the curve.

Wall meltdown

Social media is currently a walled universe from the rest of the internet. Imagine if this wall were to disappear. Gear up for this reality as all that social content becomes searchable. Mindboggling. The social network is no longer a framework or inanimate. It has a life and sentient intelligence of its own. Brands and people will plug in and out. The form factors will change but this intelligence is here to stay.

Jason Mander, head of trends, GlobalWebIndex

In the 10 or so years since Facebook first came to prominence, social networking is a behaviour transformed. The days of sharing everything with everyone have long since disappeared as we have become more and more aware of the need to manage our digital footprints. We are no longer so enthusiastic about 'poking' each other or competing for check-in badges, but have been quick to embrace mobile messaging apps and content-sharing services. We have waved goodbye to many local platforms – remember Hyves in the Netherlands? Or the once much-fancied Orkut? We have witnessed global players such as Twitter and Facebook making in-roads into more and more markets, supported by a series of acquisitions designed to ensure their long-term success.

Specific behaviours or platforms have been evolving, then, but the underlying popularity of social networking has remained a solid constant. By the middle of 2014, GWI's data in fact shows that 9 in 10 online adults aged 16–64 are users of networking sites, the vast majority on a regular basis, with Facebook the first-choice destination in 29 of the 32 countries we surveyed (being displaced only in China, Russia and Japan by Sina Weibo, VK and Twitter respectively).

Against this context, it is hard to dispute that social networking has established itself as an ingrained and impressively global behaviour. Although it is popular (and headline-grabbing) to talk about the 'death of Facebook' or speculate about our imminent abandonment of social networks as we come to tire of the activity, the simple truth is that networking is too embedded within the fabric of our online activities for this to happen. It is right to expect further, potentially dramatic, changes, though. By the middle of the 2020s, we will still be using social, but will we be engaging with platforms like Facebook and Twitter in exactly the same ways as we are now? Absolutely not.

Fast-growth markets

Some of the changes discussed above are already taking place and have been widely recognized, with the ongoing migration to mobile being the biggest case in point. Far less discussed is the continuing shift in momentum from mature to fast-growth markets. At present, the latter typically receive (by far) the lowest levels of digital investment because they have relatively low internet penetration rates (while 90 per cent or more of adults in countries such as Sweden, the

UK and Canada are now internet users, the equivalent figures remain below 50 per cent in markets such as Indonesia, India and China, and often significantly so). However, these national rates are showing very strong year-on-year growth levels, meaning that millions, if not billions, of people will come online for the first time during the next decade.

In relation to networking, this has profound implications, as it is in fast-growth markets where the enthusiasm for all things social is strongest. Users are not only the most likely to be using all of the platforms tracked by GlobalWebIndex, they are also carrying out the widest range of social behaviours. If we look at the percentages who visited Facebook in a single month in 2014, then, despite one or two local nuances, it is not hard to see the general pattern here: it is the fast-growth markets that top the list. And while India might have one of the lowest internet penetration rates of all (still below 20 per cent of the population), size really does matter: the 90 per cent of its online population who visited Facebook in a single month in 2014 represent more users than in the whole of the European Union Five (France, Germany, Spain, Italy and the United Kingdom) combined. India has in fact seen a 60 per cent rise in the numbers visiting Facebook in the two-year period 2012–14, compared to equivalents of 20 per cent or so in most mature markets (Table 9.1).

This trend makes it fairly clear that in the next 10 years all of the major social networks have the potential to see huge levels of growth in emerging markets, something that underlines the rather Westernized perspective of those ready to talk about any imminent demise in social networking. It also shows why digital investment strategies will need to evolve to respond to this new reality; if the history of networking to date has been a very US-centric affair, the next stage will see a lot of focus shifting from the West to 'the rest'. Indeed, it is worth noting that across the 32 markets tracked by GlobalWebIndex, mobile networking is already most established in the regions that contain the most fast-growth markets, with the current (let alone future) size of the audience in the Asia-Pacific (APAC) giving clear pause-for-thought (Table 9.2).

Elsewhere, the ongoing shift to mobile will continue to see social networking becoming more specialized and, in places, more passive.

TABLE 9.1   Comparison of Facebook users

	% who visited Facebook in a single month in 2014		% who visited Facebook in a single month in 2014
Mexico	92%	Canada	77%
Philippines	92%	Spain	77%
Malaysia	90%	Ireland	77%
Argentina	90%	Poland	75%
India	90%	USA	75%
Thailand	89%	Sweden	74%
Vietnam	88%	Saudi Arabia	73%
Turkey	88%	UK	72%
Indonesia	88%	Australia	69%
Brazil	87%	Netherlands	68%
UAE	87%	France	67%
South Africa	86%	Germany	63%
Singapore	83%	South Korea	58%
Taiwan	82%	Russia	50%
Hong Kong	81%	China	26%
Italy	79%	Japan	25%

TABLE 9.2 Comparison of social network users via mobile

	% who used a social network via mobile in a single month in 2014	Universe (millions)
Latin America	77%	96.66
Middle East and Africa	76%	27.08
Asia-Pacific	71%	627.61
North America	65%	131.47
Europe	62%	169.59

While we might once have used a site such as Facebook for most things social, we have become increasingly likely to turn to platforms that fit a particular activity (Instagram and Pinterest for photographs, messaging services for instant chat, and so on). In short, we have been moving away from the one-site-fits-all model of networking to embrace a more fragmented approach where we visit different services for different activities.

Just look at the growing numbers outside of China using WhatsApp each month and it is clear that many of the conversations that used to take place via SMS or inside social networks proper are migrating to this space (with WhatsApp's impressive performance in fast-growth markets in particular also helping to explain its price tag) (Table 9.3).

All this does not mean that we have left Facebook, though, or that we will do so in the future in any serious numbers. We might be using the main site itself more passively or less frenetically, but Facebook is continuing to transition itself into the glue that holds together all of our social activities. As its list of purchases makes clear, it wants to become a general portal for our online activities, maintaining a social emphasis but incorporating content, purchasing and more besides.

TABLE 9.3   Comparison of mobile users of WhatsApp

WhatsApp	% mobile audience using it each month
Q2 2013	30%
Q3 2013	33%
Q4 2013	36%
Q1 2014	39%
Q2 2014	40%
WhatsApp: Top 10 Markets in Q2 2014	
South Africa	79%
Argentina	75%
Malaysia	73%
Hong Kong	69%
Singapore	69%
India	67%
Spain	65%
UAE	64%
Mexico	64%
Netherlands	62%

Essentially, it will be the gateway for many of our online behaviours, even if far fewer of these are hosted on its main site compared to in the past.

In a sense, then, 2014–24 will see social networking becoming both more fragmented and more unified at exactly the same time. The Facebook of the 2020s will still be highly recognizable, but the smart money says it will have found ways to facilitate a far broader range of our online activities and behaviours.

Lauren Friedman, head of social business enablement, Adobe

Almost anything in life can be exciting simply because it is *new*. Think about new relationships, a new job, or a new TV series. People love things that are new. They thrive on the thrill that is all part of that initial discovery phase.

When social media first emerged, it was all the rage with technology early adopters and the millennial generation. In 2014, some of that generation's parents and grandparents are using social media platforms. The importance of social media today cannot be disputed. But, that importance is no longer simply because it is new. This shift, from being novelty to purpose, will transport social media to a whole new level in the coming years.

We have already seen many shifts in the way we use social media. We have moved away from focusing on 'viral campaigns' and towards creating more meaningful engagements and relationships. Facebook is not the only big player in the space any more (and some younger folk would probably say that Facebook isn't a player at all). Brands are participating in conversations and building relationships with their customers (and their customers are letting them!) instead of purely using social media as a marketing and advertising tool.

Corporations are now faced with some major decisions. They can either choose to be social, or stick with their traditional, 'old-fashioned' ways. Brands are now faced with adapt-or-die decisions and the best way to come out on top is to embrace social completely.

Infuse social media into every aspect of the way you do business

Social media started out as another marketing and advertising platform that brands used to push out their messages, campaigns, announcements, and more. However, it quickly became apparent that social is much more than the magazine ads or billboards that brands were used to. Instead, brands are able to get real-time feedback on campaigns, switch out content and imagery regularly, and be more agile. But, what's next? What are companies supposed to do with the feedback they receive? How can they capitalize on the direct inter-actions with their customers? The days of using social media purely for marketing are over. Now, brands will begin to infuse social media into every aspect of their business – not just within their marketing department. Here at Adobe, I work to integrate social media into every aspect of the way we do business, not just marketing and advertising. Employees in different job functions can use social media to achieve their core business objectives. So, what does integrating social media into every aspect of the business look like? Figure 9.1 shows this in action.

FIGURE 9.1   How social media integrates every aspect of business

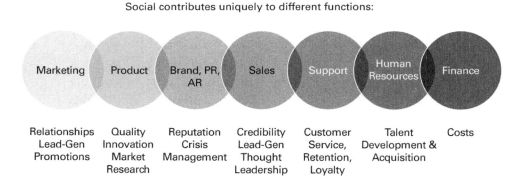

Social contributes uniquely to different functions, and different functions across an organization can use social media to achieve their

specific business objectives. By integrating social media into every aspect of the way a brand does business, the opportunities are endless:

- Sales can use social media to generate leads.

- Human Resources can use social media for talent acquisition.

- Product teams can use social media to do market research and understand customer challenges in order to drive product innovation and development.

- And finance is happy because social media can help to cut costs (by cutting down call centre volume, for example).

Working cross-functionally to establish integrated social media strategies across the entire business will drive real business results.

Enable, empower and educate your employees to be social on behalf of your brand

Many companies are still afraid of social media. They don't want their employees, who are tied to the company, to be irresponsible on social media. Companies provide a list of dos and don'ts for their employees on social media, which deters them from talking about even the positive experiences they have in their job. This, too, is shifting.

In the 2014 Edelman Trust Barometer, it is very clear that employees are trusted more than anyone else within an organization – in fact, the average employee is trusted two times more than a chief executive. Empowering, enabling and educating employees to be active on social media on behalf of your brand is the future. Social media training is quickly becoming mandatory for an ever-growing range of companies, and elevating a company's employees to act on behalf of the brand is extremely powerful. Of course, part of this training is to educate employees on what not to do in order to protect themselves and the brand, but it should also be focused on how employees can get involved and impact a brand's social universe and customer relationships. Adobe's Social Shift social media training programme does just that. It is a healthy mix of examples of where employees went wrong and how all of our employees can get involved and interact with our customers online.

Be where your customers are... on their phones

Mobile has transformed the way we use the internet. For starters, mobile has doubled the amount of time we spend online, with 593 per cent growth from 2010 to 2013 (comScore at **www.comscore.com**). Both Facebook and Twitter users spend more time using those networks on mobile devices than they do on traditional computers or laptops.

Optimizing for mobile is crucial. Ensuring your website is responsive and looks clean on a mobile screen, or building a mobile app when appropriate, will help to make the mobile experience for your customers a good one. If you are not optimized for mobile, you are failing.

When it comes to internet traffic, Facebook is still the king of referrals with an estimated 21 per cent of distribution (followed by Pinterest at 7 per cent then Twitter at 1 per cent). If your customers are clicking through to your websites from Facebook on their phones, they better have a great experience.

Social media plays an important role in mobile device usage and that role is amplified even more when combined with other mediums: 84 per cent of mobile owners use their devices while watching TV (source: Nielsen). What are they doing? Some of the top activities are surfing the web, shopping, checking scores, or looking up information about what they are watching. And the more devices the user owns, the higher is their engagement.

Targeting – getting it right

It is important to target the right people, at the right time, on the right device, with a personalized message.

The customer journey has become incredibly fragmented, moving across numerous channels and devices, and flooded with more messages than ever. As a result, it has never been more necessary for brands to target and personalize customer messaging. Luckily, social profiles, CRM data, web analytics and loyalty programmes contain an abundance of detailed information about your customers.

Targeting and appropriately segmenting your customers is crucial to your success on social media. Ideal social media content is always timely, resonant and relevant. It capitalizes on conversation trends, audience interests and brand priorities (source: Edelman Digital). Personalization is key in building lasting relationships on social media.

Identifying your community is the first step. Once you know who they are, where they are active, whom they trust and how they currently engage with you, you can begin to segment your community in order to reach them with timely and relevant content that will resonate with them individually.

How you can target today:

- Demographic: age, gender, income bracket, education, job, cultural background.

- Lifestyle: social class, lifestyle, personality, interests, opinions, attitudes.

- Behaviour: online shoppers, brick and mortar customers, brand preference, prior purchases.

- Geography: continent, country, state, province, city and so on.

If you actually talked to people in the way that most advertising talks to people, they would punch you in the face. Personalize and target your messages.

Remember the root of social media: connecting people to people. Even as social media evolves, the root is still the same. Social media enables us to connect with other people in ways that were not possible before. It may not be *new* any more, but the future is full of opportunity.

Paul Armstrong, FORTH/WITH

We often think of technological change as new emergences on the scene such as drones, cryptocurrencies (aka Bitcoin) – but the majority of real change being seen currently comes from established platforms pushing new boundaries in privacy, content creation and sharing functionality. As known and unknown disruptors loom on the horizon, the future of social remains a regular topic of interest, asked about by clients and prospects looking to create a resilient business. Whether it is new technologies such as Bitcoin or established ones such as social networking, the one constant remains: change.

The future is still TBD

Many years ago I created a framework that enables anyone to evaluate emerging platforms or re-evaluate an existing platform for fresh campaign work. It is a concise tool that surrounds the phrase 'to be determined', or TBD:

- T stands for *technology* (can the technology do what you want/are asking it to?), where the user writes down a clear description of what the technology can do and what it cannot do. A good example of a tricky platform is the ephemeral messaging app Snapchat. Whilst the technology is there, many do not understand it en masse.

- B is for *behaviour* (will our target do what we want them to do?), where we evaluate the friction that stands between the user and the desired outcome. After this, the framework then examines the likelihood that this friction will be overcome; the willingness to complete if you like.

- D stands for *data* (will enough people do what we want them to?). In this section we explore the realities of the platform or area being researched. It is here where we list out everything we know about the platform (and area) in order to evaluate it on the correct criteria such as unique users, time spent etc. This section is often the longest and most detailed, as it is often the key determiner for action.

Once you have this laid out before you, perspectives begin to change and often a brand's risk acceptance comes into play, but the framework can help to avoid spending on risky propositions, or at least create a timeline of reconsideration.

But isn't mobile the future of social?

In many ways mobile is the *now* of social rather than its future. With 70 per cent smartphone penetration in the UK (and similar numbers in the United States) mobile has firmly arrived and it is clear that many apps now grow via newer networks (WeChat, ProductHunt, Flipboard) as much as existing ones. The intertwining of social and mobile undoubtedly will increase. However, it is always beholden to the technology infrastructure that surrounds it, so progress, whilst quick in some areas, will stay slow in others and other solutions will be required.

Dark social will lighten up

Arguably, as any technology or industry progresses, so does the ability to measure it. Social is no different in this respect, although it continues to prove difficult. Despite the numerous new metrics available, the old ones remain, and in recent years the issues surrounding 'dark social' (or the hard-to-attribute traffic that everyone has) has grown increasingly concerning. RadiumOne now estimates that 72 per cent of sharing remains copy-and-paste related. This number is a clear concern for anyone in marketing, as it becomes difficult to justify spend and correct strategy if you are trying to hit a moving target. The future must, therefore, be a measured one, a future that laser-focuses in on accountability and a desire to measure not only the traffic you get but to improve your whole business with the data and information available.

People will refocus on the realities of social

It is easy to think that people spend their entire lives on Facebook and Instagram but the fact is they do not. It simply appears that way. Remembering the 90.9.1 rule (where new content is created by 1 per cent, 9 per cent then edit this into new forms, which are both then consumed by 90 per cent of the community) rarely fails a brand when looking at how information is consumed in their industry – and this is unlikely to change.

Distribution will become a staple part of all strategies in the future

Understanding the rule above is a key part of the future, as it will be increasingly important to maximize the ever-diminishing free distribution platforms currently on offer. As Pinterest adds unique pin types, Twitter evolves into a new timeline and Facebook's organic reach dips even further, it is clear that the platforms are ready for their pay days. Therefore, strategies for the future must include one of two things: some form of paid distribution if success is to be seen (... or work is to be seen at all) and some form of data capture that serves the brand or marketer directly and therefore decreases future reliance on paid media.

So that leaves us with?

Context. With the introduction of Google Glass, smartwatches, iBeacons and additional sensors in everyday objects such as fridges and cars, context becomes the next big area for technologists, advertisers and marketers to grapple with. In a way it has always been in front of us, but now with the addition of technologies such as GPS, facial recognition, online privacy settings and public levels of sharing providing real experiences and useful information, this seems within our grasp and less on the creepy side of things than ever. The ability to achieve this, however, is not straightforward and mistakes will be made, but the ability to achieve greatness is equally high.

As always, value is the key to the future of most things. If the value for the person on the receiving end is too low, the desired action is increasingly unlikely to be completed, as people have more options, less perceived time and decreasing attention spans – marketers need to understand this, whether it is the reduction of friction when creating apps and experience or simply just helping users. One thing about the future of social that is increasingly clear is that success will not be seen by those who focus simply on the screen alone.

Simon Kingsnorth, digital marketing director

Before we leap into making predictions that would make Nostradamus jealous, it would be a useful exercise to look back at the last 10 to 15 years and review the journey we have all been on since the turn of the 21st century.

The early days of the internet saw Friends Reunited try to bring lost schoolfriends back together – with some initial success, but it never really captured the simplicity necessary to grasp global domination. Myspace followed but, again, the user experience was not intuitive and so it failed to gain the popularity it probably deserved. Then came Facebook. Launched back in 2004 at Harvard University by the now infamous Mark Zuckerberg, memberships were initially restricted, but as these were lifted the explosion was quick. Within two years Facebook had 6 million users, two years later that was 145 million and just 10 years after launch it exceeded 1.3 billion. Twitter likewise grew to 200 million active users in less than seven years and similar growth has been seen for WhatsApp, LinkedIn, Pinterest, Google+, Tumblr, Instagram, Weibo and many more that have over 100 million users signed up. The reason for these explosions in growth is simple. Humans are sociable animals. We have always existed in communities of various forms and social media is simply a community on a vast scale for the modern world. We love to share, talk, laugh and learn, and social media is a simple, accessible way to do that with the people we care about. That is why we cannot doubt that social media is here to stay. One other thing we can say with a good degree of certainty is that whilst it is here to stay, it will certainly not be in the form it is today, so let's explore some of the changes we may see over the coming months and years.

First, there are some trends that are out there for everyone to see and that are set to grow significantly in the short term. The two that are probably the most significant are mobile and video.

The growth of mobile

Mobile is another area that has grown exponentially in the 21st century, so much so that even the internet has struggled at times to keep up.

Social media, however, is part of the mobile revolution, with the vast majority of Twitter users interacting via mobile devices and a significant percentage of Facebook users too. We can expect this to become 100 per cent in time as mobile becomes an outdated concept – by this I mean that we are continuing to move towards a society where *everything* is mobile. Tablets are outselling desktops and new connected devices such as Google Glass, Cars and even Fridges are beginning to come onto the market. It won't be too far in the future that the concept of mobile will be laughable, in the same way that we no longer see television programmes advertised as being 'in colour'.

The growth of video

Video is becoming increasingly commonplace. It is now quite rare to go online and not come across a video of some form, whether you are shopping, learning, socializing or simply browsing. Video streaming is becoming an increasingly common way to watch your favourite shows with companies such as Netflix seeing strong growth. YouTube is considered to be the second largest search engine behind Google (who also own YouTube, of course) and so we will continue to see increasing volume of video in our searches. Google is already very good at predicting when we might want a video to answer our query, something I was personally grateful for just a few weeks ago when I needed to know how to lay turf. We may, however, see some sites become more video than text, and the rest begin to grow video to a much higher percentage of their overall content. In recent years a new trend has arisen through apps such as Vine, Tout and Snapchat – micro-video – the concept of sharing video but in short, simple form. Taking social messages and forcing them to be punchy is a trend arguably started by Twitter that has now made its way into video. You should expect to see more of this as we become increasingly time poor and content hungry.

The growth in location-based technology

Another trend we should expect to grow in the short term is an increase in location-based technology. We already see this integrated into a huge number of apps. Some of the more obvious are maps, but there are plenty of opportunities here for businesses to take advantage of. For example, recognizing whereabouts in your store the customer is standing, therefore knowing what product they are looking at, or communicating with regular customers who you recognize are passing your store, or even sending consumers messages when they are shopping for something at another store that could use your service, eg a car loan. This does have the risk of becoming increasingly intrusive, of course, and there are likely to be cases of this in the near future. It is a great opportunity for businesses and consumers alike but, as always, the strategy that sits on top of the technology has to be right. We should expect social media to become heavily integrated into search in the coming years. When you are searching for something why wouldn't you want to see any relevant tweets, for example, especially those from your network? How Google use Google+ or work on their relationships with other social sites to deliver this is yet to be seen.

Non-Western-based social media

When people in the United States and Europe think of social media we tend to think first of Facebook and Twitter. The two biggest, right? Well there is a site that is a hybrid of the two and has over 250 million users. Sina Weibo is China's most popular social media site and is not yet open to the world. There are obvious language issues that cause some difficulties that English-language based sites do not have in their international growth strategies, but nonetheless we should expect Weibo and/or other sites from Asia to begin to create a splash on the international scene over the coming years.

Social media – not just a channel for youth

Another thing to be aware of as we move further into the 21st century is that people are growing up. I know that sounds obvious but I have personally heard many people (some who should know better) make such statements as 'people over 60 don't really use the internet and wouldn't understand social'. We have to keep in mind that the internet has been around in society for about 20 years now and those people who are 60 were 40 back then. I don't know many 40-year-olds who are complete technophobes, most are able to pick up new technology very easily. Of the many people I know aged over 60 almost all have a mobile phone, most use some apps and most use Facebook. In just 10 years from now the 60-year-olds will have been 30 when the internet began to become mainstream and I have every confidence they will all be able to work a computer, use the internet and most will have at least one social media account. It is important to bear this in mind as we make judgements about social media being a channel for the youth, as this will increasingly be wrong.

The new face of customer service

One use of social media, as mentioned earlier in this book, is of course customer service. Consumers now have a direct form of communication with a company and can air their grievances very publicly. Handling this correctly is key to success. As with any customer service experience, turning the negatives into positives is one of the ultimate goals. I would expect this use of social media to continue and to expand. I would expect social channels to start to create specific mechanisms for this that pull the customer service away from the main feeds and timelines, as this would be a better customer experience and an advantage for the business.

Forecasting further ahead

Looking further ahead is always difficult and we can all hypothesize about what this could look like. If we continue to believe in Moore's law, which has proved itself reliable to date, then we can expect significant increases in computer and internet connection speed over the coming years. If we consider Google's Loon project we can also expect the number of internet users to grow as internet penetration grows. If we assume that consumer confidence in the internet also continues to grow then we can expect more people to shop online, and if we look at Amazon's delivery drones then we can see this becoming the norm.

All of the above indicates to me that there are several directions that social media will take, and so I will conclude by making some bold forecasts. Biz Stone, co-founder of Twitter, recently stated that he believes social media is 'just getting started'. So there is a long road ahead and I would encourage you to try to expand on this list:

1 Social media will make all of its content, including individual posts, searchable via Google.

2 Shopping will become more common on social media channels.

3 Social media sites operating within specific verticals will have increasing success, such as sport, finance, automotive, music, film and other large-volume opportunities.

4 Social pages will become more conducive to enabling customers to respond directly without creating potential brand damage.

5 Creating and sharing media will become increasingly easy as wearable technology becomes mainstream.

6 Businesses will get smarter about how they use social. No longer shouting about their greatness, they will develop strong content strategies and have unique strategies for each social channel, only operating on the channels that are relevant.

7 Everything will be mobile. Responsive and able to work on any device will be the norm. Pinching and swiping to try to read content will disappear as a concept. Social will be at the heart of this as it reaches 100 per cent mobile usage.

8 People will use social media more to partake in crowd-based activities with individuals that they don't know but do have things in common with. Crowdfunding and peer-to-peer lending opportunities will grow. The world will increasingly become one community.

9 SMS text messaging will virtually disappear, perhaps only remaining for emergencies, as messaging apps take over.

10 Cloud content will increase as people become comfortable with the concept and begin to release their psychological attachment to ownership. This will further enable sharing.

Mike Berry, Mike Berry Associates

Social media was something that barely existed 10 years ago (when Facebook was newborn in 2004 and Myspace was preparing to dominate the social world), but what might be the state of social media in 10 years' time? Well, the reality of course is that it is anyone's guess, but I hope that it is possible to make a few informed predictions. Let's consider the possible futures of social media under the following five headings:

1 Social media will not be 'un-invented'.

2 But the 'usual suspects' may well change.

3 Social media will be increasingly enabled/facilitated by technological advances.

4 Social listening will become increasingly sophisticated.

5 The end of the social media fail; brands will increasingly get their act together.

Social media will not be 'un-invented'

We have come too far for that. Erik Qualman, in the latest version of his much-viewed and shared series of videos (#Socialnomics) (**https://www.youtube.com/watch?v=zxpa4dNVd3c**) claims that 53 per cent of teenagers (actually 'millennials') would prefer to lose their sense of smell than their tech (I think we need a few more details on this one) and, moreover, that more people in the world own a mobile phone than a toothbrush (!) – two rather worrying statistics. All over today's increasingly connected world, many people cannot imagine life without Facebook, or Instagram, Twitter, Tencent/QQ or Sina Weibo. It is getting tough to distinguish between mobile messaging apps and true social networks (WeChat anyone?). When marketers talk about 'the Digital Revolution' they are probably referring to the rise of social networks, or mobile phones, or most likely both. These two phenomena have been truly transformative with respect to their impact on society, business and specifically marketing. And there is no going back.

But the 'usual suspects' may well change

The recent rapid growth in Instagram (which gives a great experience on mobile – go figure!) and the levelling off in some more developed markets of the growth of Facebook, reminds us that social media is notoriously fickle. Maybe the megabucks that Facebook paid for Instagram (US $1 billion) and WhatsApp (US $19 billion) were well spent after all? The threat to the established players is that history tells us that social brands can very suddenly fall out of fashion and favour. When the music stops, the party can move on to somewhere else. So we should put our incredulity aside and recognize that in five or ten years' time the major players may not necessarily be Facebook, LinkedIn, Twitter and YouTube. After all: how many of today's social media-addicted teens remember Myspace, Friendster, Orkut and Bebo, all of which were leaders in their day? Social media has moved on and will continue to do so.

Depending on where you are based, we should turn our eyes to the East: Chinese brands (Tencent, Sina Weibo, Alibaba/Taobao, Lenovo and Huawei) are eyeing international expansion and we may find that the US brands in social and mobile become less dominant globally.

So let's learn about social media by getting involved, testing and establishing what works and what doesn't. Even if the names of the key social networks for our brands (ie for our customers) are different in 10 years' time, my bet is that there will be many similarities with today's social megabrands in terms of function and how content is shared.

Social media will be increasingly enabled/facilitated by technological advances

And, of course, technology. It is logical to include this, since technology is where it all began, way back in the 1990s. Google Glass is currently looking like a game-changer, even if it turns out *not* to be the dominant technology of the threatened (and seemingly imminent) 'wearable era'. Whether it is glasses or watches (but not, please, 'smart wigs') possibly combined with the trusty mobile (btw: isn't it time we started calling them 'communicators', or maybe even the German 'handy'?). Futurists deserve no prizes for forecasting that the future of social is mobile (after all, it is the future – and increasingly the present – of digital!). However, Google is talking about faster broadband. *Much* faster. The Google Fiber project (**https://fiber.google.com/about2/**) delivers broadband speed approximately 100 times faster than current average basic broadband. And it is starting to roll out now. It is hard to imagine how that will transform how we share and consume video, in particular, using the next generation of mobile devices. No more going to a desktop computer and patiently logging in to our social media account; with wearables and superfast mobile internet, it's all going to be right there – in our face (maybe literally!).

Social listening will become increasingly sophisticated

The new 'industry' of social media has spawned several spin-off sectors: eg social media management (Tweetdeck, Hootsuite, Sprout Social etc) and social media monitoring (Salesforce Radian6, Sysomos, Brandwatch and others). Of course, it makes a lot of sense to listen before we talk: eg imagine you (or your brand) arrives at the party and rather than immediately shouting at people, you quietly attach yourself to a group before making a relevant contribution and gradually joining the conversation into which you are welcomed, because you are sharing interesting/useful things, ie adding value. The more intelligently we can analyse the buzz (considering shades of sentiment and watching for trends) the better we can contribute and positively influence conversations going on 24/7, 365 days a year, among our target audience about our brand and their wants and needs; indeed, in social media that is the most we can realistically hope to achieve. The key is to listen well, which means using high-powered tools, correctly configured and operated by skilled practitioners; this is (gradually) becoming the case, thanks to the emergence of the above platforms and others, plus a lot of hard work coupled with some bitter (and sometimes very public) experience!

Which leads us naturally on to the last point.

Brands will increasingly get their act together

We have had a good few years now of 'Schadenfreude', sniggering at how big and small companies have got it horribly wrong in social media (and secretly being thankful it wasn't our brand), but now the laughs are drying up; basically, brands are growing up and the fails are increasingly being 'nipped in the bud' (or should that be 'headed off at the pass'?). What was required, of course, was for senior (and middle) management in organizations to engage with the process, without either being scared of the technology or dismissing it as silly/irrelevant ('not proper marketing'); to be honest, one just needs suitable controls in place to stop any employee from well-meaningly tweeting about politics, war or sex. And, of course, time if nothing else will fix this; the 'digital natives' are growing up and will be adopting increasingly senior roles in businesses.

In many organizations, social media directors and managers are being appointed; some might have had from five to eight years' social media experience (which couldn't have been the case five years ago!) and most are intelligent and competent. This means that organizations are getting more professional with their social media and bringing to bear on social media the same thorough, professional approach that they apply to procurement, sales, customer service and, yes, marketing. And, surprise surprise, it isn't actually rocket science. To cut a rather long story short, professional social media management is essentially about deciding which social channels you are going to: a) monitor (ideally all); and b) engage in (realistically the ones where your customers/potential customers predominantly hang out). Then you determine what technology you need, set up your structure with the right staff, the right training in the right locations, configure/deploy the technology and, finally, let the professionals get on with it (subject, of course, to periodic checks and reviews).

A social media operation is more science than art; the creativity can be supplied by the 'content architects' (producing the necessary blog posts, infographics and, of course, video to populate the various social media presences). This may sound easy. It's not.

But much of it is common sense and essentially it just requires the thorough and consistent application of a policy to every element of the 'social media machine' so that it functions optimally, remembering to pull it in for maintenance every now and then to keep it running smoothly. Not easy, not free, but certainly not impossible and not necessarily very expensive as compared with other things the organization already spends money on (eg IT, customer service, TV advertising). And right now many organizations are rising to this challenge by building a professional social media operation supported (and funded) by engaged senior management.

So: there are likely to be increasingly slim pickings for the annual 'social media fails of the year' roundup videos/blog posts, but the upside is that there will be more effective social media marketing and management and better ROI from social media (along with advances in actually measuring that ROI!), all of which will certainly be welcomed by chief marketing officers pitching for more budget from the chief finance officer...

Chapter conclusions

Biz Stone, co-founder of Twitter, recently stated that he believes social media is 'just getting started'. With this in mind, thinking by the seat of your pants is the new name of the game. Be ready to embrace rapid change as the focus shifts from mature to fast-growth markets. In 2014 we are moving away from the one-site-fits-all model of networking to embracing a more fragmented approach where we visit different services for different activities. As our options diversify, perhaps we will also become a more cohesive social world community.

CASE STUDY   BNP Paribas/Tweet & Shoot

Client

BNP Paribas.

Project

Tweet & Shoot.

Overview

BNP Paribas is passionate about tennis and a long-standing sponsor of Roland Garros, the French Open; 2013 marked a 40-year partnership between the bank and the tournament and BNP Paribas wanted to mark it by doing something remarkable and groundbreaking, demonstrating its passion for innovation and for tennis. It was decided to use a social media first.

The approach

On 23 May, three days before the French Open, BNP Paribas would invite tennis fans across social media to play in a unique game of tennis: to train Jo-Wilfried Tsonga, the French number one and world number eight, through Twitter. Using Twitter as the platform, we created the 'Tweet & Shoot' application – revolutionary new technology that allowed fans to train Jo-Wilfried themselves, using a simple Twitter mechanism and a social media-controlled robot. Participants logged on to the Tweet & Shoot website, then dragged-and-dropped a tennis ball on a virtual on-screen tennis court, adjusting the position and trajectory of a three-shot combination to challenge Tsonga.

These selections were encoded into simple hashtags, sent via tweets to the social media-controlled robot, which was connected to the internet and Twitter via 3G. Fans could also add a personal message of encouragement to Tsonga.

On 23 May, Tsonga took to the tennis court to take on Twitter users via the robot, which fired out fans' shot combinations whilst a commentator read the accompanying tweets. The event was live streamed, allowing fans to tune in and share the fun.

We also kept tennis fans updated about Tweet & Shoot through the 'We Are Tennis by BNP Paribas' platform, a digital community created by BNP Paribas, where people globally can share their passion for tennis.

Results

Over 2,700 tennis fans participated, with people from all around the world challenging and encouraging Jo-Wilfried Tsonga. There were 5,865 tweets sent using the #tweetandshoot hashtag (25 million impressions) and 183,600 views of Tweet & Shoot – which is 12 times the capacity of Roland-Garros's Centre Court. There were 110 global pieces of press coverage of the event, including *Creativity*, *Campaign*, *Brand Republic*, *Campaign Brief*, *Fast Company*, *Contagious* and *GQ*. Tweet & Shoot was a first in sport and social media history, breaking technological boundaries.

Links to campaign

http://www.bnpparibas.co.uk/en/

Risk assessment and risk management in social media

OUR CHAPTER PLEDGE TO YOU

When you reach the end of this chapter you will have our experts' visionary responses to the following questions:

- What are the key dangers I need to look out for when creating a social media programme?
- How can I keep my company safe?
- How can I protect my employees?
- What tools are out there to help me?

Play safe to stay in control...

In this short, but maybe not so sweet, concluding chapter, we asked Tom Chapman at Red Rocket Media to discuss the burning issue of risk when it comes to business engagement with the social media.

Understanding Social Media has taken us on a journey across a wide sea of issues that you will have to deal with when implementing a social media strategy for your business: from planning your programme to planning your budgets, from choosing a team to creating your message, from building relationships with your clients to analysing the data you get back from them.

The arena is exciting, or might I go as far to say, addictive, for marketing communicators. We have increasingly sophisticated tools at our disposal. The opportunity to implement great ideas with impact is growing by the day. We know more about our consumers than ever before. We can communicate business to peer (B2P) directly and in real time. We have access to endless data and our analysis of it is becoming pin-sharp, almost forensic. Security, protocols and brand management have never been more crucial. To stay in control of your social media presence, you must understand the dangers and implement safeguards to protect your business. Social media can make you but it can just as easily break you. Tom Chapman tells us more.

Tom Chapman, content specialist, Red Rocket Media

Since the early days of social media, individuals have been preaching its benefits, claiming that it can help to channel business growth, reach potential customers and better communicate brand messages. Although all of this is certainly possible, the risks are almost ignored in favour of the advantages.

Proof of this can be seen in the way that businesses are incorporating social media into their policies. In 2014, Marketing Profs reported on a study conducted by LinkedIn and undertaken by TNS Global, which reported that more than 80 per cent of SMEs were using social media to encourage growth (Nanji, 2014). Moreover, it was revealed that almost 95 per cent were using it for marketing purposes.

However, advisory body Grant Thornton published a survey that same year, which revealed that just 33 per cent of companies had a social media policy in place (Thompson, Herzberg and Sullivan, 2014). Even worse, just 18 per cent of respondents stated that their organization had conducted a relevant risk assessment.

Much like any businesses decision, social media contains an element of risk. Just setting up an account and randomly posting is an extremely bad idea, potentially leading to lost revenues and even legal action. Consequently, companies must implement a plan to minimize these dangers.

How is social media dangerous?

Writing for the online *Huffington Post* in 2014, security and identity-theft expert Robert Siciliano identified several areas where social media could pose a threat to businesses (Siciliano, 2014). During his analysis, he reported similar findings to the study conducted by Grant Thornton, showing that most firms did not have a dedicated policy to deal with these risks. He expressed concerns that institutions were in danger of suffering severe security issues.

For example, Siciliano stated that companies had to be aware of:

- *Confidential information leaks.* In the majority of cases, this will be caused by hackers looking to break into company records and disseminate information. However, these people can also hack into social media accounts to spam customers and generally cause problems. Alternatively, disgruntled workers or former employees can use social media to spread company secrets around the internet.

- *Social media having a negative impact on a brand's reputation.* Although social media can spread a company's message, it also has the potential to create bad PR and offend customers. When this occurs, this message can spread like wildfire, reaching forums and, in the worst cases, could even be picked up by news organizations. As a result, seemingly innocuous posts can quickly ruin a company's reputation.

- *Intellectual property theft.* Although criminals use the internet to commit identity theft on a regular basis, it could also be argued that firms are at risk from other companies stealing their ideas. For instance, an organization that posts a promotion online may see their deal copied by a rival.

- *Legal ramifications.* Posting information on social media must always be done with care. Potentially, even messages written months or years ago could be used by a court or someone seeking to bring litigation. Consequently, it is essential that those in charge of these accounts are well versed in media law.

These dangers are not the only threats out there, but the better prepared a company is to tackle these risks, the safer it will be online. Fortunately, to help employers prepare for the hazards of social media, Siciliano also recommended a range of safety measures, as detailed below.

Create a social media risk assessment

Although there are risks associated with using social media, companies must not isolate themselves from it altogether. Simply put, social media is the future – and savvy employers can use it to greatly benefit their organization. Therefore, business owners could use the following tips (Siciliano, 2014) to keep themselves safe online:

- Implement a social media policy, ensuring employees know how to act and behave while online.
- Train staff members in media law and ensure they understand the risks of social media.
- Invest in internet security and ensure these defences are up to date.
- Above all, do not ban all aspects of social media. It needs to be embraced, not prohibited.

The methods described by Siciliano should help to keep companies safe against most threats. However, they arguably fall short when a company needs to minimize the effects of bad PR. To really prepare for the dangers of social media, firms must implement a strategy to handle bad press. One of the best examples to learn from is that set out by Federal Express (FedEx), as detailed below.

How FedEx handled a social media crisis

FedEx is a renowned delivery service; common sense dictates that the overwhelming majority of its packages need to be transported safely and arrive promptly. However, in 2011, the organization suffered a devastating social media crisis when one of its employees was caught on YouTube throwing a customer's computer monitor over a fence – reportedly breaking it in the process (Goobie55, 2011).

Despite this obviously being an isolated incident, the video turned viral. Within a few short days, millions of users had watched the clip, while others cloned it. Moreover, the comment section quickly started filling up with other customers sharing their complaints about FedEx. Although the recipient of the computer package was arguably justified in uploading the video, his grievance now threatened the very credibility of FedEx.

Fortunately, the company responded to this problem almost immediately, acting responsibly and professionally. In another video posted online, the vice president of the company, Matthew Thornton III, apologized to the YouTube community for the actions of this staff member, confirmed that the employee was facing disciplinary actions and reported other measures that the company was taking to remedy the situation (FedEx, 2011).

Similar to the original video, other users started weighing in on Thornton's apology, sharing positive examples of FedEx's service and commending the organization for admitting its mistake. This example demonstrates how quickly incidents on social media can spread – but also shows there are ways to minimize the damage.

What can we learn from FedEx?

If a company finds itself in a similar situation, the first thing it should do is to take measures to remedy the matter as soon as possible. Ignoring it simply is not an option. However, as evidenced by FedEx's timely response, the organization likely prepared for this situation far in advance – as professionals in crisis management often recommend.

For example, one specialist organization, PHA Media, suggests a range of measures to prepare for a PR disaster (PHA Media, 2014). It states that companies should:

- Anticipate every possible disaster and adequately prepare for it.
- Find the right spokesperson and back them up.
- Train individuals in social media.

- Have a communications team ready to tackle social media disasters.
- Have a 'Frequently Asked Questions' (FAQ) document and develop key messages.
- Gather all the facts about the incident before commenting.
- Communicate with staff, stakeholders and customers about the incident.

Do not fear social media

Although this chapter contribution illustrates the dangers of social media, it should not be ignored. After all, social media is now a vital part of our society and is unlikely to just go away. Instead, companies should embrace this medium and use it to get their messages across. That said, going in without any preparation is foolish – and this reckless approach could easily cripple the reputation of any business. By all means use social media... just be aware of the potential risks first.

References

FedEx YouTube Channel (2011) [accessed 1 August 2014] FedEx Response to Costumer Video, *YouTube* [Online] https://www.youtube.com/watch?v=4ESU_PcqI38

Goobie55 (2011) [accessed 1 August 2014] FedEx Guy Throwing My Computer Monitor, *YouTube* [Online] https://www.youtube.com/watch?v=PKUDTPbDhnA

Nanji, A (2014) [accessed 1 August 2014] How SMBs Use Social Media, *Marketing Profs* [Online] http://www.marketingprofs.com/charts/2014/24547/how-smbs-use-social-media

PHA Media (2014) [accessed 1 August 2014] Top ten ways to protect your company from a media crisis, *PHA Media* [Online] http://www.pha-media.com/insights/crisis-reputation-management/top-tips/

Siciliano, R (2014) [accessed 1 August 2014] 7 Small Business Social Media Risks, *The Huffington Post* [Online] http://www.huffingtonpost.com/robert-siciliano/7-small-business-social-m_b_4846083.html

Thompson, T, Hertzberg, J and Sullivan, M (2014) [accessed 1 August 2014] Social media risks and rewards, *Grant Thornton* [Online] http://www.grantthornton.com/~/media/content-page-files/advisory/pdfs/2013/ADV-social-media-survey.ashx

Chapter conclusions

The better prepared a company is to tackle the risks posed by social media, the safer it will be online. Fortunately, to help employers prepare for the hazards of social media, there are a range of recommended safety measures you can follow. Stay safe and social media will become an increasingly powerful, positive channel that is destined to become increasingly integral to every business strategy. Good luck!

CASE STUDY   eBay/[a•mo•bee]

Client

eBay.

Agency

[a•mo•bee].

Project

eBay #MyMix fashion campaign.

Overview

eBay understands the importance of attracting mobile customers, and selected [a•mo•bee] to execute the mobile portion of the #MyMix campaign. To showcase the hottest bloggers and trend-setting stylists from around the world using the #MyMix tagline [a•mo•bee] created a mobile campaign that celebrated UK women's individual 'mix and match' approach to style.

Rather than using traditional models, the #MyMix mobile campaign featured women recognized for their individual style, which allowed users to explore the featured clothing items and check out additional styles using the eBay app.

Execution and use of media

[a•mo•bee] extended the #MyMix experience onto mobile using rich media to create an interactive experience in which users could browse and buy the spring/

summer looks in the virtual magazine on their mobile devices. Users could read more about the featured bloggers, access behind-the-scenes footage, and even go straight to purchase. Users had the ability to mix, match and create their own outfits and share their fashion finds with friends over social media using the #MyMix hashtag. Additionally, users could read more about the featured bloggers, access behind the scenes footage, and even go straight to purchase on selected items. Within the virtual magazine, users were given the option to download the eBay mobile app. Using augmented reality technology, users pointed their devices at eBay print magazine ads to access the virtual MyMix magazine, offering behind-the-scenes stories and videos from the five featured style-setters.

Additionally, the augmented reality ad provided a direct link for users to download the eBay app. The eBay MyMix ads were placed in popular magazines, including *More!*, *Reveal*, *OK*, *Grazia*, *Stylist*, *Look*, *Marie Claire*, *InStyle*, *Glamour*, *Elle*, *Cosmopolitan*, *Company* and more.

Results

The MyMix mobile campaign performed exceptionally well, achieving over three times the objective click-through rate: 0.99. Because consumers were given the ability to go straight to purchase on a range of selected items within the MyMix mobile campaign, mobile purchases soared. In fact, eBay's revenues jumped 23 per cent to US $3.4 billion in the second quarter of 2012, with a large portion being generated from mobile transactions.

Links to campaign

Download our mobile app

View fully functional examples of our award-winning creative work, including 3D mobile ads, only from [a•mo•bee]:

www.amobee.com/adshowcase

CONTRIBUTORS' BIOGRAPHIES

Contributing Editor

Miranda Glover

Miranda Glover has worked in digital communications for more than a decade, initially as a content producer, then as the UK account director at international consultancy Icon Medialab, M&m Partnership and FMI Group. Key accounts have included The European Commission, Unilever Bestfoods Europe, LG Mobile Europe, Sony, Prada and Motorola US. Miranda now works independently as a communications strategist and content marketing producer for SMEs, corporates and start-ups. She specializes in brand communications, PR and social media campaigning. She is also a three-time published novelist with Random House and often appears at literary festivals.

Contact:
miranda@mirandaglover.com; www.mirandaglover.com

Chapter 1

Danielle Ryan

Danielle Ryan is Digital Channel and Conversion Manager at Ryanair.

A marketing graduate from DIT Ireland, Danielle is an e-commerce and digital marketing professional from County Wicklow, who now specializes in digital channel management and conversion optimization. Her career to date includes work in the luxury retail and telecoms industries, but more notably in the airline industry, where she has worked on digital marketing and e-commerce strategy for AerLingus Regional, CityJet and now Ryanair, Europe's largest airline. She loves the travel and aviation industry and also finds time to put her hand to some flying at the weekends.

Contact:

ryandanielle@gmail.com www.ryanair.com

Richard Costa D'sa

Richard Costa-D'sa is Managing Director of a leading, fast-growing, award-winning digital agency called Jam. Particular recent highlights include adding global accounts such as Samsung and Xbox, as well as developing their UK roster, which now features brands such as Unilever, Nestlé and Tesco. In 2014 the agency won several significant international awards and, more importantly, has been recognized as the agency most respected by its peers.

Jemima Gibbons

Jemima is a social media strategist, writer and blogger. She works with agencies as a white label consultant, and delivers a bespoke programme, the Social Media Launch Pack, to start-ups and SMEs. Jemima's book on social media and business, *Monkeys with Typewriters*, was published by Triarchy Press in 2009.

Contact:

jemimag@gmail.com

Chapter 2

Joseph Morgan

Joseph Morgan is Director of Strategy, Head of Planning at MOF, Brand Interactions agency. His role and remit at MOF is twofold: first, to cultivate client partner relations, providing top-level support where needed; and second, to translate such insight into key strategic and creative output that drives significant business change.

His knowledge of strategy across the spectrum, combined with his experience in data-driven lead generation, analytics and CRM make him a key part of the senior management team.

Joseph is a published author in the *Journal of Brand Management*, noted colloquium speaker, and was shortlisted for the ADMAP/ WARC Essay prize 2012 and a Cannes Direct Lion 2014.

Contact:

www.matterofform.com
joe@matterofform.com

Elaine Lindsay

An international speaker and media consultant, Elaine's a Kinda Bionic PollyAnna who chooses joy. Her goal is to inspire you to seize joy. When Elaine speaks, trains and hosts her show *Business BanterPlus TV*, she discovers passion: yours and her own. Elaine lives her passion – you can too. Her main focus is Google+ including Hangouts on Air, YouTube, LinkedIn and the integration of search and social. She is Dean of Digital Media Social Buzz U, a certified Relationship Marketing professional, a G+ evangelist and early adopter.

Contact:

troolsocial@gmail.com

Alice Roughton and Über agency

Alice Roughton is Social Media Manager at integrated creative agency Über, where her main focus is on the development of strategic social media-led digital campaigns for clients.

She has experience working across a wide range of digital, social and online PR projects for clients including Topman, Crabtree & Evelyn, Harveys Furniture, Warner Brothers Studios, The Hobbit Film Franchise, London College of Fashion, Arts Council England and Meadowhall Shopping Centre.

Mike Zeederberg – Safe and Well online team

The Safe and Well online team responsible for creating '@ppreciate a mate' consisted of: Barbara Spears, Carmel Taddeo, Alan Barnes and Tony Daly representing the cohort arm of the study, operating out of the University of South Australia; Phillipa Collin and Teresa Swirski, of the University of Western Sydney, led the youth participation aspect of the campaign; Bernadine Brewer, Mike Zeederberg and Valentina Borbone led the project from a digital strategy perspective, on behalf of Zuni Digital Arts Network, a renowned digital creative agency that provided the creative ideation for the campaign and helped to bring the media promotion to life.

Chapter 3

Laurent François

Laurent is Executive Creative Strategist and co-founder of Re-Up, a London-based boutique creative and digital agency, specializing in social media and digital activation. Re-Up regroups veterans of the advertising industry, creativity marketers and artists. In 2010, he launched a business unit within

Roularta Group (a media group that owns L'Express in France), called SocialERS, dedicated to implementing a new value chain and new sources of revenue for online media and publishers. Previously, Laurent was the first head of 360° Digital Influence for Ogilvy in Europe (now 'Social@Ogilvy'). With his team, he has been implementing social media strategies for clients such as Tom of Finland, Vodafone, Grazia, IBM and Nestlé.

Laurent also teaches at ESCP Europe and writes for *Social Media Today*. He regularly gives conferences on social media and innovation (*Social Media Week*, Digital Shoreditch etc).

Laurent also blogs on fashion for Hit Bag and Le Boulevardier, which, he says, are great hubs for creative projects.

Contact:

www.thisisreup.com

Trina Albus

Trina is the founder of Magenta, a social media agency with primarily fashion and beauty clients in Los Angeles and New York City, including W Magazine and J Mendel. Before founding Magenta she worked at PriceWaterhouse, Discovery Communications, Time Inc and BeachMint. She balances her time running the agency, teaching social and digital marketing workshops and courses at General Assembly, and presenting at conferences, including the Lucky Magazine Fashion and Beauty Blogger (FABB) Conference.

She is very active in the Los Angeles tech community, serving as a mentor at Launchpad LA and as an advisor to start-ups. She is a contributor to Financial Times Press's *33 Million People in the Room: How to create, influence, and run a successful business with social networking*. She has been involved with *Social Media Week* since 2009, serving as an Advisory Board member and speaker at Social Media Week New York and Los Angeles. Trina stays current within the tech and digital space by participating at conferences, including SXSWi and TED, and was invited by Google to become one of the first Google Glass Explorers.

Contact:

www.magentaagency.com

trina@magentaagency.com

Ema Linaker

Head of the Social Centre of Excellence, Middle East and North Africa, Leo Burnett/ Holler, Ema has over 18 years' experience in international markets, including her most recent assignment in Dubai, where she founded and built Social@Ogilvy in the Middle East region, Ogilvy and Mather's Social Practice. It is now a regional powerhouse of social experts spanning eight countries delivering social, digital and mobile solutions to a variety of local, regional and global clients. Previously, Ema held a number of leadership roles, including five years as the Corporate Communications and Public Affairs Manager for Google.

She is a very outspoken and passionate thought-leader on social media and communication in the MENA region, and you can learn more about her thoughts about social media practices with a specific Middle East perspective on her personal blog.

http://emalinakeruae.tumblr.com.
www.leoburnett.com

David Barker

David Barker works for [a•mo•bee] providing state-of-the-art, end-to-end mobile and digital advertising solutions for global brands and agencies. He is Senior Vice President and Managing Director EMEA, Advertising Solutions. His role involves overseeing the delivery of their products throughout EMEA such as Amobee 3D – their innovative ad creation platform, Amobee DSP – an advanced programmatic marketing platform for mobile and digital advertising and Amobee LTV – designed to provide detailed insights into app engagements in order to increase ROI.

www.amobee.com

Chapter 4

Magnus Jern

CEO of Golden Gekko, one of the pioneers in the mobile app market, Magnus founded the company in 2007 and has since grown the team to become one of the leaders in the industry. Today he leads the mobile Application Solutions Division at DMI (Digital Mobile Innovation) after Golden Gekko was acquired in 2013. Magnus spends most of his time travelling between offices and clients, speaking at conferences and sharing his insights and thoughts about trends and best practice.

Contact:

www.goldengekko.com

Adolfo Aladro García

Adolfo is Chief Operating Officer at ADTZ, Madrid, responsible for the R&D network, creating smart systems for advertising management. He has previously worked for Orange-France Telecom, Espana, YA.com Internet Factory (T-Online Spain part of Deutsche Telecom) and Telefonica Moviles. He has a degree in computer science from the Universidad Politécnica de Madrid, qualifying with distinction in the Department of Applied Mathematics (1997) for his paper on 'Internet, education and new information technologies: expectations and future'.

Contact:

www.adtz.com

Conor Lynch

Founder of SocialMedia.ie, Conor has over 15 years' online marketing experience gained through working with a wide range of organizations including many global brands such as Sony, Allianz, Guinness, Coca-Cola and also SMEs and start-ups. He manages a top Irish specialist digital agency to be found at SocialMedia.ie and Connector.ie.

Conor has worked in senior roles for two of Ireland's top digital marketing agencies, as well as Ireland's first internet-only bank RaboDirect. He is an honours graduate of DIT, Trinity College and the UCD Michael Smurfit Business School. He is also a course designer and has worked as a lecturer at Maynooth University.

He judges various awards, and has himself won Irish Internet Association's 'Best Use of Social Media' in 2011 and was voted the IIA 'Internet Marketer of the Year' in 2005.

Contact:

www.connector360.net

Ivan Adriel

Head of Creative Strategy, Connector.ie, Ivan is a prodigious digital creative professional whose talent came to national prominence in Brazil when he was only 14. This was when he developed a Harry Potter blog that got over 10 million page views per month.

Since then he has had a successful career creating digital strategy for global brands while working in Brazil and Europe. He loves to help brands to understand what motivates, engages and drives consumers to interact with content and experiences in order to establish and foster both loyalty and advocacy.

Ivan also travels the world seeing the sights and mapping trends to help brands such as Citibank, Allianz, Sony and 3M.

Alpesh Doshi

Principal and co-founder of Fintricity, Alpesh has worked in business-focused technology projects over the past 17 years. His experience with using internet technologies stems back to 1996 where he worked on one of the first web projects within a major bank. His focus is on helping clients to deliver business-driven solutions to technology. Alpesh also works with clients to understand social media and helps to implement solutions to leverage for business value.

Contact:
alpesh.doshi@fintricity.com

RBBI: Harvey Bennett, Mark Brown, Hani Anabtawi

Harvey Bennett is a partner at RBBI and heads the performance marketing division. His experience in the digital media industry, both in the United Kingdom and the Middle East, has helped RBBI to grow into a leading digital marketing business in MENA. Harvey enjoys pulling data apart and demonstrating relationships between seemingly unrelated events. His inspiration comes from books such as Tim Harford's *The Undercover Economist*, Steven Levitt and Stephen Dubner's *Freakonomics* and Ben Goldacre's *Bad Science*.

Mark Brown is Account Director at RBBI. Until June 2012 he was the region's official Facebook reseller and was instrumental in launching the original Connect Ads sales team for Facebook. His skill set ranges across devices and into the mobile display industry. He is a key member of the RBBI mobile team and has helped launch Addictive Mobility into the region (a socially powered mobile ad network available through RBBI).

Hani Anabtawi is a data analyst at RBBI. He joined from Rocket Internet in November 2012. Hani prepared the meta-analysis and was responsible for the integrity of the data. Together Hani, Mark and Harvey have developed a unique understanding of how consumers interact with their brands on Facebook.

Contact:

www.rbbideas.com

Katarzyna Czyrnek

Katarzyna Czyrnek is a graduate of Marketing, Management and Sales Management and from the very beginning of Positive Power Sp. z o.o. has served as Vice President, Sales Director. Passionate about e-commerce, she specializes in implementation of complex e-commerce, m.commerce projects and works for key clients – well-known brands in Poland and all over the world. She is responsible for co-operation with brands such as 8a.pl, Mitsubishi Electric, High Sky Brokers and Kler SA, co-ordinating work of the Sales Department and developing the sales strategy.

Contact:

katarzyna.czyrnek@positive-power.pl

Chapter 5

Ana Jesus

Ana Jesus is the EMEA Marketing Manager for Shoutlet, a social media monitoring platform. She is responsible for driving Shoutlet's marketing and communications strategy to meet local needs within the EMEA region. Ana is a Chartered Marketer with over eight years' experience in international marketing within the technology, finance and property industries and holds the CIM's Postgraduate

Diploma in Marketing. In her spare time she is the author of a reference London blog for immigrants and tourists and has contributed to several books and press articles on the topic of emigration.

Contact:

www.shoutlet.com

James Eder

In 2005, James Eder, aged 22, founded website StudentBeans alongside his brother Michael. By 2014 Student Beans has gone from an idea to a nationally recognized brand, reaching millions of students every month. Now known as The Beans Group, the company employs a team of over 40 people and was named Digital Business of the Year 2013 at the National Business Awards. Today a media and technology company, StudentBeansID, their digital student-verification platform, is expanding to work with retailers around the world.

James's drive and passion led to him winning a number of awards in 2013, including Social Media Entrepreneur of the Year at the Great British Entrepreneur Awards, being named one of Future 50 and graduating as a Marketing Academy Scholar.

Jenna Hanington

Jenna is Marketing Content Specialist at Pardot, a salesforce.com company, where she specializes in content creation and copywriting. Her articles have been featured on the Pardot, Salesforce, ExactTarget, B2Community and Capterra blogs, among others. Off the clock, you can find Jenna with her nose in a good book, hanging out at a lake, playing soccer, or unsuccessfully attempting to parallel park her car.

Contact:

www.salesforce.com

Molly Hoffmeister

Molly is Marketing Content Specialist at Pardot, a salesforce.com company, where she specializes in content creation and social media marketing. Since joining the team in 2011, Molly has built and managed Pardot's social media presence as the company grew from a 50-person start-up to a division of one of the world's largest SaaS companies.

Contact:

www.salesforce.com

Mark Walker

Mark Walker is the Content Marketing and Social Media Manager for UK and Ireland at Eventbrite. Mark regularly blogs and speaks about the events industry, digital marketing and business strategy. You can read more at the Eventbrite blog, follow him on Twitter (@jfdimark) or connect on LinkedIn.

Contact:

@jfdimark

Kieran Kent

Kieran is Managing Director of Propeller PR and has overall responsibility for leading, managing and driving Propeller's PR business. He has over 15 years' experience running UK and international communications programmes for technology, marketing and media businesses including the likes of Adobe, NEC, Disney, Quantcast, Oxygen8 Communications, Maxymiser and Tripwire. Prior to joining Propeller, Kieran was Client Services Director at Tech PR agency ITPR, which was voted one of *PR Week* magazine's 'Most Rated Agencies by Journalists'.

Konrad Feldman

CEO of Quantcast, Konrad Feldman co-founded the company with the aim of transforming the consistency and performance of online advertising through science and scalable computing.

Quantcast is a digital advertising company specializing in audience measurement and real-time advertising. As the pioneer of direct audience measurement in 2006, Quantcast has today the most in-depth understanding of digital audiences across the web, allowing marketers and publishers to make the smartest choices as they buy and sell the most effective targeted advertising on the market. Today, Quantcast directly measures more than 100 million web destinations, collects well in excess of 500 billion new data records every month and routinely processes as much as 30 petabytes of data every day.

Konrad has 18 years' experience in applying machine learning to the analysis of massive data sets across a diverse range of industries including banking, insurance, telecoms, utilities and retail.

Prior to Quantcast, Konrad co-founded the software company Searchspace, which helped the global financial services industry to detect terrorist financing and money laundering. He holds a BSc in Computer Science from University College London (UCL), where he subsequently spent three years as a researcher investigating the use of Artificial Intelligence in the financial services industry before founding Searchspace.

Chapter 6

Marc Duke

 A consultant specializing in B2B marketing, primarily with emerging technology companies, Marc has over 15 years' marketing experience helping businesses to grow through generating brand awareness by understanding their products/technologies, while providing the marketing know-how to reach their customers in a focused and cost-effective way.

Marc offers companies a mix of strategic and tactical marketing, covering areas such as analyst/influencer relations, PR, social media marketing, copywriting, competitive analysis and profile-raising activities such as speaker opportunities. He also runs training courses on analyst relations and marketing to help entrepreneurs and companies. He is happy to work on a project or on a retained basis.

He has worked with accelerators, start-ups and established vendors including IdeaPlane, PNMSoft, QualiTest, Ensighten, Demandware, Palmtree Technology, Celltick, Celaton, IronPort Systems, Clearswift, Adobe, HP and CSC Financial Services. He also has a wealth of agency experience having worked for Lewis Communications, Hill & Knowlton, Porter Novelli, Brands2Life and Sunesis. Marc is a Chartered Marketer with a CIM Postgraduate Diploma in Marketing; he speaks French and Hebrew fluently and is a graduate of Imperial College, London, with a degree in Chemistry with Management.

Marc's emphasis is on creating opportunities and delivering results quickly. His strength as a consultant is that he is removed from the day-to-day running of the company and provides a fresh perspective.

Isabelle Quevilly

Isabelle is an independent digital strategy director who says: 'Challenging convention is daunting, but I believe it can also be rewarding and exciting. I create solutions that rethink how a business is designed to make it braver, relevant and futureproof. I'm an entrepreneur at heart, but I also want to make a positive difference in the world. I love turning ideas into something real, getting results, and iterating them.'

Contact:

www.brilliantnoise.com

Neil Witten

Founding partner, CTO and product owner at StoryStream, Neil is an evangelist of new technology and is passionate about the positive impact that it can have on the world. He is a seasoned entrepreneur with a true appreciation for the unique formula required to realize a technically challenging online proposition while delighting the end user. Previously, he founded Bite Studio, an award-winning digital agency with a wealth of experience in creating fantastic user experiences online, for brands and inspiring start-ups.

Neil's background is in large-scale, user-centred design of online software, utilizing the latest technologies. He has over 15 years' experience in architecting, designing and developing cutting-edge web-based systems. He has experience in digital strategy, technical consultancy and project management and development of a wide range of applications for blue-chip clients across multiple sectors.

Contact:

www.storystream.it

Ellie Mirman

Ellie Mirman is Director of Marketing at HubSpot, an inbound marketing and sales software company. Get more tips on marketing and sales best practices at **http://blog.hubspot.com**.

Paul Handley

Director of Hit Social Media, Paul Handley has worked in social media and online marketing for many years. Hit Social are providers of social content and specialists at increasing social network's fan counts.

Contact:

www.hitsocialmedia.co.uk/
paul@hitsocialmedia.co.uk

Omaid Hiwaizi

One of the industry's hybrids, Omaid studied mathematics and got a job as a graphic designer on *i-D* magazine, before entering the industry as a creative and then metamorphosing into a strategist. Having founded two agencies (Hubbard Hiwaizi McCann and Crayon) and transformed several planning departments, he has the most diverse mix of marketing expertise, gained on UK and global business across the widest range of marketing disciplines. This gives him a unique perspective on today's complex world.

At Geometry Global, Omaid is responsible for driving the journey marketing approach through a mix of data, analytics and behavioural insights across all channels and contexts.

Adrian Nicholls

With a 20-year line of digital and integrated positions, Adrian has created campaigns for the likes of Audi, Toyota, American Express, McCain, Allied Bakeries and Pizza Hut. As one of the industry's digital innovators, Adrian brings a unique set of skills to the role. Prior to Geometry Global UK, he held positions as Business Lead at CMW, Executive Board Member and Client Services Director at DraftFCB London, Managing Director at Blue Barracuda, Deputy Managing Director at Good Technology and Group Account Director and New Business Director at Glue London.

Adrian joined Geometry Global to help further integrate digital into the heart of its omnichannel offering. He has also an internal education role and is responsible within the agency's Digital Council to help deliver next-generation ideas in an environment that is evolving at an extremely rapid pace.

He firmly believes that to engage with the 21st-century shopper, one needs to understand their behaviour, which is not constrained by platform, and use digital techniques to target consumers across purchase decision journeys.

Peter Simpson

Peter is a CMO and Strategic Alliances Executive with experience of building programmes and managing teams to deliver revenue acceleration. Currently at Reevoo, a social commerce company, prior to Reevoo he built highly successful partner programmes at Secerno (acquired by Oracle) and Cramer systems (acquired by Amdocs). He has 12 years' experience in the IT industry and 12 years' experience in strategic alliance and channel management.

Contact:

www.reevoo.com

Peter Cameron

Managing Director of Dam Digital, Peter has been providing digital solutions for over 14 years and is a pioneer of the UK internet industry. One of the founders of the agency JKD, which became one of the largest new media companies in the UK, he has led the user experience elements in all of these projects, working with clients and their customers to understand their requirements and ensuring that these are integrated into all elements of the project.

Contact:

www.dam-digital.com

Olivier Choron

A channel marketing and technology veteran, Olivier Choron is the CEO and founder of purechannelapps™.

Olivier spent his early career developing industry-first SMB initiatives in EMEA and globally with 3Com and Nortel Networks. Moving into the Partner Relationship Management (PRM) space with Allegis Corp/ClickCommerce, he was responsible for a number of key accounts including Microsoft Europe, GE Finance, Subway and BT Ignite.

After launching and running a full-service UK-based channel marketing agency for six years, in 2011 Olivier founded purechannelapps™, a social media and e-communications software company. Customers of purechannelapps include leading brands such as Microsoft, Adobe, SAP, Avnet, McAfee and Mountain Hardwear.

Chapter 7

Lee Wilson

Service Manager, Red Rocket Media, Lee has worked in digital marketing for over a decade, since completing a degree in business management and communications in 2003. For a large chunk of his career he has specialized in helping companies increase their visibility online through search, working with start-ups and SMEs through to multinational and global brands. He currently manages a team of search specialists, content specialists and outreach experts.

Red Rocket Media is a specialist social media and content marketing agency with offices in Portsmouth and London. Services include: social media strategy, management and analysis, content marketing strategy, content creation by professional journalists (articles, blogs, infographics, e-books, white papers, videos etc), content promotion and performance analysis.

Contact:
www.redrocketmedia.co.uk

Mazher Abidi

Head of Social Media at Initiative, Dubai, Mazher is a marketer with particular interests in digital and social media marketing, marketing using new technologies and implementing integrated marketing communications. He is a published academic researcher, writer for *The Guardian* Media Professionals network and ad-hoc university lecturer/speaker on social media. Mazher is a previous winner of the Journalist of the Year award, having held the position of Arts Editor at Student Direct.

He leads the social media team at Initiative in Dubai. Initiative are part of the Middle East Communications Network (MCN) – the regional holding company of key media, creative and PR agencies owned by the NYSE-listed Interpublic Group (IPG) including Lowe, MRM, McCann, Magma and Weber Shandwick.

Contact:
www.initiative.com/

Chapter 8

Jack Cooper

Jack Cooper is a digital marketing evangelist and content outreach specialist at Red Rocket Media. He writes about trends in the digital marketing scene and stays active in exploring new platforms at the forefront of the industry.

Contact:

www.redrocketmedia.co.uk

jcooper@vldigital.co.uk

Jim Dowling

Jim is Managing Partner at Cake in London, responsible for day-to-day leadership of the agency. He oversees the delivery of work to clients from strategy, creative to execution. His main clients include IKEA, vinspired, Magners, Carling, Sainsbury's and BUPA.

He began life as an account lead on Cake's early flagship clients, and then became the company's first Planning Director in 2001. In 2005, a stint with Ogilvy PR in Asia-Pacific, based in Hong Kong, as the region's planning director, saw him develop global insight as well as digital expertise, launching the network's social media practice. In 2008, he returned to London and Cake as Head of Planning, and then within the year became Managing Partner.

Contact:

www.cakegroup.com

Laura Crimmons

Social and PR Manager at Branded3, Laura heads up the Comms team to develop creative strategies to get clients talked about online in all the right places. With a wealth of experience and qualifications in both traditional and online PR as well as search marketing, Laura has an in-depth understanding of how PR feeds into SEO strategies and is regularly invited to talk on the subject at industry conferences.

Using her range of media contacts, Laura can work with clients in any industry and has delivered fantastic national coverage for clients.
Contact:
www.branded3.com

Mathew Sweezey

Manager of marketing research and education at Salesforce, Mathew is the head of thought leadership for B2B marketing for the company. A consummate writer, he authors a column for Clickz.com on marketing automation, writes for multiple blogs and has featured in publications such as *Marketing Automation Times*, *Mashable*, *DemandGen Report*, *Marketing Sherpa*, and is the author of *Marketing Automation for Dummies* (Wiley, 2014). Mathew speaks more than 50 times per year around the world at events such as Conversion Conference, Dreamforce, SugarCon, and to companies including Microsoft, UPS, Dell and Resturants.com, to name a few.
Contact:
www.salesforce.com

Ithamar Sorek

Ithamar Sorek is a business development enthusiast with a broad range of international sales experience on a variety of platforms. He started his career in banking and finance, followed by a move into technology, working for Wildfire, which was acquired by Google.

At Google, Ithamar was responsible for driving new business, market strategy and establishing trade through the SEEMEA (South and Eastern Europe, the Middle East and Africa) region. Sorek is an experienced team leader, with experience in sales management, new business procurement and operation management. His reputation is for building strong, long-standing business relationships with large networks and individuals across the globe.

Robin Skidmore

CEO of Shackleton PR, Robin is the company's founder and a leading digital marketing entrepreneur. He has helped some of the UK's biggest brands to transform their visibility, enhance their reputation and grow their business online.

Also co-founder of digital marketing agency Epiphany, he developed Shackleton as the PR and social media arm of the business to ensure it would share the same philosophy of creative marketing rooted in solid analysis. He recognized that PR agencies were often unable to demonstrate the impact of their work to clients whilst struggling to adapt to the changing digital landscape. He also recognized that social agencies often limited the potential of their campaigns by focusing exclusively on digital channels and content.

Contact:
www.shackletonpr.co.uk

Chapter 9

Anil Nair

Anil is the CEO and Managing Partner of one of India's leading digital engagement agencies, L&K Saatchi & Saatchi. He helps leading Indian brands to make their transition to click and mortar, helping them digitally reengineer from the inside out.

L&K Saatchi & Saatchi are pioneering a 24/7 always-on approach to communication with initiatives such as 'Live Creativity', which prepares a brand to be ever ready to respond to changing environmental flux.

He is based out of Mumbai, India, where he lives with his wife who is a fiction and travel writer.

Contact:

anil.n@lkdigi.com or follow him **@tattertale**

Jason Mander

As Head of Trends at GlobalWebIndex, Jason oversees all of GWI's content – producing trends on key digital topics and authoring the company's flagship quarterly reports on social networking, mobile/tablet usage, e-commerce and brand engagement. Jason also manages the Market Report series – analysing trends in each of the 32 countries surveyed by GlobalWebIndex – and has released a number of Audience Reports examining behaviours and attitudes among high-interest target groups such as teens, influencers and parents.

Jason is a regular public speaker as well as a frequent contributor to articles, news stories and TV coverage across such titles as BBC News, *The Guardian*, Bloomberg and NBC. Prior to GlobalWebIndex,

Jason was Head of Insight at Future Foundation; during his time there, he launched the company's US service, oversaw its Beyond 2020 innovation series, managed its Quant, Intelligence and Forecasting departments and served as Account Director for a number of global brands.

Jason first began working with trends as a Research Fellow at the University of Oxford. Building on a PhD in social sciences, he published a book through Cambridge University Press, presented at a number of international conferences and was fortunate to visit more than 100 different cities in the name of research.

Contact:

www.globalwebindex.net

Lauren Friedman

Lauren Friedman is a social marketing authority with extensive experience working with brands to create their social personas, nurture their Facebook and Twitter communities and curate their social conversations.

As Head of Social Business Enablement at Adobe, Lauren runs the company's enablement infrastructure programmes and partners cross-functionally to establish integrated social media strategies that empower business functions to meet their respective objectives, ultimately elevating Adobe as a social business.

Contact:

www.adobe.com

Paul Armstrong/HERE/FORTH

HERE/FORTH is an advisory service that helps business leaders decide how best to use rapidly changing and emerging technologies to create resilient businesses for HERE (today) and /FORTH (tomorrow). Before this he led the social team at Mindshare (media agency) and worked in-house at Myspace HQ during his seven-year stint in Los Angeles, where he worked for some top international brands including Sony, Activision, 20th Century Fox, DreamWorks and Yahoo! amongst others. Paul also created @themediaisdying Twitter network and regularly writes for outlets including *The Guardian*, Reuters and Cool Hunting. He can frequently be seen on the BBC when industry news breaks.

Contact:

www.paularmstrong.net/hereforth

Simon Kingsnorth

A Digital Marketing Director, Simon Kingsnorth has worked client-side for a wide range of businesses including start-ups and market leaders across many sectors. He has built a number of successful digital marketing strategies both nationally and globally and consulted for companies across the world. He is also a contributing author to the book *Understanding Digital Marketing*.

Mike Berry

Founder of Mike Berry Associates, Mike started his career in sales and marketing at Procter & Gamble, leaving to join DM agency EHS Brann (now EHS 4D), then Wunderman (the direct/digital marketing arm of Y&R) and was promoted to the board as Group Account Director. In the 1990s, he was Director of Direct Marketing and Sales Promotion at Kevin Morley Marketinl. In 1996 he joined Bozell Worldwide (now DraftFCB) as Senior Vice President for European Integration. He launched Bozell Marketing Services where he was MD and his main client was Commercial Union (Aviva). In 2002 Mike got together with two partners to launch SPIRIT, a Central London-based integrated/digital marketing agency. In 2008 Mike moved to Jack Morton Worldwide, the interpublic experiential network, as Head of Digital for Europe, Middle East and Africa. His clients included Nokia, Shell, HP, Toyota and COI (DCSF and the Army). He left in July 2009 to pursue a consultancy and training career, drawing on his extensive experience of online and offline marketing and working with a range of clients in B2B, B2C, public and charity sectors.

Mike is the author of *The New Integrated Direct Marketing* (Gower, 1998) and is a Fellow of the Institute of Direct Marketing for whom he trains regularly (IDM Diploma in Digital Marketing, complete digital marketing); he is also a member of the editorial board of the *IDM International Journal*. He is Course Director on the Digital Marketing Workshop for ISBA (Incorporated Society of British Advertisers) and is Lead Adjunct Professor on the Master of Digital Marketing degree offered by Hult International Business School and Econsultancy. He regularly teaches the CAM (Chartered Institute of Marketing) Diplomas and trains for the Internet Advertising Bureau (IAB).

Contact:

www.mikeberryassociates.com

Chapter 10

Tom Chapman

Tom Chapman is a content specialist for Red Rocket Media and an expert in risk management strategies for social media, as well as crisis PR. He has written extensively on these topics and continues to expand his knowledge as the social media industry evolves.

Contact:

www.redrocketmedia.co.uk

CASE STUDY
INDEX OF SUPPLIERS

ADTZ

We focus on quality, dedication and customer service. We help you to maximize Facebook's potential as a marketing channel. We began with social media marketing and it is in our DNA. We bring all our knowledge and experience to make your Facebook investment profitable. Our constantly developing intelligent platform takes the creation, optimization and analysis of your Facebook campaigns to the next level. Within Facebook Ads' Preferred Marketing Developer program (PMD), we have the greatest presence in Spain and Latin America. We have offices in Spain, Brazil, Mexico, Colombia, Argentina and Chile.
Contact:
http://www.adtz.com/
spain@adtz.com
T 00 34 912 240 111

[a•mo•bee]

[a•mo•bee] offers an industry-leading digital advertising platform for advertisers, publishers and operators to achieve unparalleled results. Uniquely, we have the deep expertise and technology to provide a comprehensive suite of solutions for key stakeholders. Advertisers need our platform to create the most captivating campaigns and buy the best inventory that reaches the right consumers at the right time. Publishers, mobile network operators, enterprise companies and developers need [a•mo•bee]'s platform to get the most value for each impression.
Contact:
http://www.amobee.com
T +44 (0) 203 301 5555

BBH London

BBH is a full-service creative agency for the digital age, providing strategic brand ideas, integrated communications and pure play digital solutions for some of the world's best-loved brands. The agency's work for Audi (Vorsprung durch Technik), Johnnie Walker (Keep Walking) and Axe (The Axe Effect) are some of the most enduring campaigns ever. At the heart of the agency is a strongly held belief in 'high performance creativity' that maximizes the value of our ideas for clients. This demands world-class creativity designed to solve real business problems and deliberately deployed and optimized. BBH delivers this with best-in-class tools and resources such as user experience, digital CRM, interaction design, social strategy, community management, web build, brand identity, high-end film and fast-turnaround web video.

The business was founded in London in 1982 and employs 1,000 people across eight offices: London, Singapore, New York, São Paulo, Shanghai, Mumbai, Los Angeles and Sweden and is part of Publicis Groupe [Euronext Paris FR0000130577, CAC 40] – one of the world's leading communications groups.

Contact:

Carly Herman, New Business Director, Carly.Herman@bbh.co.uk

www.bartleboglehegarty.com

Dam Digital

Dam Digital was created in 2011 by four experienced digital practitioners. The four founders have jointly over 50 years' experience of delivering digital projects for brands such as John Lewis, Waitrose, PayPal, Casio and Universal. All four of us have worked together at previous agencies and we have handpicked staff from these agencies to form Dam. Our strength is delivering digital solutions for clients that meet real challenges they have and to add real value to their businesses.

Contact:

www.dam-digital.com

info@dam-digital.com

Digital Arts Network (DAN)

DAN is the global digital network of TBWA, covering teams in six continents and 23 offices; DAN Sydney led the charge on the creative in this campaign. DAN is a formal global structure for how TBWA approaches digital and integration, rooted in TBWA's media arts philosophy that everything between a brand and an audience is media and that, increasingly, those touch points are digital. The core competencies of TBWA/ DAN include creative technology, UX, e-commerce, social media, content, mobile, IP and platforms, analytics, search, audience behaviour and production.

Contact:

http://digitalartsnetwork.com/

Glow Digital Media

Glow, whose flagship product is called Glow Machine, gives advertisers tools to create and optimize multiformat ad campaigns, track and build engagement, and view data dashboards and analysis across social media channels. Glow is a Facebook strategic Preferred Marketing Developer (sPMD).

Contact:

Ithamar Sorek, VP Business Development, ithamar@thisisglow.com

www.thisisglow.com

hello@thisisglow.com

Google

Larry Page, our co-founder and CEO, once described the 'perfect search engine' as something that 'understands exactly what you mean and gives you back exactly what you want'. Since he said those words, Google has grown to offer products beyond search, but the spirit of what he said remains. With all our technologies – from search to Chrome to Gmail – our goal is to make it as easy as possible for you to find the information you need and get the things you need to do done.

We provide a variety of tools to help businesses of all kinds succeed on and off the web. These programs form the backbone of our own business; they have also enabled entrepreneurs and publishers around the world to grow theirs. Our advertising programs, which range from simple text ads to rich media ads, help businesses to find customers, and help publishers to make money from their content. We also provide cloud computing tools for businesses, which save money and help organizations to be more productive.

The web has evolved enormously since Google first appeared on the scene, but one thing that has not changed is our belief in the endless possibilities of the internet itself.

Contact:

www.google.com

Positive Power

Positive Power is a software house, providing support and effective solutions for business clients for over 12 years, constantly evolving and branching out. Since 2014 Positive Power has been a part of Indata Software SA group, associating almost 200 professionals and IT passionates, listed on NewConnect market of the stock exchange. Positive Power is focused on implementing technologically advanced: e-commerce platforms (both dedicated and based on Magento), dedicated B2B systems and applications, innovative web and desktop solutions as well as native mobile solutions. Among our partners you can find: Onet.pl, Intersport Polska S.A., Tikkurila, Benefit Systems, SnowShop.pl, 8a.pl, Pfleiderer SA, Mitsubishi Electric, Fjord Nansen, Nixon Car Parts and many others.

Contact:

http://www.en.positive-power.pl/

purechannelapps™

Founded in 2011, purechannelapps Inc. helps customers to drive business growth through better enablement, communication and collaboration with their sales teams. The company delivers enterprise-class targeted e-communications and social media amplification solutions that help organizations to reduce communication costs and amplify their social media messaging through their brand advocates. With offices in Texas and the United Kingdom, purechannelapps is privately owned and funded.

Contact:

visit **www.purechannelapps.com**

Richard Rogers +44 (0) 20 3540 6585, info@purechannelapps.com

Quantcast

Quantcast is a technology company specializing in real-time advertising and audience measurement. As the pioneer of direct audience measurement in 2006, Quantcast now has the most in-depth understanding of digital audiences across the web, allowing marketers and publishers to make the smartest choices as they buy and sell the most effective targeted advertising on the market. More than 1,000 brands rely on Quantcast for real-time advertising. As the leader in big data for the digital advertising industry, Quantcast directly measures more than 100 million web destinations, incorporates over 1 trillion new data records every month and continuously processes as much as 30 petabytes of data every day. Quantcast is headquartered in San Francisco and backed by Founders Fund, Polaris Venture Partners and Cisco Systems.

Contact:

Konrad Feldman, co-founder and CEO

https://www.quantcast.com

@Quantcast

Queensland University of Technology (QUT)

QUT is a highly successful Australian university with an applied emphasis in courses and research. Professor Judy Drennan is Director of the Services Innovation Research Program in the Faculty of Business within the Faculty of Business at the Queensland University of Technology. Her qualifications include a PhD from Deakin University and a Masters of Education from the University of Melbourne. Judy provides valuable expertise from a marketing perspective.

Contact:

https://www.qut.edu.au/

Red Blue Blur Ideas JLT (RBBI)

RBBI is a specialist digital marketing agency. Our focus is on interpreting user behaviour and translating insight into actions for brands to leverage. RBBI understands the complexity of the modern user journey, from discovery to on site user experience through to conversion. This gives RBBI a unique ability to understand the various components of a brand's digital footprint, and positions the agency as a regional thought leader and pioneer in digital marketing. Our core services are usability, UX/UI, performance marketing, SEO, mobile advertising and analytics. Since 2012 RBBI have helped large brands to establish and improve their digital business.

Contact:

Harvey Bennet, partner, heading up the performance marketing division: **www.linkedin.com/in/harveybennett**

Twitter @RBBideas

http://rbbideas.com/

T + 971 4454 2608

Reevoo

Reevoo has pioneered a measurably better approach to ratings and reviews based on independent validation. The company helps clients to harness the voice of the customer to inject trust and buyer confidence across the entire multichannel purchase journey. Their Amplify™ methodology provides rich and well-structured content to drive increased revenue and customer-driven insight.

Contact:

www.reevoo.com/contact-us

Shackleton PR

Based in Leeds, Shackleton is a social PR consultancy set up in 2012 by one of the original founders of parent company Epiphany, sharing the same philosophy of creative marketing rooted in solid analysis. The consultancy prides itself on creating and delivering activity, as well as subsequent measurements, that is specifically designed to demonstrate a tangible impact, while embracing the changing digital landscape. The Shackleton team comprises expert PRs, journalists, analysts and campaign planners working closely with Epiphany, one of the UK's leading digital agencies, to ensure that it remains at the forefront of digital strategy.

Contact:

www.shackletonpr.co.uk

Shoutlet, inc.

Shoutlet is an enterprise-class, cloud-based social relationship platform that empowers brands to build meaningful customer relationships by harnessing the power of social marketing. More than 600 brands and agencies in 50 countries use Shoutlet to publish, engage and measure social marketing campaigns that gather consumer data to drive measurable business impact. Headquartered in the United

States in Madison, WI, Shoutlet has additional offices in New York, San Francisco and London. Current customers include 3M, Regus, Corinthia Hotels, Best Buy, NASCAR, Canon, Shutterfly, Norwegian Cruise Line and Cloetta.

Contact:

www.shoutlet.com/

T +44 (0) 20 7025

Über

If you are going to call yourself Über you are going to have to work very hard every day to live up to your name. Your service has to be over and above, your ideas have to shine brighter and your results need to be consistent. It means that winning awards is a by-product not a goal. It means taking your work seriously and yourself not so. It means learning and understanding exactly who your clients are, exactly what they do and exactly who their customers are. It means only providing a service when you can provide it impressively. You have to be passionate, knowledgeable and love what you do.

Contact:

Hello. We are Über.

Founder and MD, Richard Benjamin, Richard@uberagency.com

Client Services Director, Alan Baker, Alan@uberagency.com

Head of Digital, Nic Jones, Nic@uberagency.com

Über Agency 0114 278 7100

Twitter @uberagency

Facebook **https://www.facebook.com/UberThinking**

www.uberagency.com

University of South Australia

The University of South Australia (UniSA) conducts research and consultancy with an emphasis on application of knowledge in collaboration with government, industry, the community, the professions and other community groups. Dr Barbara Spears is a leading nationally and internationally recognized researcher of girls' bullying and cyberbullying, and is/has been chief investigator on several national projects related to cyberbullying and mental health. Dr Spears was the lead researcher on the case study project.

Contact

http://www.unisa.edu.au/

University of Western Sydney

The University of Western Sydney (UWS) is a confirmed research leader in Australia. UWS nurtures a distinctive, high-impact research culture and has proven research excellence and depth. Dr Philippa Collin is a Research Fellow at the Institute for Culture and Society, University of Western Sydney. Philippa completed her PhD on youth political identity and the internet in Australia and the United Kingdom (University of Sydney, 2009). Prior to her appointment at UWS, she was the Managing Director of Research and Policy at the ReachOut. com by Inspire Foundation (2002–10) where she worked in various roles in programmes, policy and research. Philippa was the driver of our youth participation and engagement process.

Contact:

http://www.uws.edu.au/

We Are Social

We Are Social is a conversation agency, a new kind of agency that combines an innate understanding of social media with digital, PR and marketing skills. We are entirely focused on innovative, creative and effective social media marketing and communications and we like to think we are getting rather good at it.

With an international team of over 500 and offices in New York, London, Paris, Milan, Munich, Singapore, Sydney and São Paulo, our mission is to put social thinking at the centre of marketing.

We work with clients including adidas, Heinz, Kimberly-Clark, Mondelēz, Heineken, eBay, Jaguar, Intel and Expedia on global, regional and local projects.

Contact:

http://wearesocial.net/

Zuni

Zuni is a leading digital strategy and marketing agency, specializing in digital strategy, implementation, optimization and training. Zuni helps clients to create a more meaningful, sustainable and profitable engagement between themselves and their customers through digital and other channels. Zuni have worked with many of Australia's blue chip companies helping them to realize their business objectives.

Contact

http://zuni.com.au/

Mike Zeederberg, Managing Director:
mike.zeederberg@zuni.com.au;

https://www.linkedin.com/in/mikezeederberg

Valentine Borbone, Client Relationship Director:
valentine.borbone@zuni.com.au;

https://www.linkedin.com/in/valentinaborbone

INDEX

Note: The index is filed in alphabetical, word-by-word order. Numbers within main headings are filed as spelt out. Acronyms are filed as presented. Page locators in *italics* denote information contained within a figure or table; locators as roman numerals denote material contained within the book's preliminary pages.

CPSIA information can be obtained at www.ICGtesting.com
Printed in the USA
BVOW08s1722290315

393697BV00004B/5/P